Thoughts From A
High Plains
Pundit

Greg Hansen

THIS BOOK IS DEDICATED TO

SCOTT GORDON
WINONA, MN

ABE4 USN USS CONSTELLATION CV 64

BELOVED BY MANY

CONTENTS

INTRODUCTION

I AM A CHRISTIAN AND A CONSERVATIVE.

THIS BOOK IS COMPRISED OF JOURNALED THOUGHTS AS I REFLECTED ON NEWS STORIES, MOST OF WHICH WERE SHARED BY POSTING THEM ON A WEBSITE AND ARE IN THE CHRONILOGICAL ORDER OF EVENTS.

I WAS ENCOURAGED TO SHARE THEM IN BOOK FORM LARGELY AS A FORM OF ENTERTAINMENT BUT ALSO BECAUSE IT MAY BRING INTO THE FRAY OF POLITICAL DISCUSSION SOME DIFFERENT THINGS TO CONSIDER. THE BOTTOM OF MANY COMMENTS IS THE TITLE OF THE RELEVENT STORY IF I THOUGHT IT WAS NECESSARY TO CLAIFY WHY MY THOUGHTS WERE SO ARROGANTLY WARRANTED..

COMMENTS, EXISTING AS THEY DO IN THE JUNGLE OF INTERNET POSTING, AN EXPECTATION OF FLAWLESS GRAMMOR ETC...WOULD LEAVE THE READER WITH A HANDFUL OF THOSE TINY BITS OF POTATO CHIPS FROM THE BOTTOM OF THE BAG.

THE BOOK STARTS OUT WITH SOME EARLIER THOUGHTS AND JOINS UP IN THE 2ND CHAPTER AS THE 2016 PRESIDENTIAL CAMPAIGN HAS GAINED STEAM...GAINING IN LENGHTH AND INTENSITY AS TIME MOVES ALONG.

KEEP IN MIND THAT I'M NOT A FANCY AND EDUMACATED PERSON AND THAT I HAVE A HABIT OF WRITING WITH A PAINTBRUSH INSTEAD.

Foreword

I would like to see folks avail themselves to the area of The Declaration of Independence where we take the King of England to the woodshed for abuse of the People…of all things concerning our history, that one area is sorely neglected and as such, bravery eludes many citizens.

Whereas the overt expression of the diminishment of the powers of Tyrants are insulting to the tyrannical, wrapped up in all of the political discourse in these times exists the war between powers that be against the powers of the People, to whom the Constitution belongs and as such...

that certain bravery of the People to stand again against the original and current obstruction of Liberty can only be achieved by being equal in proportion to the degree of the humbling of themselves to the Providence's of Almighty God.

-Greg Hansen

Folks, politics is a rough business…

expect not a pretty thing.

CHAPTER 1

EARLIER THOUGHTS

If we were to imagine that the United States government consisted of only the White House, Capital, Supreme Court, Pentagon and one other building that housed the very few bureaucracies necessary to operate Federal governmental functions that consisted of only things necessary and fundamental, and I mean bare bones basic…we would have a united population.

In that scenario, what could someone standup and propose as a law that would start dividing the people? If we were to look closely at that law we would discover that it does not follow the admonition of "Love thy neighbor as yourself" but was rather established from a selfish place.

Now, times that above selfish act by thousands…that's what explains the wide division we have today in this country.

Nov 25, 2011 5:57 am

And the head waiter, upon seeing this, exclaimed "who ordered the really, really fresh turkey?"

15lb Wild Turkey Dies After Crashing Through Restaurant Window…on Thanksgiving

Dec 4, 2011 7:58 am

Well heavens to Betsy, they shouldn't let a great opportunity go to waste. Take that bomb out in the desert somewhere in the Middle East, let the terrorists sniff it out and then tape themselves to it and then when it's all full of terrorists like fly paper shoot the bomb...it's called a "Jihad disco" ...it's fun!

Dec 7, 2011 6:15 am

If the Supreme Court sides with Obama Care the simple notion of liberty will no longer exist. It really would undo the entire premise of the Constitution and render the Bill Of Rights to cute poetry. In one small act we would all effectively be a part of a commune because the premise of Obama Care is that this has to be done for the "good of the whole society" thus they will be able to mandate that we buy anything "for the good of society". We won't have to give them any ideas, there will be a deluge of mandates. And there will be a civil war.

Dec 7, 2011 7:03 am

60 minutes is trying to frame the whole problem on "evil corporations" only. What has happened is that the Government has imposed its regulatory self onto corporations for decades to a point where a corporation's conduct has become indistinguishable from the conduct of Government. Corporations, by force, have essentially become bureaus of the Government. It's called Fascism. This was Mussolini's vision outlined in his manifesto.

Dec 7, 2011 7:59 am

We slaughtered our own chickens growing up and I was always amazed that upon removal of the head chickens become world class gymnasts and acrobats. Then it occurred to me, their small minds were a hindrance to their full potential!

First bill of rights "Congress shall make no law respecting an establishment of religion, or prohibiting the free exercise thereof..." This means that the Government CANT prohibit it ANYWHERE!!!! Not in government buildings, Churches, homes, parks, bars, cars, schools, streets...NOWHERE!

Mr. Trump, just run. Jump in now. Yeah, not everyone will agree with some social issues but Government shouldn't be in the business of social engineering anyway.

Nonsense is a healthy diversion from the weight of life. Isn't that right Jerry Lewis and Carol Burnett?

Oh, Communist societies are constantly partying and having colorful parades with balloons and stuff aren't they? I mean sometimes right? Maybe once? Ok, Ok...I think there was a clown in Russia once before they executed him.

Target and most of the other large retailers' profit margins typically fall in the range between 3-4.5%. That means if you stood on the street corner selling apples all day for a dollar a piece that you would have to sell 1000 of them to make $37. And then imagine someone calling you a rich greedy Capitalist.

Hey geeks, we love ya but don't get into over-thinking. It just gets messy when one tries to apply binary algorithms to the dynamics of nature.

Wow, I didn't know that engineers are "driving" trains. Heck, all he would have to do is crank the steering wheel and simply drive around the Occupied With Wall Street...things.

Occupy Portland Mother Places 4-Year-Old Daughter on Train Tracks During Protest to Shut Down Port

Say what you will about Trump but for a billionaire he sure has a humble office and a working office.

Liberal 10 Commandments:

1. Thou shalt love the Lord thy earth and not sin against her. Think green.

2. Thou shalt consider anything deemed immoral to be deemed as normal.

3. Thou shalt not have any mind of thy own, the "collective soul" is thy Holy Ghost.

4. Do not honor thy Mother and thy Father, thy public school are those things unto you.

5. Do not let thy selves be tempted by infidels eating cheeseburgers, thy Soylent Green is sufficient.

6. Everyone is the same.

7. 2+2 can equal 5, there's nothing wrong with being wrong.

8. Do not want, the Government provideth thy needs.

9. The "Community" is the meaning of life.

10. Thou shalt pity thyself and cry often, for thou art small and meaningless.

By design, they don't want students educated. They would figure things out. Hush, hush...it's perfectly fine to abide in the blue.

Efficient or not, it is insanely horrifying that Government would (and has) make a law that changes your natural inclinations because it's "good for you". It's the position that they are the parent and you the child...and these knot-heads are our employees!!!!!!!!!!!!!!!!!!!! For those who don't understand that, here's another way of saying it;

THE STUPID IDIOTS WE HIRED TO CLEAN THE TOILETS AND SWEEP THE FLOORS ARE IDIOTS WHO NOW THINK THEY ARE THE BOSS--------FIRE THEM!!!!!!!!!!

A Texas rancher and a Nebraska rancher were having a conversation about large spreads and the Texan says "I can get in my pickup and drive all day and still never reach the other side of my land"

The Nebraskan lowers his hat and says 'Yep, I had an old pickup like that once"

'So I was in the jungle the other day and all of the sudden these baby Gorillas were grooming my hair and the huge Silverback male mas standing 3 feet away, staring at me point blank. No I wasn't scared, we were doing mushrooms'.

Wild Gorillas Groom Man During Park Visit...as Huge Silverback Watches

Corporations were absolutely civic minded in the past, they were after all staffed with ordinary Americans. That was before Government imposed socialist bureaucracy on them through laws and regulation which took the heart out of them.

The internet is not public domain (Or shouldn't be). When a person goes to a website on the internet they are experiencing nothing more than a private phone call with pictures. The Government should not be in the business of regulating ANYTHING about it. The internet is not like public airways or public streets. 99% of internet activity occurs on privately owned servers. Don't let them get anywhere near regulating anything about our privacy (the internet). There are laws already that deal with piracy, child porn etc...they can use those laws to prosecute.

"Good evening America, this is CNN and we are all 13 year old's."

The difference is that the internet does it by using pictures and sounds on CSS sheets. It's not a Right in the sense that a Government benevolently grants it or denies it. If a person wants to go out and buy a computer and pay for the services of an Internet provider then they are exercising their God given Right to engage in commerce...unless, God forbid, it becomes illegal to own, buy or sell computers and internet servers. The idea that the Internet is somehow a public domain is ridiculous. It's not like public parks and streets...it's not public property.

The Founding Fathers never ever imagined Government being this authoritative monster that it is. If they were to somehow all show up today and look around for a day or two, the only thing they would say is "Just two questions, when were we invaded by the Enemy and where do you keep the guns?"

What's a King doing with a desk?

Letter Discovered in Louis XV Desk at Versailles

The Bible says that we can't even begin to understand God's existence. We are like a brick wall trying to understand the mason...can't even begin.

Hey, he ate some funky Kung Pao chicken and was trying to get home real fast. "Get out of way... before pants filled up"

Raw Video: Stolen Car in China Hits 13 Vehicles

Religion: A man-made dogma of rules and rituals that, upon adherence, makes one feel that by their own might they have achieved righteousness.

Religion makes oneself feel pretty self-empowered. Kissing cups or rugs, lighting candles and incense, doing dances with wolves, yelling your head off at the moon and burning sticks upon the equinox, banging bells, gongs and the dirt, running away as fast as you can and believing that your own feeble self, that will one day die, and has the natural ability to conceive what truth is, is what is called "Religion"

Heavens to Betsy! That's amazing that anyone survived that wreck!

"Hi Honey, how was your day?"

"Oh, we were driving along the freeway and a truck smashed us into the guardrail like a tin can and then we plunged over the side and burst into flames...but were fine.

BTW, where's the Jim Beam?"

Firefighters Rescue Mother & Daughters From Smashed Car Dangling Perilously Over Bridge

111000110010011100101100010111101001010101010010101001... That's what I think.

IBM Creates World's Smallest Magnetic Storage Device From 12 Atoms

The one thing that animates Germans the most is incompetence at work. They are confounded by someone doing their job poorly and they also get loud about it, LOL.

The way they were caught was because they were dragging their butts whenever they went anywhere in the airport.

At first everyone thought they were just trying to be funny but then one official said "Wait a minute, I bet they have something heavy in their butts!" and then everyone laughed.

Ironically, it turned out to be true.

Eight S. Korean Men Arrested for Trying to Smuggle Gold in Their...Butts

Frida has been exposed to huge amounts of radiation but that's okay by her, she's just glowing with pride.

X-Ray Art? Here's How the Stunning Photos Are Made

What's funny is, after she screams the Zebra is like "oh crap, I bit a human...they are really gonna shoot me now!" LOL

Slo-Mo Freak Out: Woman's Reaction to Zebra Bite Goes Viral

I think that it's ridiculous that people would think that global warming would cause coastal flooding from melting ice shelves, ice bergs etc.. Think of this; only 10% of an ice shelf is above water, the other 90%! is under water. We all have done this, left a glass full of ice and whatever beverage only to come back later to a glass with no ice and a significantly decreased volume. Ice creates a "void" in water that itself cannot fill upon melting. Global warming would be very good!-----think terrarium. It would be wonderful, crops growing in once desolate areas, a more stable atmosphere and thus less violent weather brought on by extreme weather cashes, year- long outdoor swimming pools and palm trees in North Dakota!

Here's what transpired upon its first test:

Gurimov, test pilot #1 : I'm not gonna fly that dang thing! Have Yagoslav do it!

Yagoslav: I ain't flying that piece of crap, besides it's Zorzy's turn!

Gurimov: Zorzy got dirted-out when he had to fly the Kopnager, the plane that can fly both directions at once...it vaporized...

Commandant (holding a pistol): Both of you idiots better knock off all the yammering and get your sorry asses in that damn thing and give it a try before I shoots you both!!

Want to See the Soviet Union's Massive Nuclear Equipped Super Plane?

Jan 27, 2012 8:56 am

Microwave ovens use microwave (tiny wavelength) radio frequency bounced back and forth very quickly that produces friction inside the object you are cooking thus heating it.

Things cooked in a microwave are heated from the middle-outward because the clash of microwaves occurs in the center of the oven.

35 years of being time tested (and mother approved) has made microwave ovens a safe alternative to cooking over campfires (NOT mother approved)

So go ahead, don't be afraid. Heat yourself up a big bowl of chili with onions and cheddar cheese and see for yourself today! LOL

Jan 27, 2012 9:25 am

You can be assured, farmers are certainly not going to follow the guidelines of useless bureaucrats. They are going to follow the current weather patterns of any particular year for planting, ground temperature etc...

Jan 28, 2012 6:00 am

Pre-reconstruction work, phase one, complete sir!

Giant Cargo Ship Carrying Rocket Parts Smashes and Collapses Kentucky Bridge

Jan 28, 2012 6:37 am

You know what...these goofy liberals are gonna have pretty big eye's on the day the "Sleeping Giant" awakes again.

We have been too kind and tolerant and now the enemy has gained more strongholds in conquering our nation. To you liberals; consider your ideals. Did the founding fathers think like you? How about the American people in the 1800's? Or the 1950's? You liberals are alien to this country.

Jan 30, 2012 8:20 am

What would be funny is if it does turn out to be an alien spacecraft. The aliens would be so embarrassed that they finally got caught...sitting there all red-faced.

Deep-Sea Explorers Still Baffled by Unidentified Object on Sea Floor -- Can You Name It?

Feb 9, 2012 7:07 am

Wait a minute you meathead Liberals! What about your precious equal protection? Why isn't it demeaning for ALL the other groups represented by mascots?

Cornhuskers, as if Nebraskans still shuck corn by hand, that's insulting!

Cowboys, why heck, they are the ones that beat all the Injuns up!

Trojans, insulting to the gay community!

The Fighting Irish, what, making fun of all the people who died in the potato famine fighting for their lives?

Sooners, making fun of people waiting for Government grants.

Volunteers, doesn't that insult Obama's civilian army?

Gophers, what are the precious wolves gonna eat after everyone goes out with a garden hose and bat and kills all the gophers? etc...etc...

Defiant University of North Dakota Brings Back Fighting Sioux Nickname

There is such a thing called "reaching" and that is what we see here. Like a door to door vacuum cleaner salesman that see's the appropriateness of applying two extra layers of Hai Karate aftershave before making his rounds.

Nicki Minaj Performs an Exorcism on Herself, Speaks in Tongues & Levitates During Grammy Performance

No, no, no!...the dolphins finally got fed up with these giant fat-cat whales beaching themselves and getting all of the attention so they decided to join the occupy fad and created the "occupy the beach" movement.

The crabs were said to be grinning from claw to claw as the dolphins were being consumed.

Why Are Hundreds of Dolphins Dead on Peruvian Beaches?

Either that or some whale cut an awful, awful fart off the coast of Galapagos from eating some bad krill (after which the whale gently apologized) The thing was so stinky that the dolphins' only conclusion was that life had no meaning.

Yeah, now that I think about it, that's probably what happened.

A lot of people throw the word Fascist around to merely describe an ugly form of government. It is shocking, however, to read Mussolini's Fascist Manifesto and discover how similar it is to aspects in our government today.

One of fascism's main points is the control on the people it exerts by the governments marriage to businesses and corporations, Obamacare being the latest example.

I saw a news story that they are banning smoking at NASCAR events except in designated areas...so the other non-smoking people can better enjoy the non-stop breathing of toxic exhaust fumes.

Announcer: "Here we go folks, 3 seconds left on the clock as Masters approaches the top of the key with the ball. Wait a minute folks, there he goes again, Lin snatches the ball from Masters hand exposing a chink in Masters armor and is driving erratically down the court, stops short of the key, and shoots. It's a three pointer folks!

That's the end of the game folks. Lin has railroaded the Barons once again! I have to squint to even see what's just happened here! Wanton disregard for ball handling by Masters! Lin's chop sticks it to them again and gives the Barons a second take-out in the last month in the last seconds of the game.

Boy! the laundry list of accomplishes by Lin lately has given the Barons' a season that can only be described as sweet and sour!"

Here's the Deal With Reporting Guidelines on Jeremy Lin From the Asian American Journalists Association **(By the way, I like Chinese very much :)**

My, My come to find out that not only do we find out that Rush wasn't picking on an innocent young girl, but now we discover that she's also a Feminazi...don't Rush's advertisers who bailed out look silly now!! LOL

A reasonable company should know they aren't going to gain anything if they publicly abandon Rush's show but instead they will indeed lose the patronage of millions of Rush fans. I am one of those millions who have suspended or canceled any relationship with companies that have left his show...I don't like doing business with weak and sickly companies that empower the political correctness agenda.

These people were referred to by other tribes of the day as the Gunyalo or "Goons" but most notably as the original "nut jobs" because they only ate whole nuts, shells and all as they were too stupid to crack the shells.

They were known to only have 4 words in their vocabulary, "uk, um, do, fu" (left,right,up,down).

One day in 9,534 BC one of them stood up and said "Uk" and they all just walked into the ocean and were never seen again.

'Red Deer Cave' People May Be New Human Species

How awesome God is! Even though he wiped out the world with Noah's flood, he made sure that the dead dinosaurs and vegetation would be combined and pressurized underground, giving us a holistic and natural source of fuel because the "tropical paradise" that was the World, was going bye-bye.

Gee wiz, the tornado was so talented and tricky that it opened the back door of the bus and then slammed it shut!

Watch From Inside a School Bus as Deadly Indiana Tornado Strikes

Apr 4, 2012 5:15 am I think what they should have done is lowered a dog down by tying a rope onto its hind legs and when the dog got to the boy yell "fetch" so the dog would grab hold of the boys shirt and then they could lift them both out.

iPhone Used to Help Rescue Toddler Stuck in a Well

Apr 27, 2012 6:14 am

"The strongest reason for people to retain the right to keep and bear arms is, as a last resort, to protect themselves against tyranny in government." -- (Thomas Jefferson)

May 2, 2012 6:38 am

Amazing that so many people across the world actually want a tyrannical Government to make their lives miserable...I guess that matches how they already feel about themselves. I think it's that simple.

Oct 31, 2013 7:40 am

The first part was a beautiful ascent and flight over the majestic prairies on the wings of an eagle, but the last part is the eagle getting shot and doing a barrel roll down and through a grove of trees to the ground...all the while passing gas.

What Happens When a Champion Beatboxer Meets a Violinist?

May 12, 2015 5:08 am

If this guy were to win the next Presidency or Hillary for that matter, we will know for an absolute certainty that fix is in place by some very, very insidious powers. It will unmistakably, and almost literally, establish the line in the sand that separates the Government from the People and erases any doubts.

Megyn Kelly Presses Jeb Bush on Common Core Critics: 'Are They Wrong?'

You know, it's just incredible that Satan has managed to position a certain kinky sex act as a determination of a society's moral and doing so by the anti-Christs that have somehow worked their way into power positions in our country.

While ordinary citizens have been busy with their occupations, evil people have been busy boring their way into the woodwork. Look at the utter, utter chaos that will come if the Supreme court does something so stupid and so immature as to actually take serious...some group of peoples' kinky sex life. Because what about: S&M people Swingers Role reversal Players Bestiality Aficionados infantilists etc... I don't think that very many people have thought about what is going to happen when the standard of equal protection under the law is asserted with regard to all of these other peoples' kinky sex lives.

It's just stupid kinky sex and these people with the maturity of 7th graders are seemingly running the show. Dianne Sawyer is sitting poised in a lovey blue dress across from the President of the most powerful country in history and with a straight face asks a most important and pressing question " Mr. President, I'd like to ask you about how you feel about these dudes' kinky homo style sex life"

Let's see here. "Imagine there's no Heaven" Well, you just experienced it in real life Friday...like it?

Watch As Pianist Pays a Touching Tribute to Victims of Parisian Attacks Outside Theater

Hillary married up to the Trailer Park Trash class but now she's gotten old. It's time to change her name to Madge, give her a heavy eyebrow pencil and orange lipstick then give her that long coveted job as a waitress at the run down truck stop on the outskirts of town. She can then joke with the boys about never having had much sex in her life as the ashes fall from her cigarette into their coffee.

'I Will Not Stop Talking About This': Fox News Contributor Unleashes On 'Fake-Feminist' Clinton

CHAPTER 2

FEBRUARY 2016

Jan 1, 2016 9:02 am

I'm not saying that everybody is either on one side or the other but the only war being waged in this country is this; Christ vs anti-Christ I don't believe that politics is what divides this country. It's disguised to look that way but what we are witnessing in these days is an full blown assault by Satan to take down a Christian Nation.

Jan 17, 2016 7:07 am

Well, it kinda sounds like someone having an argument with the Lord...if that is so, do you think that you will win? And if you win, what do you plan to do with all of the stars (the ones in space)?

Jan 28, 2016 7:06 am

Do you have gas? A little pressure, bloating and sometimes burning sensations? Then go ahead, let it go! With gusto and fervency! Fart! Blow your tank and fart proudly!

'Like a Missile': N.J. Garbage Truck Explodes, Rips Hole Through Home, Damages Others

Feb 6, 2016 5:24 am

Folks, the only true outsiders are Trump and Carson...period. I believe Trump will go viciously at what he says (in particular what he promises in public) he will do because of his ego and reputation and more importantly because he is half German and Germans are a tenacious bunch...we just now need to hear his litmus test for judges in public. You have to think about this, would Trump allow all of the media to make fun of him for not doing what he said he would do?

Feb 6, 2016 5:57 am

The only two devastating elements that can permanently undo this country and bring it to another civil war is the Supreme Court loaded left and an electorate loaded left, third world voters.

Feb 7, 2016 5:38 am

What in the Sam Dickens do you expect? Trump, Cruz and Carson are not very good at attending political prom queen coronations. People who have actually done physical things in their life and have tangible results to show for it, are more baffled by venues organized by people who only make laws for a living.

Feb 9, 2016 8:00 am

It's amazing to see how many people look to politicians as some kind of savior. I want a dude that's going to go in there with a big axe and start swinging away at intricately designed social structure of human failure called politics. A pretty, smooth and sweet politician. An articulate one. A really, really smart one...one who you give permission to make decisions for your life, I want nothing to do with.

For those of you who don't know, every soldier who served his Country was a dirty, rotten, cussing, tobacco spitting, mean SOB that secured your liberty...commonly referred to a man of valor.

Feb 9, 2016 8:18 am

People who are not governed by the Lord can be ruled by anyone.

That looked like it was produced by a 9th grade drama class with a super 8 camera, a $200 budget and a bag of snickers minis that everyone got an equal portion of. After the final cut, each of the participants got a pack of Double Mint gum as a participation trophy.

Surprise Donald Trump Movie Drops One Day After New Hampshire Victory — and You'll Never Guess Who Plays Him

Well, she's noisy. But just as long as she doesn't crap on the floor, I guess we'll let her play human for a little while longer.

Hillary Clinton Literally Starts Barking Like a Dog During Campaign Rally

There's only one reason why libs don't like guns or even the sight of one and that is because it's only weapons that have defeated them in past, starting with the Revolutionary War, and it's the only thing standing in the way of their desire to destroy this Christian nation now or in the future. The only real war that has ever been fought on Earth is that between Christians and anti-Christs...everything else has been battles.

Be honest, have you ever been sitting around with the guys talking and acting the caveman when all of the sudden a woman walks in the room...does that suddenly change the atmosphere? The desire to put women in combat with men is to disrupt and prevent camaraderie...one of the MOST important elements of combat.

Now ask yourself, how come no one has ever suggested separate female combat units? How come they always have to be mixed in with men if they are so able to do the same things? Ask women, what would be so wrong about top to bottom female units? Why not give them their own Carrier group that is entirely staffed from the top Commanders all the way down to the AA's? With NO guys? Why not?

Navy SEAL Who Shot Osama bin Laden Shocks Fox Host with Opinion on Women in Combat

Bruce, I think that you need to just go back and return those taters and get your money back. You shouldn't let yourself get so out of control, kinky and horny.

Caitlyn Jenner Says She's 'Gotten More Flak' for Being Conservative Than for Being Transgender

Radiocarbon 14 decay: Their "savior" Scientists are stuck with the fact that the rate of carbon 14 decay in our present day can only be established by looking at objects that we know FOR CERTAIN are X number of years old. For instance, we can walk back the age of an ancient piece of pottery by observing the materials used, any art work displayed, method of manufacture etc... So scientists take a manmade object that they can date back to ancient China, determine that it is about 3,000 years old, and say "Oh, the rate of carbon 14 decay is thus"

When they find a dinosaur bone they attribute that same rate of carbon 14 decay and determine that the bone must be much, much older.

Here's the problem: They don't know for CERTAIN the rate of decay at 6,000 years because there is literally nothing to compare it to...we don't have a manmade object or any living thing that old, so nobody knows.

Here's the answer: When God cursed the earth, the structure of living things rapidly descended...that is until God ceased its decay or we would have all been long gone. Observe the rate decline in the ages of historical figures in the Bible.

I like how the Rino thinks twice about ramming it again "And don't you ever come back! Or I'll ram you again!...Oh, my head hurts. What the heck is that thing made of anyway?"

Video Shows the Moment 3,100-lb. Rhino Violently Rams Tourists' Vehicle

I just thought of something...Trump/ Pres. Cruz/ Supreme Court.

Trump is not going to get tricked into a boring policy detail debate...this is exactly how idiots in the past have won...by being the biggest BS policy promise makers.

'Now He's Repeating Himself': Watch What Happens When Rubio Repeatedly Demands Trump Lay Out His Plan on Health Care

Now, examine this...how these stupid little TYPICAL arguments of traditional campaigns try to rise up. Really? We want weeks of being lulled to zombie status watching the media pour over the details of a stack of tax returns?

'Release Them Tomorrow': Cruz Calls on Trump to Publish His Tax Returns Immediately

Now Rubio's strategy is to try and imitate Trump?

CHAPTER 3

MARCH 2016

When Trump say's that he loves the poorly educated he's speaking about the people coming out of college...he's going after the youth vote.:)

We are not electing a pastor...we are hiring a hit man, a gun slinger...Pale Rider. Yeah, might not be pretty but it's going to be a rough job to reverse the power of the Political Ruling Class.

Looky, stop begging for compassion. We are sick and tired of people who wear their kinky sex lives on their sleeves and expect everyone else to bow down to it. Think of this, if a politician uses the term "gay" on TV and you then ask them to describe that sex act, would they do it?

I think Judge Napolitano said that it's a felony if she only just gave the dude that set up her server the state dept. pass code...something along the lines of treason.

Mar 10, 2016 6:25 am

Oh, they discussed it...until they concluded that by doing so it would end up at the Supreme Court. That is, evidence would be brought forth!!

AG Lynch Testifies: Justice Dept. Has 'Discussed' Civil Legal Action Against Climate Change Deniers

Mar 10, 2016 6:34 am

Didn't the polls say that the coughing, rusty chainsaw voiced Hillary was going to win Michigan? And the news hosts were saying "Oh my, dear me...lets have another one of those cookies. Isn't that something else?"

Mar 10, 2016 6:45 am

Let's examine an equal application of this judges logic: Guy gets drunk and breaks into another guys house: Judge says drunk guy not responsible because he say's "Oh gee, I thought it was my friend's house"

Guy gets drunk and rapes a woman and guy says "Gee, I thought she was my wife!"

What says you Judge?

Man Who Shot Home Intruder Never Thought It Would Amount to This

Mar 10, 2016 6:51 am

Don't be a sissy Ben! A real man should never get caught, especially in public, talking like a girl complaining that some horrible, hairy, beastly man was shoving you around. I think you should take a year off and do some lumber jacking or something.

Breitbart Editor-At-Large to Trump: Fire Your Campaign Manager for Roughing Up Reporter

Yeah, lots of cameras! Come on media, if it really happened, you should have lots of proof! I thought when this first came out that it was off to the side or something...not in the middle of a crowd.

Breitbart Spokesman Quits As Video Emerges Appearing to Show Trump Manager Grabbing Reporter

I have always wondered this, the Supreme court said "yeah, it's your body, you can do with it what you want" But how was that right extended to anyone else...like a Doctor or some lady in a rundown apartment with a coat hanger that performs abortions?

Heavens to Mergatroyd, I hope that all of this bitterness between Trump and Cruz supporters is basic trash talk between rival "sports teams" and that after the cage fight (which is and should be very nasty) is over that we all join up and demonstrate a mutual respect and brotherhood and band together for the greater cause.

We all like to see sportsmanship after a tough football game and see the players shaking each other's hands, let's commit to act likewise.

Is anyone else freaked out by Kelly's robotron personage? She comes off exactly like robotic hologram like reporters in futuristic science fiction movies. I keep waiting for the moment when a staffer has to rush to her while they are live and has to replace a circuit panel in the back of her head or something.

Mar 16, 2016 4:58 am

I would like to ask if anyone out there has the money and means to create a new party...American Party would make for a perfect name and this for the purpose of a political lifeboat. Both Jeb and John have both creepily said "Donald Trump will never be president" with that political establishment confidence because THEY ARE PLANNING FOR A BROKERED CONVENTION and Trump or Cruz won't be the one chosen. The combined voters of Cruz and Trump will make sure...YOU ESTABLISHMENT REPUBLICANS WILL NOT BE PRESIDENT...PERIOD!!

Mar 16, 2016 5:03 am

Hey! Trump won the North Mariana Islands too. What's wrong with including them in the results? Geesh! Mariana never gets any respect!

Mar 17, 2016 5:09 am

I'm thinking that Trump would nominate Cruz and the Senate would confirm to get him out of their midst. I'm hoping that deal gets struck between Trump and Cruz as the convention draws near.

Mar 17, 2016 6:46 am

I knew a guy from Topeka who put his willy under a press thinking it would stretch it out and make it bigger. He now makes a living unlocking car doors with it as a "Slim-Jim"

Mar 18, 2016 5:05 am

He had "glass breakers" in his back pack...you mean...rocks?

Mar 18, 2016 5:21 am

They say marriage is like a tornado. It starts out with lots of sucking and blowing and by the time it's over, you lose all your possessions except for your pickup.

Mar 18, 2016 5:34 am

What would have made the act even more entertaining would be if he was wearing a hat with un-popped popcorn glued to it.

'Everything Just Went Crazy': Shock Video Shows Stunt Performer Catch Fire During High School Rally

Mar 23, 2016 5:33 am

The Pledge of Allegiance is not just some cute thing kids do at school, it ought and did mean something serious. If a Muslim, not just an Arab, but a Muslim was practicing Sharia as such in the early days of our Country he would have been kicked out of the Country!

Muslims are by the very teachings of their cult, expressly anti-American! Same goes for people like Bill Ayers, Black Panthers and squirrely white libtards who burn and stomp on the American Flag protesting our Country. And for that matter, Bak Abunga too! It's not just a Republican/ Democrat thing anymore. We are being invaded by Anti-Americans!

Mar 24, 2016 5:54 am

I hear a lot about some coming Civil War 2...well, we are in the middle of it.

Whereas this Country has always been inhabited by a vast majority of Christians or at least agnostics respectful of Christians, we are now under a full blown assault by anti-Christians and they want nothing more than to destroy us. You see, Satan hates the fact that of all of the horror in history, all the war and violence, all the brutality, all of the poverty, America, a Christian founded and populated Country shines as the opposite.

People that live in this Country that are not Christians are and have been becoming more and more ANTI and that's much different than being indifferent. Trump supporters are OK if Cruz wins, but to Evangelicals, Trump is perceived as a hired gun for the expressed purpose of stopping the importation of a permanent voting block of anti-Christians.

Mar 24, 2016 6:09 am

Isn't that cute, He's feeling left out so Abunga is having his own cute little political campaign for President of ISIS.

Obama on Socialism Versus Capitalism: 'Just Choose From What Works'

Mar 25, 2016 5:15 am

Doesn't this just show exactly how unmindful the people in Congress have become?

Even after a couple of months of very serious threats by the voters and leading pundits that an option other than Cruz or Trump WILL cause mass revolt, they still are still arrogantly dancing with their delusional thoughts.

Let me try to explain this to you brick-heads in Congress. We now know that you only arrogantly Represent the ones who financed your political life. It is now VERY DIFFERENT! Yes, revolt, yes Tea Party, Yes Trump or Cruz, Yes, DON'T GET IN OUR WAY!!

Mar 25, 2016 5:33 am

Specifically, he never sides with anyone during the Republican Primary's...he lets that play out. I might add though, that even though we basically have gridlock now, look at what Obingo (or whatever his name is) has managed to do on his own, turning the Military into a gay bathhouse, an invasion of third world minded future voters and the strengthening of our sworn enemies. Let's be noble sportsman and let's be wise and not let them win... Trump or Cruz.

Caller Repeatedly Asks Limbaugh Why He's Not 'Warning' Listeners About Trump – Here's His Answer

Mar 25, 2016 5:50 am

Every time I hear her, I have this flash back to Fred Flintstones' Mother In-Law but with a shrill...

Newly Discovered Email Contradicts Clinton's Claim About Private Server

Mar 25, 2016 6:16 am

I appreciate where the Cruz supporters are coming from but who would you hire to do some remodeling to your home, a Pastor who might be unable to get the job done or a bonafide guy with a successful reputation? I'll gladly vote for Cruz or Trump...GLADLY!

Mar 25, 2016 6:30 am

We are not hiring a pastor, we are hiring a hit man. And hit men are about as pretty as the butt crack of a plumber but they get the work done.

Mar 29, 2016 5:04 am

What Unbako (Or whatever the weirdos name is) was trying to do was to keep them from comparing Capitalism to Socialism...because they are already in Socialism and if they start comparing them there is a chance that they might have a change of mind.

White House Tells TheBlaze What Obama Really Meant in Talking Socialism Versus Capitalism

Mar 29, 2016 5:36 am

The reason Trump poll numbers have high negatives is that there are Republicans that are willing to stay home if he gets the nod. These Republicans are, most literally, (insert your favorite Republican candidate here)/ Hillary supporters...period. If you stay home this year, you will be acting perfectly as Satan desires.

Of all of the kinky sex acts that people engage in, why is it that the kinky sex act called kinky same sex has somehow become a personage? And why is it that this kinky sex life has to become so prominent and protected?

I don't see swingers running around crying for rights. I don't see role players, bdsm, latex etc…asking everyone else to bow down to them.

I can hear it now "How dare you say that! It's so much more than peener in butt!"

Which, to that I say, what other differentiating factor is there?

CHAPTER 4

APRIL 2016

One of the quickest ways to break tempered glass is to use a scratch awl or an automatic center punch (Any hard sharp point), poking directly at it.

I'm gonna name my private lake "Hey freak, you can't have our country lake" Change that name.

Initiative Aims to Eliminate Offensive and Racist Geographical Titles from Washington State

The wonderful potato.

I'm just hoping that after a nominee is selected that Conservative/ Republicans strongly unite behind the winner. If we don't, Satan will be rolling on floor laughing as a once great Country elects our own enemy...once again.

"What?...what? I don't understand one syllable of what you are saying I'M A TIGER... HUNGRY!

I'm telling ya, all that whispering has me thinking of bacon sizzling...plus... those nice eggs! Alright, I've had enough... BREAKFAST!"

'Tiger Whisperer' Dies After Mauling at Florida Zoo

And it's exactly why Liberals are always forcing PC trough blame. Liberalism is a God-despising hateful soul.

I easily predicted that their choice would be Trump...they come out of prison hating Government and forced social structure. Hillary's Maude like voice, bulging eyes, jerking neck and craggy pointing finger makes them want to freak'n RUN!...Like any man!

We Talked to Five Ex-Felons Whose Voting Rights Have Been Restored — They All Plan to Vote for the Same Person

I love Ted Cruz...everything about the guy. If he would have won the nomination, I would have happily voted for him but I'm a Trump supporter and here's why.

We are getting schnookered [emphasis added]. All of us, left and right. The only way to socialize or communize a great and mighty Godly Nation is to divide it first...while simultaneously putting it back together into a tidy New Order.

Here we go, first the Left gets a law made that has a blanket effect on all, offending the Right.

The left again deals a blow, the Right retaliates and wins. The left protests the Right defends. The left wins, the Right protests. All the while, the mother sow that has everybody rushing to it for milk (or political victories) getting bigger and bigger and ever more important.

The fallout remaining is an all-powerful Government imposing a bleak and tasteless neutrality of Political Social Order. That's why is difficult to discern the difference between Democrats and Republicans on Capitol Hill and they are viciously defensive of their profound power. As recent as the early eighties in SW Nebraska the drinking age was 20 in Neb, 19 in Kan, and 18 in CO (3.2 beer) Now...all uniform.

This is just one tiny example. Think about how much freedom of individuality has been trickling away to Political Social Order. Uniform, uniform, uniform for all! The Government should be nothing more than a room full nerds in black glasses sitting in front of little tables, a tablet of paper and pencil.

Apr 29, 2016 6:12 am

Donald Trump breaks the fancy dignity and allure of Political Social Order and undermines its power. Think of what's happened. Something as dumb as a drag queen wanting to take a poop in a woman's restroom in Frisco is now a matter of great National importance!

Meanwhile, the Great Sow is thinking and will be dispensing it's solution in time...and we still stand divided when the solution comes...the Sow, even bigger and more important.

It ought to be legal to have a homo parade in Frisco but serious jail time maybe in Nebraska, or as each locality prefers. That's liberty...and individuality and it would be hard to discern the all mighty power of a centralized Government in that scenario.

Let the earthquakes crack where they do and let the rain caress the oceans of wheat on the high plains. We won't demand any of their rubble and they can't demand any bread.

You may have never been in business before and don't what it means to place the most effectual people in areas that need it most, disregarding pedigrees. Sure I know that Cruz is a born again, principled Constitutionalist! but as President I fear that he will get as far with these establishment people as he did in the Senate.

Think of this; It's the Supreme Court that has made two recent decisions that has had more social and financial impact on the Country than all of the legislation rendered since the goofball obangy (or whatever his name is) was elected. If Trump wins, there will be a huge clarion call to select Cruz to the Supreme Court vacancy. That doesn't get us just 8 possible years of principles in Government, that gives us 40! In the place that has the most effect!!!!

For now, we need someone who WILL get the wall built. We have to get the SCOTUS leaning right again! I don't believe that Cruz will be able to muster the support to build the wall...just simple.

CHAPTER 5

MAY 2016

Folks, I love Ted Cruz but if Trump wins, at least, why not give him a chance? Trump has that ego and that "German Tenacity" If he makes a public stance and especially a promise to do something he's really, really going to fight to make that happen. He better know, if he starts drifting to the center and starts "growing" HE'S TOAST in the general.

The summery is that he won't let himself be embarrassed by publicly failing to do what he says he will do. For those of you that hate him...just wait a second till after the convention. Cruz supporters do really still have all the power in this election because without Cruz supporters, HE"S TOAST. He won't say it now, but just wait. After the nomination he will shower praise on Cruz and he will indicate that Cruz would be a perfect choice to fill the vacancy at the SCOTUS which, really, is where Cruz can be way more of a blessing to the country long after a Trump Presidency.

Trump WILL assemble a cabinet dream team involving many of the other candidates. Christie, AG, Carley, EPA, Carson, VP or surgeon General, Rubio, VP or Secretary of State, Cruz, Supreme Court. Remember, he has to bring along the Cruz wing...you can still win the argument with Trump as President because he won't get caught dead being seen as a liar and a failure.

May 4, 2016 5:58 am

I often wonder if indeed, these are the last days. The Bible teaches that in the last days the contrasts between those guided by the Holy Spirit and those guided by Satan will become even more stark. So, who's motivating you? Those who stay home, vote for Hillary or a third party candidate are acting as the very hand of Satan in putting this Country "away". It will be you that forever loads the Supreme Court Left. You can stand in the future soup lines and complain about any and everyone else but it will be only you're doing. The crappy part is that Satan won't even reward you.

May 4, 2016 6:14 am

Mr. Levin...settle down a little bit. I love ya man but give this a a little room...you're gonna really like his Supreme Court nomination! We're gonna have a wonderful Constitutionalist in the place where it matters most!

May 4, 2016 6:17 am

Oh, just to add...nobody thought Trump would win the GOP nomination. He'll mop the floor with Hillary...there's no way that crooked hag is gonna win if everyone gets behind Trump...each having their own reason why.

May 5, 2016 6:04 am

As Trump will put Cruz at the top of the list for SCOTUS, Cruz fans will have something of their own election...something to vote for.

May 6, 2016 6:34 am

I understand what's going on here and like always, the political class has good American people fighting with each other again. Forget ideology. These current political elites are absolutely horrified that Trump will destroy their power and corruption. When any current or former Republican Politician comes out against Trump, keep in mind that the only thing they really care about is clutching their bags of money that they got from there donors and lobbyists.

I can see opposing the war but then after we go in, you're obligated to support our effort as a Country.

I happened to be watching that last night and it quickly turned into journalistic eroticism. I about barfed and had to switch over until her show was done.

Michael Moore Reveals to Megyn Kelly What 'Worries' Him Most About Clinton: 'My Fear Is...'

To you good folks that are negative about Trump please keep in mind that he is at war with the same corrupt Politicians that care more about their lobbyists than they do, or did, about us.

Good for you N.C.!!! An example for every other State. What is the centralized Fed's gonna do if we all stand our ground?!!

N.C. House Speaker Defies Justice Department's Order on Bathroom Law: 'We Will Take No Action'

Something to remember about Trump is that he grew up in the midst of laborers working on his Fathers construction jobs. His business is constructive by its very nature. Constructive! It makes money and employs people! They are nice places to go to.

And now to know something about Politicians. So-called "Conservatives" in politics toss out the red meat to the constituents and after they get in office, the only thing they care about is supporting Wall Street, Bankers and insurance companies...that's where their dough comes from. Wall Street has nothing to do with our economy. That's why even though the economy hasn't bugged since 2008, the stock market has gone up. Wall Street is just a casino. They don't care if Carrier goes to Mexico and people lose their jobs, they only care about the bets they made on Carrier.

These people who want to start a third party know that it would only get Hillary elected because that would protect the current system that both parties are entrenched in.

May 6, 2016 7:52 am

LOLOLOLOL...I love this guy, Trump! You ain't gonna butter him up and certainly not buy him off.

Former Mexican President Vicente Fox Apologizes to Trump — Now, See How Trump Responds When Asked If He Has a 'Message' for Him

May 6, 2016 7:55 am

Bye, bye little sniveling brat...go get a job and do something constructive instead of nursing off of your lobbyists.

Paul Ryan: I'm 'Just Not Ready' to Support Trump, Despite Him Being Presumptive GOP Nominee

May 7, 2016 6:59 am

I say we need some patience here. I'm confident that Trump will give conservative-conservatives plenty to vote for in the coming month...because if he doesn't, even those who voted for him will reject him.

I would like to provide some things to think about regarding Trump. I was talking with a friend that was trying to make a point that Trump has no details when it comes to how he's going to solve specific problems. My answer was this: "You know that I'm a Master Upholsterer, If someone came into my shop with an old Queen Ann Tufted sofa that needed refinishing and the springs needed to be totally re-tied, wouldn't it be strange that the customer would start drilling me on all the details of how I'm going to accomplish all of that? You have to either trust me based on my reputation or go somewhere else."

"The same is true of Trump. We need a practical and business like solution...not a political one. Draw the parallel, Trump in the Oval Office and Trump sitting at his board room table.

Trump as President will have under his authority all of the various bureaus and agencies. All of their waste and even more importantly, all of their un-elected powers of making laws and regulations. Trump looking at all of that nonsense as if he's sitting at his boardroom table will not, in fact could not, let all of that continue. We're talking about the IRS, BLM, EPA, Department of Education and on and on.

Have you noticed, the tons of pressure on society by so, so much Socialism imposed that is not the result of laws being passed? We don't hardly even debate specific laws anymore because we are too busy being attacked on all sides by un-elected whatevers. Trump literally won't stand for it.

Really? Full grown adults in positions of power taking time during their day to empower kinky 14 year old boys masturbating while wearing their Mothers dress? Really? What horny perverts LOL

White House Spox Says Obama Admin's Transgender Bathroom Directive Is Just 'Guidance,' Not a 'Threat'

May 14, 2016 7:15 am

Businesses that face similar situations need only tell the customer that they simply don't know how to do it. Don't refuse, just say "We don't have the knowledge and experience to do that...we don't know how to do that. Sorry, we don't have the ability to do everything on the planet."

'Dramatic Intervention': Christian Bakers Who Are in Court After Refusing to Make 'Support Gay Marriage' Get a Major Boost

May 17, 2016 5:29 am

I remember reading a quote one time that went something like this "If all of the people in the world demanding world peace were to gather together, their first order of business would be to take a vote on how to kill everyone that disagreed with them"

May 18, 2016 6:24 am

Have they taken in the fact that there are more physical assaults against officers by these new self-entitled spoiled brats that grew up with no discipline?

May 19, 2016 5:14 am

Remember when everyone thought "Oh my, a really rich guy for President?" when Romney was running? Well now, by contrast to Trumps success, Romney looks like a janitor and that's the real reason why his panties are in a wad. He lost his mantle as "The smartest businessman who can solve all of the nation's problems".

May 19, 2016 5:29 am

You know, it's pretty simple. There has to be something terrible and horrible going on in the heart (or lack thereof) of anyone voting for Hillary. There has to be something terrible and dark going on in the mind of anyone who allows Hillary to win just out of spite. If we have that many awful people in this Country that Hillary wins...ufta.

I have always thought about how lame and drab and uninspiring, in appearance, the GOP conventions were. Remember that wide side shot of McCain alone on that huge, plain blue stage yelling "Help me, Help me!" There wouldn't be one darn thing wrong with having some TV professionals involved in making a television event look appealing to the viewers. I say let Trump have at it! We are just going to have to move beyond looking like a bunch of people in black glasses, plaid suits and broomsticks duct taped to our backs.

This is fun...taking the Country back. It's fun!

They'll get on board as soon as they figure out that they are missing out on the party that the party is having!

Poll Shows Republican Voters Want Party Leaders to Unite Behind Trump — and By a Big Margin

In the remote Vermont countryside, Bernie pulls into the gravel driveway in his 1944 Mercedes Grosse almost as slow as he can walk. A weathered and weary hand pushes open the handmade wooden door...it creaks, of course.

"Hey you, I'm home!" He hangs his vintage wool top coat on the railroad spike that he had driven into wall in 1963. Jane pretends not to hear him but grudgingly acknowledges his presence as she turns to put supper on the table and mutters "Food's ready, sit down"

They comfort themselves before the wood block table adorned with a single homemade candle and tattered cloth napkins. Bernie reaches to the loaf of bread only two hours old and tears off a warm piece and thoughtfully dips it into his bowl. "Split Pea soup?...without ham? How come everybody else gets split pea soup with ham but I don't get split pea soup with ham? How come I don't get the ham?!!"

Jane slowly looks up, chewing carefully to avoid that certain painful tooth. "You're Jewish, you moron!" The only cat in the house that was sitting nearby eyeing the feast realizing that no scraps would be coming from that table, yet again, gets up and quietly strolls away into the darker parts of the room.

May 20, 2016 5:41 am

Does anyone remember Zap comics from the 70's? Well, that's the Obama administration.

May 25, 2016 5:49 am

After his speech, which was great and a lot of fun, Trump looked out the window at the chaos going on and remarked " Look at that Cory, I don't even have to pay anybody for visual aids to make my point about the wall!"

New Mexico Mayhem: Chaos Unfolds As Protests Break Out At Trump Rally

May 25, 2016 6:37 am

For who are still against Trump, may I ask you something...be honest, are you still addicted to the dressed up platitudes that phony politicians have been feeding the public over the years? Are you still fooled into thinking that it's possible that beautiful sentiments can fix the country's problems?

The Government is not a sanctuary. It's not church. It's not wise. It's not thrifty and 90% of the people in it care absolutely nothing about you. The Government is a damn thing and it's gonna take one tough, crude, no holds barred son of a buck to go in there and start swinging that sledge hammer around and taking out the walls and under-girding.

The things that need to be done and the eventual rewards achieved, as always, are only reserved for those who are willing to sweat. And that may not look so pretty.

Ok, Boss Maude (likened of Boss Hog) you really got Trump that time, huh? You really think that people want to listen to an annoying leaf blower with rusty, squealing bearings all the time. If you're a man and you vote for this thing, you will be officially banned from watching John Wayne movies from now on.

Clinton: Trump 'Could Bankrupt America Like He's Bankrupted His Companies'

It amazes me how this dude has spent his adult life so ardently pursuing a fake identity. He actually tries to outdo himself at being fake to a point where one starts to wonder if the only thing he's really after is that he thinks if he try's hard enough, he will one day become a glorious plastic statue (recycled plastic, of course)

Al Gore Declines to Endorse Either Clinton or Sanders, Says He Will Support Nominee

It's pretty impressive how absolutely consistent a person can be for so many years. I don't think that you're gonna be able to trip Rush up anytime soon...the more people try, the wiser he gets.

Listen to Limbaugh's Response When a Persistent Caller Presses Him to Endorse Trump

If it ain't in the Constitution it's for the States to decide...period. Let each State pay the price for their decisions.

If a State wants to start masturbating along with everyone's particular sexual kinks then let then be only ones who have to pay for it. These people want it to be a national issue because if they get everyone to agree that their particular sexual kink is OK then that absolves them from being sexually perverted...which is just dumb because everyone is a sinner. Are we going to just keep doing this for every sin that everyone has?

It's a 6 year old child's mentality that we are capable of using stupid humanistic tricks to avoid God's Laws.

Here's Trump's Response When Asked What's the 'Right Thing' To Do About Transgender Bathrooms

May 27, 2016 6:56 am

Well, why don't the libtards make a special about the Clintons? As the opening scene music they could use "Liar" by the Sex Pistols.

May 27, 2016 7:24 am

I'm over 50, not married, no kids anywhere and I'm not offended. I'm offended by smelly diapers though...and arrogant thought police reporters.

Washingtonian Editor: People Shouldn't Say 'Start a Family' Because It's Offensive

May 27, 2016 7:35 am

It would be the greatest political event ever! I hope they do it because, most importantly, it pronounces the American political rebellion of 2016, on both sides, against the elite political ruling class. They would fill an arena, bust all of the dress down norms and Hillary would look like such a bum...the last pathetic remnant of the ruling class.

MSNBC Host: Proposed Debate With Sanders Is a 'Hat Trick, Grand Slam and Slam Dunk' For Trump

In one fell swoop, Mr. Rubio matures by 10 years...now Big Marco!

Rubio Does a 180: I Will Attend GOP Convention, Speak on Behalf of Trump if Asked

I wish that the Republicans in all offices across the Country would just start asserting that they aren't going to legislate peoples private kinky sex lives.

At least just say that you don't want to make children sick at breakfast time by talking about hairy adults' sex lives.

In these days, either the Holy Spirit is guiding a person or Satan is.

To understand the mindset of someone who embraces tyrannical forms of Government needs only to look at spouse abusers. Despite all reality, they somehow think that they can abuse love out of people...which is the same for American Liberalism.

That little skip in the worlds' rotation last night was caused by two billion shot gun blasts of rice from the mouths of Chinese seeing this.

Chinese Detergent Ad Gets Over 2 Million Views in One Day — for All the Wrong Reasons

May 28, 2016 6:51 am

This might be a little off topic but it made me think of something that I always thought would be a great idea. Lure manufacturing companies back to the U.S. by creating enterprise zones in urban areas.

They would have to play a big role in developing parks, schools etc... but operate tax free for a period. The only thing is that the Libs would say "Oh, big business making slaves again" because the Dems need the ghettos. Trump loves to develop, it might be a good effort to put forth.

May 28, 2016 7:12 am

One who um have tent post, pee by tent, one who um have beaver pelt, pee behind tree.

Indian Tribe Passes New Transgender Bathroom Policy — and Activist Group Is Left 'Very Sad and Disappointed'

May 31, 2016 5:32 am

For the most part there are smart people, people who can remember facts, and then there are intelligent people. This dude is not the latter.

Famed Physicist Stephen Hawking Weighs in on Trump: 'He's a Demagogue...'

CHAPTER 6

JUNE 2016

They thought it would never happen. As long as they verbally gave the public what the public wanted to hear, they could perpetually exist in their political bio-dome.

But now an unexpected horror this way comes as a dark and fatal cloud, not unlike that of the Pharaoh's self-induced plague, penetrates what was believed to be sanctuary. They were the entitled after all. The smartest ones by far and the only ones capable of keeping control of the unruly Americans, the debaucherous romance between the press and the political ruling class is exposed and rejected as an authority. The loudest wailing coming from the most guilty.

Never-Trumper Bill Kristol Is Eyeing This Conservative Lawyer For a Third-Party Run

Hmm...all the education. All the time and money spent for the study of voids. The smart will say "I must be superior, look at my math thingy"

The intelligent say "It's a common preoccupation of them that have the least of capabilities in the real world to live in one of their own creation"

First of all, Hillary ain't the one actually typing these out...some aide is. Second, Marco Rubio was still in quite a strong position in the primaries until he did something that absolutely wiped him out immediately…he tried to imitate **Trump. Have fun Crooked Hillary.**

'He's Trying to Scam America': Clinton Rips Page From Trump Playbook in Epic Twitter Rant Against Presumptive GOP Nominee

Trump should really point out the fact that she is trying to imitate him and the specific way she's doing it for the people who aren't very discerning.

As if his Presidency didn't prove his ineptitude enough, Obama seeks the assistance of Trump to better explain it. People who hate guns should never show up to trap shooting competitions.

I wonder what the heck is wrong with this little kid…did someone steal his pop-gun or something?

Mark Cuban Isn't So Sure Donald Trump Is a Fellow Billionaire

I wonder if the all the male liberals have considered the possibility that they are actually the virgins to be given to the radical Islamist's.

Those that get into a twist about Trump are just going to have to get used to not getting a daily fix of positive platitudes from politicians. If that's your kick then Hillary will sufficiently supply those for you but Trump isn't going to prematurely delve into topics that are months away from being on the plate.

It's time that the well-deserved women in the U.S. Military are given their own branch with air and sea divisions. Every female officer and every female service member transferred from the standard military and staff every position in their own branch. The dirty, nasty, dudes will just have to do without them in the regular military.

Newly Crowned Miss USA Is an Army Reservist. Check Out How She Responds When Asked About Women in Combat.

Jun 9, 2016 5:37 am

The Clinton's have a troubling secret that they are really fearing Trump might bring out. In the recent tell all book by Dolly Kyle, who had affairs with Bubba from way back, she describes how racist both Clintons are. They fear that all of the cross-validations from others will come out.

Jun 10, 2016 8:59 am

Doesn't that just comfort you anti-Trumps? Dear, dear...the big caring Liberals have come to your rescue and made you feel better? Kiss them back and let them wrap you in a fuzzy blanket. There, there... that naughty, naughty Trump won't ever hurt your dedicates anymore!

Jun 11, 2016 6:27 am

Well, if you all want to know how Hillary's crime spree started, I'll tell you.

It all started in a small, haphazardly arranged trailer park. Billy was sitting on their Mediterranean style couch with Hurculon fabric...orange plaid, I believe, and it was splitting along the patterns exposing the crumbling foam. They could never figure out what those yellow crumbs were that was always sticking to their polyester shirts. Billy had his arm around the portly neighbor girl who's trailer was situated perpendicular to theirs.

The Dukes of Hazard was on the TV that had a small pair of vice grips hanging from the channel changer...the knob had long ago been lost. Hillary was in the kitchen, dragging on a joint fashioned with green paper by the window with a fan in it. By the time she went into the living room, Billy was already in the back bedroom humping violently the now wide-eyed, freckled girl.

Hillary, sitting on the edge of the couch with her forearms on her knees, started to become engaged in the answer to life. Her mouth was agape and there was a membrane of saliva across her lips that moved in and out slowly.

Alas, never before had she witnessed such intelligence! And never before had she witnessed the most gleaming example of success and prosperity! It was at that point that she forever vowed to emulate her newly discovered hero...Boss Hog.

Jun 11, 2016 6:37 am

Oh, he will eventually endorse the Lady Who Wears Drapery As Clothes because he doesn't want to die crumpled next to a pine tree on the black slopes of a ski resort...knowing that the press would never question why in the heck an old man who barely gets around walking and has never skied before, was there.

Sanders Supporters Offer Surprising Responses When Asked to Consider Trump-Clinton Race

Jun 12, 2016 8:29 am

Hillary is now desperately heading to Orlando...to check cash registers for unattended money. Update at noon to see how much she found.

49 Killed in Orlando Night Club Massacre, Making It Worst Mass Shooting in American History

I love seeing Mr. Trump unscripted...always his best appeal. Reality is desperately needed in this country...yes, more important than social thoughts that never amount to more than people arguing.

You cannot actively suppress Christianity while simultaneously promoting humanism and making a god out of Government and expect something other than what the worst of humans are capable of dishing out.

Oh, that they won't be beguiled anymore, oh, that they rebel...our money! Power! Slipping away from our jagged and mossy fingernails...we, we just have to utter our dying words!

Trump Chastises Republican Party Leadership: 'Just Please Be Quiet'

When we look at anything in the world regarding plants and animals, the paradigm is that the best examples of any organism are the ones that pro-generate...not the mutants.

If some critter thought it necessary to change and adapt in order to keep its species going, and that change takes time, how did it keep surviving until it was complete? And then, why did it ever change or adapt if it was able to survive in the first place.

Show anywhere in the fossil records of a particular species a set of just 3 subsequent subtle adaptations or changes...a particular species now. How did the irregular and very, very deep valleys of the ocean come to be? Where in the Sam Hill did ALL of the water come from? How in the Sam Hill did plant matter mixed with animal matter get trapped beneath the crushing weight of the ocean floor?

Lastly, how come only Earth gets to have a nifty celestial clock that our rotation is in perfect synchronization with? If you can answer that short quiz with facts, then you will pass logic class and earn some credits. If not then you will be referred to the class of "Self-indulgent & wishful thinking as a way to assuage guilt" because feelings are not allowed in science class.

Most of us here have had the misfortune to be around an obnoxious or negative person once in a while...it fills the atmosphere with a depressing spirit. Now just imagine spending even one day with Hillary. It has to be exactly like being in the presence of some vicious drug lord or hanging around with Charles Manson. She has to be one of the most successful Sociopaths of all time.

The surest way to provide support for the self-righteous heart is for them to express seemingly untouchable moral platitudes. They believe that this isolates them from judgment...in their minds, their set of morals supersedes even the Lord's.

The United States, as the Founders well knew, came to be by the provenance of God. Our prosperity has been able to fund most of the world's evangelism...we are the hub of evangelism.

Without this Country, the Gospel would hardly make a whisper to the world. It's Satan's fervent desire to destroy us for that very reason. The Southern Baptist Convention here, has decided that emotional self- feel-good-ism is more important than protecting our freedom to share the Gospel. We are under a full blown attack and invasion of third world people who we know will always eventually vote for those very anti-Christs in our Country that are helping this invasion.

It might be the very key aspect of the apostasy of the Church to allow their own demise.

Hasn't God warned his people enough times throughout history about allowing the enemy to infest? A refresher course of the events throughout the Old Testament are very much warranted here!

Evolutionists, explain to this crowd how the Platypus came to be. An otter with a ducks bill, a mammal that lays eggs and is a mammal with venom in its talons.

For extra credit, explain the process whereby a beetle has developed two chambers in its rear end each filled with a separate, basically inert, chemical that when combined creates a burning acid when forced out of the back of the beetle with the aid of very specific mechanisms...meet the Bombardier Beetle.

Hillary Clinton walks into a bar with a bullfrog on her head. The bartender says " where in the heck did you get that thing?" The bullfrog says " Well, it all started out as a wart on my ass!"

For those who are never Trump. You may not like him but consider the credentials of those closest to him. First, do you really think that his two very bright and articulate sons are fakes?...either one of the two would alone make great candidates for any office. They wouldn't be out there supporting him if he was some closet lib or a nut.

Second, look at his political advisers and power supporters...do you think Jeff Sessions would support someone who's off the reservation? In November, if Trump hasn't at least partially won you over, at least go vote for the judges alone because after the election there will be only two crowds standing apart. Inactivity doesn't count, which one will you be standing in? Hillary's?

helo, i is a voter to the hilleri...i wents to da colege and iz most, most smart. i has self kofidens bekos obamama rubbed my nipplors reel nice. i no dat der is dum trumpets hear so i say sumpting, dees mexicos are even smartor dan you and me and we need more uz dem. obamapajma boy and the loud wart hog da call hilary is say so. beliVE me i iz moRe smert tan you iz.

Never has a candidate with the fervent support that Trump has ever lost and with Clinton barely winning the Democrat nomination, if she wins we will know the utterly heinous nature of the establishment. The only way she wins is if there is all out Republican/ Democrat fix. These ruling elites will be completely unaware of the physical, manifest revolt they will have on their hands.

All throughout the more rural parts of the Country, the older guys are always like this to young men...and young girls too. It's the way men are attempting to beef up the younger guys. It's meant to give them some hoo-ra. The thing is it's not going to come from some weasel dude. Johnny cash sang in a gospel song "A child won't hold a trembling hand" I'd like to see Badink Abinga (or whatever his name is) make a man out of a young boy.

British Actor Daniel Radcliffe Shares the Advice Donald Trump Gave Him When He Was 11

Sitting in the jail: " How in the world did we get caught, we worked on our women outfits all night?"

"Habib...look at our legs. We freaking forgot to shave our legs!"

Islamic State Terrorists Reportedly Use Disguises in Escape Attempt — and Their Chosen Outfits Should Get You Giggling

Jun 22, 2016 5:32 am

I see these days that Hillary is trying to play this refined, in control and measured politician. She's trying to hide the bawdy, mean old Mother-in-law voice but wait for the debates...he's gonna shred her!

Jun 22, 2016 5:40 am

Think of this, if Crooked Hillary were to win and other countries decided to attack with ICBM's or the like, Crooked Hillary's only thought would be "Oh, I bet I'll get a high up position when the enemy wins...I'm in bed with them after all."

Jun 24, 2016 5:38 am

The States against homosexual "marriage" should just simply change the name...there's nothing in the ruling that says the NAME has to be the same, just the FUNCTION

Hey, there's a motorcycle license and a CDL...different licenses but same function. . You see, that would drive people who do homosexual sex insane because it's not about the function, it's about undoing a Godly Country and Gods tenants.

Jun 24, 2016 6:27 am

Here is my solution for the need of low level migrant workers while keeping them away from being able to vote. The Migrant Billet System.

In the Military every rate (job) only has assigned a predetermined number of Billets (personnel). If you want to go into a certain rate you have to strike for it...sometimes waiting a while for a vacancy of Billets. We could use that same system with immigrants. Put 3 designated centers near the border...say, Florida, Texas and California. Let every employer who needs migrant help go before a board, giving reason for Billets to be assigned for their company/

farm. After Billets are assigned , There is a specific identity for each individual Billet...its own number etc... Next, we announce thus many Billets and offer them to foreign workers only as a vacancy occurs.

All appropriate taxes are taken, we have a much better idea of who's here and where and it would be a big deterrent to those wanting to come in since everyone will know of any or no positions available. And then hastily deport all illegals without a Billet. Oh, and yes, the Wall.

Jun 24, 2016 6:37 am

Well, for goodness sake, getting Hillary elected sure isn't going to give you that! Is standing in the corner sucking your thumb gonna help?

Moral Majority Member: Trump 'Is the Antithesis of Everything We Set Out to Achieve'

Jun 24, 2016 6:42 am

Oh, that would be a fun trip...you could take a poop in peace knowing that everyone else can't hear you!

Man Gets on Flight Home to Atlanta and Finds Himself in the Rarest of Situations: 'It Was So Cool'

Jun 25, 2016 5:06 am

So, there is the battle of the She Dragon. The chicks reading what I'm about to say might get wizzed but here's what's happening.

When an astute person asks were does Communism come from? the answer is...it's female thinking that is not guided by the Holy Spirit. Here in this country it started out more radically in the early 70's As time has advanced, at every opportunity possible, Satan has used whatever means he can to undo the Godly Man in the U.S.. For the

Godly Man made this Country the shining light to all of the world's history with unparalleled prosperity, a nation of spreading the Gospel, a nation of charity and love.

The one thing Satan found that works best is...feminism. And, as well, especially, feminizing men. That's why all the homosexual and tranny stuff.

Now, Trump is the antithesis to the feminized dude and the feminist (remember ungodly woman). He works hard, he's successful and most of all, he doesn't cower to the She Dragon. That's why all the fems at CNN are going bats.

Jun 25, 2016 5:36 am

I remember the very moment I heard Bush 1 say "New World Order" in glowing terms. That's the precise reason that no one can't tell the difference between Democrats and Republicans...The New World order is first and its priorities are paramount.

The New World Order is important in that by all these countries being united together so tightly, they can all fall together. The crash in 2008 affected all the countries because of this tight alliance.

Every good investment adviser will tell you to spread your investments around so that if something goes wrong, you won't have all your money in one place and lose it all at once. The EU (New World Order) needs to crumble. Let's call it Economic Diversity, if you will.

Jun 25, 2016 6:00 am

I would love to see Herman Cain somewhere prominent in the next Administration...I love the guy!

Jun 26, 2016 6:56 am

How's that thumb taste, George Will? Poor dear, it used to be that half the people didn't like you, now nobody does...tisk, tisk Do you want the peas & carrots or the apples & pears for supper? Well, I'll put the jars in the water and you can decide later.

The word Fascism is loosely thrown around a lot, sort of like a bad name or something. If you read Mussolini's Manifesto and Doctrine, you'll see that the main idea was for government to be in charge of businesses yet they both acted in unison thus the facade, a fake front.

Over the past decades, government has slowly been regulating business to such an extent that you can hardly distinguish the difference between a corporation and a government bureaucracy...the facade being that corporations are independent from government. What we now call the "Establishment" is actually Soft Fascism.

This is why the government is so quick to bail them out and why corporations are quick to come out publicly against certain political issues like tranny restrooms...they are wedded. Britons decision to leave the EU is a slap to the Establishments face and even more so here, Trump is a throttling blow to the head of the Establishment.

Jun 27, 2016 11:00 am

Any of you never Trump people take freak'n heed, this crap from the Elites is about to avalanche if Clinton wins. Don't embarrass the people who died for our liberty by not voting for Trump. Be noble...war is ugly...fight for goodness sakes. Vote. Break away from your self-pity and VOTE!

Jun 27, 2016 11:17 am

We are told by the Lord in the Bible to point out sin, not what our words and opinions are but what the Lord says for judgment is for God alone. How in the Sam Hill can people repent (recognize that we are sinners and are at enmity against God naturally and need to turn away from that position) if what the Lord calls an abomination isn't said? You can be tempted, you can have performed acts, you can fail, you can have been born with a weakness and still be saved.

You know, when you really think about it the Pledge of Allegiance was not a trivial conception. Literally, if someone can't agree to "For which it stands" is a traitor and by any means should be swiftly escorted to the border and booted out...most exactly as an example are the foreign invaders waving flags from other countries.

You could surely expect that the strippers on that list are ding bats but what's up with dudes these days? Someone needs to take them boys out for a good day of cutting firewood followed by beer, a rib barbecue and a good ol' spaghetti western with Clint...good grief.

'The Biggest Farce Going on': Charlie Daniels Unloads on Fellow Musicians Asking for More Gun Control After Orlando Shooting

From way back we have compelled immigrants to go through rigorous examination to determine their allegiance to the Country. From a bare bones perspective and with complete validity, we should be seriously kicking anyone who's anti-Americans out...it's simple treason! Oh, you would hear complaining...that is, only until they are all gone.

Remember the good ol' day's when you could drive down a dirt road in an old pick up, smoking with one hand and eating a hot dog with the other and a bottle of Miller between the legs and a sweet little gal leaning up against you?

In sports it often occurs when you have a high degree of confidence that you can win, implementing a "rope a dope" strategy very often works well.

I like the way that Trump is sort of doing that now...it's good Sit back and just let Hillary's problems catch up with her for one. Another good reason why is not letting the public tire of you...Mr. Trump will do better coming in after the fact and being a breath of fresh air.

As well, stepping aside for a while, the public will actually miss him...if even just the entertainment side. A long droning message can become so common place that people just regard it as a fallacy. Let Hillary be displayed for all that she is. Let the public tire of her...because we know, there is way more to dislike in this bawdy, crooked, mean old hag.

Jun 29, 2016 4:39 am

So I've noticed that Hillary people posing as disgruntled Republicans now have a strategy to sit like vultures on web sites, waiting for a story to appear so they can be the first bombers.

What? do they pay you with every day with a used pair of Hillarys panties?

Jun 29, 2016 4:58 am

For all of you wizards who thought that Trump could never win the Republican Nomination and are now saying that he won't win the Presidency, have you ever considered that you might be in the middle of a losing streak?

Jun 30, 2016 5:34 am

Obama probably regrets that he didn't start this sabotage earlier. It's time for the fine brave woman, homosexuals and tranny's to have their own department in the Military. People make fun of them not being able to do the same as the men so give their own department to prove detractors wrong.

'We Have Reached Peak Crazy': Marines Reportedly Removing 'Man' From Certain Job Titles in Gender-Neutrality Push

Jun 30, 2016 5:52 am

People ask, what is New World Order. It's not so sinister as it is just stupid aided by personal greed. The Establishments theory is that by all of the main Country's deep alliance to an idea of Soft Fascism that it will bring the perfect, peaceful balanced notion of world peace...or Order.

The Democrats and Republicans are hell bent on this and will guard every principle Character in its implementation and furtherance...even the very Mascot of their own corruption, Hillary Clinton.

Jun 30, 2016 5:57 am

I love Ben Carson.

Jun 30, 2016 6:15 am

Well, people who really put their money on the line know that we don't practice free trade, we practice insider and corrupt trade and that as Countries reject globalism, free trade has a chance to emerge again. It amazes me that folk like Krauthammer and Will don't know the difference...but maybe they do. That would be creepy and scary. Trump knows the difference because business people are smarter at these things than typists.

What Crash? British Stocks, Global Markets Recoup Almost All Post-Brexit Losses

CHAPTER 7

JULY 2016

What's so revealing here is how unabashed they are...they don't fear anything because the top Republicans are too busy going after Trump. They gotta protect the mother ship of World Order.

State Department Wants 27-Month Delay for Release of Clinton Foundation Emails

The fact that so many returning soldiers have PTSD is from the lack of camaraderie and low morale. This might sound rough to the more delicate people here but when I was in the Navy in the early eighties drinking was applauded, girlie movies were played, crude talk was the norm, guys razed each other for being wussies, the boat made determined stops at ports specifically for the purposes of "night life with the ladies" and on Wog Day, the passages were full of stinking wet men in either their underwear or naked and there weren't any women to have to tip toe around.

Men being left to be as testosterone filled as necessary to do a tough, sometimes ugly job and it built camaraderie. And it built lifelong friends...and those are what's missing when these guys get back home, no one to relate to. Somebody that you just met that went through the same doesn't count well. A guy with PTSD doesn't have his "team". The current Military not only doesn't allow such things. They go into battle unprepared like a bunch of college kids and then boom...war! This is all on purpose. Pure unadulterated sabotage.

I have an idea, instead of prison make him perform public service by going to every big university and have events where he tells his story to an audience…for at least four years.

Ivy League Student Traveled to Syria to Join Islamic State — a Few Months Later, He Was Begging U.S. to Save Him

Just start having a conversation about ordinary everyday things…news stories, fishing/ hunting, traveling over a beer. People can't help but reveal themselves in that situation.

They must have gone to the Hillary school of "Crooked Trailer Trash Political Science, how to steal what you want"

I understand that Hillary shows up to each and every class, reaches up her Mao suit and pulls out a pair of soiled understuff and lets the class pass them around and play with them and everyone has big smiles and tears of joy.

'Never Trump' Advocates Look for Loopholes to Unbind RNC Delegates — but Will It Work?

Maria, Maria, Maria do you want more coffee.

No? Why?

Maria, Maria, Maria here, let me tie your pumps. Oh you don't have strings.

Maria, I have shoes. I have lots of shoes, do you?

Maria, Maria, do you want some more coffee…I do. I want more coffee. I'll go get us some.

Fox Business Producer, Chipotle Exec Busted After Year-Long Cocaine Sting

I'm serious here. I've never had kids but if I did I would home school and they wouldn't have access to ANY device including computers.

I learned Windows 98 at the age of 35 in about 2 months of casual use so I would just let them learn computers and internet in the second half of their senior year because really, what are they going to miss? Nothing.

While I'm at it, the only shows and movies they could watch would be the classics on DVD. I absolutely would not let any whacked out culture raise my kid. Some people are going to comment here "What are you going to do, shelter your kids from reality?" My answer is " The current Pop Culture isn't reality"

Jul 2, 2016 7:42 am

Here's what has the Trumpsters animated and here's the answer to why Evangelical Christians support him...Authoritarianism.

William Penn wrote "Those people who will not be governed by God will be ruled by tyrants." The atmosphere of authority pressure is that wickedness that has this way come. Laws and more laws. Regulation on top of laws that regulate. The things you can't say- that you can't do- on top of things that you better do.

The multitude of springs increasingly added to daily life and tightened. Working at anything from a small corporation to a large one is nothing but a futile act of survival as if one were sentenced to a weekday jail sentence.

Everything a person does now has the haunting possibility of some kind of punishment...everything, even Church of all things. This has come about because somehow there are ALOT of people who are not governed by God in this Country and the only one left to inspire them is Satan himself.

This black cloud of authority that hangs above the spirit of this Country echoes a sense of doom in its subtle thunder neglecting the reality that God's thunder is not subtle and is imminent.

Like people who live in the area of Puget Sound, Washington, Trumpsters are just looking for the sunny days again.

Jul 2, 2016 7:48 am

As he was fervently beating away under his robe...love them gay porno's baby, gotta love them sweaty, hairy dudes. Yeah, yeah, that's it baby! Gotta love me some of that action!

Judge Blocks Mississippi Law on Religious Objections to Gay Marriage

Jul 3, 2016 6:22 am

Here in Nebraska, the whole State is a gun range...

Jul 3, 2016 7:10 am

Now that thar is reaching way, way back in the drawer for some un-ripped underwear for a news story right thar!

British Comedian Caroline Aherne Dies at 52

Jul 4, 2016 10:02 am

Eris Trump is a fine, fine man and I think that lots of people are jealous that they don't have a son like him!

Here's What Eric Trump Calls the 'Worst Part of Society'

Jul 4, 2016 11:15 am

I want to say something more about the Trumps. Has everyone noticed the similarities between the Trumps and the Robinson's of Duck Commander?

Two decent, God fearing and successful family's...just ordinary people, real people. Fine upstanding parents and fine upstanding kids...all of them bright, loving and God fearing.

Everyone who objects to that is profane and abhorrent in their thinking.

How is it that you lay out all of the reasons that she's guilty yet NOT be able to prosecute? I bet you could find hundreds of prosecutors who would love to have that much to indict on.

FBI Director: 'No Reasonable Prosecutor Would Bring' Case Against Clinton in Email Scandal

Perjury to Congress at the very least...worse that she lied to us citizens, these peoples' bosses!

I hate to say this but this albatross now hanging on her, the fact that she got away with it and any thinking person knows it, might actually be at least as damaging as an indictment. This nasty, nasty cloud of inside corruption in DC plays very much to Trumps favor...sit back a little while Mr. Trump, everyone is eating popcorn and watching the "Crooked Hillary" show!

Ryan: Clinton Should Be Blocked From Receiving Classified Briefings As a Candidate

Reckless Crooked Hillary. You might want to just slowly close the door and back away if you have just discovered that Hillary is your Uber ride.

Oh, heavens! If she wins, leaders all over the world will make minced meat out of her...and us! She took crooked insider politics into a warp zone. Can you even fathom her having our nuclear codes? Can you even fathom her getting of the helicopter and there is a Marine saluting her????

Jul 6, 2016 4:33 am

I was casually watching this and stated wondering, how or why is it that everyone in key government positions are such fantastic smooth liars. It's like they all came from some school that teaches it or something. I mean, if they put me in front of a camera and was told to lie my butt off I wouldn't know how to even begin...and with a straight face, mind you!

Wow, these people are weird robotic science fiction figures!

State Dept. Spox Grilled Over Clinton's 'Extremely Careless' Handling of Classified Info — Watch How He Responds

Jul 6, 2016 4:45 am

"Never been anyone more qualified to be President than Hillary Clinton" the Barock of Kenya says. I wonder if he realizes just what that say's about himself. Hey, Barock...come on, make us laugh. Start down the list of her qualifications! Come on...something like she invented the 57 States or something.

Obama Praises Clinton at First Joint Campaign Stop: 'I'm Ready to Pass the Baton'

Jul 6, 2016 4:53 am

OK, Alan. Maybe next week you can be an Astronaut! Now go back to your room and play with your Elmo.

Al Gore Says He and Jackie Robinson Have Something in Common

Jul 6, 2016 5:20 am

Has anyone else noticed or thought about the fact that there are no more characters in the movies that ain't pretty?

Think of all the great actors that wouldn't be allowed to come close to a set these days...actors like Earnest Borgnine, Marty Feldman, Dan Blocker, Lee Marvin, Jack Nicholson, Bruce Dern just to name a few. Everyone in movies today have to look like they just came off the pages of a JC Penny catalog. Sad.

Former Marine R. Lee Ermey Reveals What He Believes Happened After He Angered the 'Liberals in Hollywood'

Jul 7, 2016 5:19 am

Now, THAT'S SOME AMERICAN'S RIGHT THERE!!! hahahahahaha Only a real American appreciates a mistake like that!

Missouri Town's Fireworks Crew Accidentally Sets Off 'Best Show Ever'

Jul 7, 2016 5:38 am

The never ending compounding laws that constantly make enemies of everyone cause this. If we were to dial back every single statue and law back to just 1970 there would be a sudden and deafening calm.

But for these days, a great pioneering Ska band had a song called "Too much pressure" as a social indication.

Massive 30-Person Brawl Breaks Out in Walmart After Teen Makes Fun of a Woman's Dress

Jul 8, 2016 4:32 am

These Clinton's are the Bonnie & Clyde of politics...just rampaging criminals!

Jul 8, 2016 5:02 am

Can you imagine meeting or knowing these people?

They are just unreal. I'm trying to imagine what the conversations would be like if the Clinton's had a barbecue with their friends...all of it would be either the crimes they are doing or how to get away with it. How could they even eat? They probably just live off of dust or something.

Now, I hope all the black folks intending to vote for Crooked Hillary make note. White crooked politician...not indicted. Black crooked politician...jail.

Dem Congresswoman Indicted After Investigation Reveals She Allegedly Used Charity as 'Personal Slush Fund'

Wow! Crooked Hillary had one too many séances when she was younger. I'm waiting for her imitation of a sprinkler when her head spins round and sput, sput, sputtering green pea soup!

Clinton Disputes FBI Finding She Was 'Extremely Careless' With Classified Data

Oblandny (or whatever his name is) is the Terrorist in Chief of these people.

He isn't doing anything other than being the voice of them as well as their cheer leader. He is the Tranny in Chief, the People Who do Kinky Homosexual Sex in Chief, the Jihadist in Chief.

He doesn't do anything unless it damages our Country. And, by gum, Satan gently pats him on the top of his walnut shaped head.

'Very Well May Be at a Tipping Point': Police Agencies on Edge, on Guard Amid Heightened Threats

This here class, is my latest example defining the word "Stupid"

Hillary? Will you please come in? Thank you...oh, it looks like someone in the back clapped a little.

Ok, so we are here to define stupid. I'm going to ask you a question and then you go ahead and demonstrate.

Hillary, being that Obamacare has been such a disaster, has made everyone's rates go through the roof and has further divided the country, what should we do about it?

Hillary: Have more of it.

Thank you very much, you can leave the room now.

Clapping.

In Nod to Sanders, Clinton Discusses Plans for Universal Health Care

Removing a statue won't stop Obshnotly (or whatever his name is) and his people from hating the honky's.

Group Fighting to Keep Statue of Former Confederate President in State's Capitol Rotunda

I never knew about Dunning-Kruger. It describes something, not only about Oblinky, but people in general. Here's their quote:

"The miscalibration of the incompetent stems from an error about the self, whereas the miscalibration of the highly competent stems from an error about others."

It is so true. I'm not just being mean. Find me a Lib political who is good at something...anything... something real. Fill up your own gas tank, cook supper for some folks, paint a shed, operate a miter saw without cutting your hand off, conduct a trial, balance a company's budget for each quarter, dance the Tango, catch a fish.

Here's where I'm going to depart from some traditional thinking on the right. I don't think that jail is an appropriate measure for illegal drug use. If we are going to jail people who have a particular moral bite in their life, then you'll have to jail compulsive shoppers,

70

compulsive video game players, compulsive phone users, compulsive...anything.

Everyone on earth has at least one compulsive bite in their moral life..."A thorn in the flesh" as the Apostle Paul said in the Bible.

Dealers, different deal.

Jul 10, 2016 7:36 am

Wow, now that's being in a hurry! hahahahahahahahaha

California Woman Receives Three Speeding Tickets Within an Hour

Jul 11, 2016 12:08 pm

If I were an adviser to Mr. Trump I would invite him to watch the 1995 college National Championship in its unrelenting entirety.

Jul 12, 2016 5:47 am

I'm fairly confident that the public has already indicted Crooked Hillary. We might want to walk carefully here. Go ahead and determine that she committed perjury but don't make the move to punish, I think the public will do that November.

Jul 12, 2016 5:58 am

Again, I'm not trying to encourage this but these folks better settle down because some very angry, wacky white guy is going to turn one of these demonstrations into a very ugly sight. It's sad that the supposed President has caused such circumstances and then fans the flames.

Motorist Sounds Off to Black Lives Matter Protestors Blocking Street. When They Surround His SUV, He Decides He's Had Enough.

Mr. Kasich, if you don't enthusiastically deliver Ohio for Trump you will first of all be hated by Republicans in your own state but be even more despised by most Republicans across the nation. Consider what happened to a long respected conservative Democrat, Ben Nelson (D) when he was the deciding vote for Obamacare...he was swiftly escorted to the Nebraska state line and hasn't been seen yet.

'The Way Is Clear': Kasich Ally Urges Former 2016 Hopeful to Challenge Trump at RNC

OK, I'll fess up. We were fishing in the area and ...well...well we had a big lunch and...I mean...I couldn't hold it in!

Dozens of Baby Sharks Mysteriously Wash Ashore in Alabama Bay

Just how horny are these people who are talking to schoolkids about some peoples kinky sex lives. You know, some people just stay at the maturity level of a 12 year old all their life.

Popular Pastor Leaves School Board Over Policy Teaching Students Safe Homosexual Sex, Abortion

Satan in his cleverness has convinced many that "diversity", or more properly, "Americans divided" is the preferred goal instead of the concept of "The melting pot"

You see, if Americans become diversified (Divided) then they lose strength. And when they lose strength of unity, the government can now more easily assert power.

Public University Now Requires 'Diversity and Inclusion' Pledge From Applicants

I see that there is some debate as to whether or not Trump should use a teleprompter. I think he should just do both...give the formal speech and top it off with his standard free-wheeling hoorah.

Mr. Trump and Gingrich are absolutely correct here! A belief in Sharia Law is a direct and pointed hostility to our beliefs and way of life...it's treason.

Now, why in the Sam Hill would Obasmy (or whatever his name is) want to have anything to do with intelligence?

Obama's Defense Intelligence Agency Director: 'I Never Met With Him Once'

I hate to say this because I really love Gingrich but I think Pense ought to be the fellow. He would be that button down balance and not distract any attention from Mr. Trump.

Trump Aides Dispute Reports That VP Pick Is Pence — Decision 'Has Not Been Made'

Smiling here, I can just imagine that Trump was sitting around with everyone advising him in every direction possible and Trump is sitting there unknown to the others and announces the VP pick via twitter...on time! He looks up at the others and says "Guess what? I just announced to the world who my VP pick is" to some very wide eyes. I love it! Problem solved!

Trump Announces Indiana Gov. Mike Pence as VP Pick

To the real Republicans on here that are against Trump, I think that you might be regretful in a few years that you weren't on board. It will be a challenge to square your stance with the fact that Trump is really making a lot of positive changes.

What some Republicans don't understand about Mr. Trump is that he's not a strict political idealog as I have come to understand. There are some very important basics about this Country that he wants to remedy that are outside the moral fights. In his naiveté, he's actually going to turn out to be a genius as President. Imagine what would happen if Mr. Trump came to find out that a group of managers at one of his properties are really screwing up. Do you think he would clean that up or just leave it?

Now, if he becomes President and a Government agency that is under his authority is screwing things up and wasting money, do you think that Mr. Trump and his ego will just let that go? While we have gotten all wrapped up in moral fights, the Government has become an absolute monster. So imagine all the relief as these agencies are cleaned up and de-powered. Monster government is the very hot water to cook the frogs.

Almost as important is the ruination of political correctness and the insipid ramifications that come with it. Political correctness is THE very foundation of their attempt at Socialism...it's a wicked passive aggressive evil. Consider that political correctness does nothing but destroy a person's liberty...if you can't be you're honest self, you will most certainly be nothing.

Mr. Trump is after some very important fundamentals that the moral fighters have become numb to. We have to, have to, have to reverse these things. The genius of Trump is that the moral things will naturally follow.

By the way, Melania was wonderful, I thought. Very, very good job! So, there are dudes out there that would rather listen to that rusty old chain saw with a screeching bearing Crooked Hillary for four years? What the dead critters is the matter with your head?

Hillary. Ain't she pleasant? Her eyes bulging, head jerking, craggy finger pointing, and sound she makes?

In the old days before sirens, they used to find a lady like her and put them on top of their fire engines so people would get out of the way...and boy did they!

It used to be in our country that even unbelievers were reverent or at least, respectful of Christians. In what might be the last days, they that are not Christians are not just skeptical of Jesus or grouchy about the Church, they are ardently marching to Satan's influence...they are the active body of the Anti-Christ, soldiers.

Whether they know what they are doing or not, what a horrible, horrible predicament they are in. Imagine judgment day and you are one of them. You are on a ball of dirt in the middle of N O W H E R E and not only the only sign of life in a seemingly never ending universe, the Earth is filled to the brim with an extravagant display of God's creativity.

We humans are the only one on Earth that has been afforded the astounding variety of foods and spices that we enjoy by light years compared to any animal. God himself has offered to bail us out of the spiritual bondage jail forever. After all of this, if someone dies still kicking and screaming at the Lord...horrible...horrible.

Oh yuck. I don't like that woman, Megan. The night that the SCOTUS ruled that dudes that do kinky homosexual sex acts can play marriage she was gushing...GUSHING! To her everything has to all boil down to feminism and she always makes sure that she inserts it whenever she can. I think she's a phony and the next one in charge of Fox News would do themselves a favor to fire that thing. When she got that evening slot she claimed feminism victory to herself, cut her hair into the shape of a bike helmet and committed a viscous act of betrayal to the very one that put her in that spot. Ugly.

Jul 20, 2016 7:24 am

You know what? I was just musing the other day about what it will actually be like with Mr. Trump as President. One of the curious things that came to mind was oddly aliens...the ones from space. Now, I don't believe space aliens exist but for the people who are the area 51 type, I can actually see Trump coming out at some point toward the end of his time there " As President, on behalf of those curious about aliens from outer space and the government keeping secrets about them, I looked into it and the answer is..." The point is, we have always been saying that what we need in the White House is one of us and well...Trump!

Jul 21, 2016 6:58 am

Accept them talking about their kinky sex lives in front of everybody, even kids, and grossing everybody else out is normal? No. Don't believe me that it's gross? Try to watch some homosexual porn while you are eating breakfast.

Montel Williams Implores Christians to Accept LGBT Community: 'We Are All Equal In the Eyes of the Lord'

Jul 21, 2016 8:02 am

What would be cool tonight when Mr. Trump gives his speech is if he addresses "you didn't build that" by asking Obama & Hillary "I didn't build that, Obama? Hillary, I didn't build that?" and then the screen is filled with pics of his property's and he goes " Like hell I didn't!"

Jul 21, 2016 9:50 am

Perhaps Trump might get together with Cruz behind the scene, patch things up and come out with a joint presser. But Mr. Cruz needs to endorse. As it is, he is still political toast.

Jul 21, 2016 12:52 pm

Something else, it was actually Cruz who started the wife fight when they thought that they would show that photo of Melania and then Trump came back with the snarl picture.

Jul 22, 2016 6:19 am

I was very, very impressed by Mr. Trump's speech. I thought at first that maybe he shouldn't go after Hillary so much but I'm glad he did! He did make a great case against her!

The 10 or 12 never Trumpsters still out there...JUDGES

Jul 22, 2016 6:32 am

I agree with him 100% I have friends who do homosexual stuff but I don't call them "gay" because to me they are just people. I really don't need to hear details about any of my friends' sex lives...I'm sure pretty much everyone has a kink and it would be a courtesy for folk to keep it to themselves. However, aside from the marriage issue which is very serious, we do get messed up in stupid issues like restrooms and the like. From an election standpoint, for this time, we need to address some very fractured structural things in our country.

Jul 22, 2016 6:45 am

Let's see what things look like a week or so from now after Hillary fires up that rusty old chainsaw voice. I think that early August polls will be the predictor because that's when those who do them have to start to be accurate to save their reputations.

If Hillary wins I will believe that the machines are either rigged or that the Republican observers in populous areas are plants or have been softened and payed off. There is absolutely NO reason, by any stretch of abstract thinking, that a person who embodies every negative aspect in a politician be elected. Obama, you might be able to explain but Hillary, no.

I'm as conservative as one can be and I have been supporting Trump since the start. The reason Trump is the nominee is because we are tired of Republicans that speak of all the conservative platitudes and then get in office only to betray.

I love Cruz' heart and mind but I think that he would have been ineffectual...I don't think that he would have been able to overcome the dislike that the Congress has for them. Moreover, I think Trump will be a lot more electable in the fall.

Nobody on the other side or those in the middle are not interested in lofty idealism, sadly wisdom has fleeted. Reagan was "The great communicator" Trump is "The great Builder" if I may say. There are many tangible things in Government that need corrected. They are things that have grown out of control while we were arguing about ideals. The tangible things that are suppressing our lives range from the flood of future Democrat voters invading our Country, Federal land grabs, States control, unfettered bureaucracy to terrorism.

The reason that this episode will not be talked about much is because nobody in the media really wants to get into pronouncing "Einkaufszentrum Mall" on air.

Munich Mall Attacker Identified as 18-Year-Old German-Iranian — Here's What We Know

78

This is a superb example of racism...real racism. The reporter was thinking like all Democrats "Now, I wonder how that dang nickra got off the farm? Who's that nickra think he is!?"

CNN Reporter's Racially Charged Question for Black Trump Supporter Backfires: 'I'm Sick of That!'

Very good class. Now for your next assignment...Jimmy, stop picking your nose!....for your next assignment go outside and find a can for recycling. That way, you will have saved the planet from mean ol' Trump.

If there were anybody left that wasn't convinced that Hillary is crooked, she picked the shiftiest looking guy in politics (except for James Carville) to accentuate the point!

That boy there just needs to go back to his shed in the hills, put the cat on his lap and listen to his wife farting and yelling at him...at the same time.

Sanders Isn't Happy 'Dictator' Trump Is Trying to Win Over His Supporters

Crooked Hillary/ Shifty Kaine 2016

What a wonderful young lady! A very valuable example for other women in this country. She is bright, humble, industrious and carries her grace very well...Mr. Trump has to be awful proud of her!

Ivanka Trump Unveils GOP Nominee Who Is 'Color Blind and Gender Neutral'

I remember sitting in a restaurant in Mombasa, Kenya with my brother and friend. It was a very simple establishment with open windows. The waiter took our order that we chose from the very short menu, half a chicken and chips each. About two minutes later, we could see through the window our waiter...chasing and catching chickens in the "back Yard" It turned out to be the best chicken and potato wedges I ever had!

No, no, no you idiot. Blowing your top is just an expression! BTW what is it about the Middle East? Is everyone who born there given a personal bomb for that future "special purpose"? How do they always manage to come up with bombs so instantly and easily...I wouldn't even know where to start!

New Details Emerge on Bomb Blast in Germany: Attacker Identified as 27-Year-Old Syrian Refugee

So, Hillary picks a VP with corruption. We then find out that the DNC is deeply corrupt at the hands of Wassy. So what does Hillary do at every opportunity there is to recruit a newly available, fellow crook? Well, you hired them immediately of course! You surely don't want rookies in your team of Bandido's when you're on your way to a bank robbery, for heaven's sake!

Hi, my name is Hillary. My Husband's semen was featured on a blue dress belonging to a White house intern and seen by everyone on Earth. I approve of this message!

Well, let's see here, this skinny little weirdo that has never lifted more than 10 pounds in his life, would be horribly baffled if he were ever faced with the challenge of having to change a tire and who's greatest accomplishment was making a few bucks from a goofy book VS a man who built a 10 billion dollar real estate development business with many wonderful property's and thousands of happy employees. What was that you were saying about being prepared? You must live in the same Alice in Wonderland that Clinton does!

Hey, if anyone ever wanted to know what it would be like to be eaten by a giant grasshopper, the next time Pocahauntus is speaking just get real close to the TV screen while a friend is slowly crunching a bag of Frito's

There is just something really freaky about her. I always imagine that her nightly meal consists of small sticks, leaves and topped with half dead moss.

I remember as a kid being intrigued and somewhat scared by the freak show areas of the carnivals that came to town. I found it odd that something so abstract was in the middle of what the rest of the carnival was all about...fun.

When in the Navy, our Carrier went to Subic Bay in the Philippines. On liberty we went into Olongapo City which was nearby. As basically a country boy and never having been to a foreign country before, I was struck with how much like it was to the freak show area of the carnival...but it was the whole town! As different as different could be, it was definitely a foreign people, foreign ways of doing things, foreign thoughts, morals and language.

I was struck again last night by the same thing, watching the Democrat convention. The reason we are perplexed by Liberals is that they are a foreign Country. I guess "Country X" is what I call them...they have yet to tell us their name. But like the Indians who have Nations within ours, these people have their own foreign nation within ours. It's different because while the Indian Nations don't attack us anymore, Country X is engaged in a full blown assault and an attempt at a hostile takeover of The United States...might weirdly be why Wall Street likes them so much, I don't know. Like Walter E. Williams said years ago "It might just be time for an amicable separation" Respectfully, Mr. Williams, that separation has occurred...we just haven't determined the borders yet.

Jul 26, 2016 7:18 am

Hey, Bernie, your usefulness to the DNC is over with now. It's probably just time for you to go back to your cabin in the woods, have a nice big bowl of warm oat germ and descend down into your turnip cellar and continue making your little bombs out of old alarm clocks and wires that you stripped from the radios that you got at garage sales while listening to re-runs of old Castro speeches on your short wave radio...the speeches that come to you from a magical distant galaxy.

Jul 26, 2016 7:31 am

Yes, yes, little Timmy real life is much different than Poke Man isn't it? There, there sweetheart how 'bout we get your favorite doll and we'll get you a fudgesicle. You can eat away at it slowly as tears of pity drip off of your sweet, tender cheeks.

'I DO NOT FEEL SAFE!': Newly Released Emails Show Liberal Students Pressured School to Cancel Ben Shapiro Event

What I think is funny is odd, I guess. For instance, I think it would be funny if a terrorist was walking down the sidewalk on the way to a bombing but accidentally trips and somehow rolls into the street and down a storm drain. A few seconds later, a quick orange flash occurs followed by a small plume of smoke but nobody notices.

I heard that when things get boring at the White House that the staff will entertain themselves by tossing walnuts at the First Lady whereby she catches them by her mouth and crunches them up whole and then spits the bits back into faces.

I'm not saying that Mr. Trump is leading it but here we go again, getting sucked up into an argument that gives power to one centralized Federal Authority.

The answer is to whittle down the ominous roll of the Federal Government. The 10th Amendment made that crystal clear in the simplest terms. The Constitution only spells out a few rolls the Federal Government plays. A good way of looking at the original intention of Federal Government's role is kind of like football...it should only provide the stadium, the security and the referees. Play Ball!

Well, she's the authority on bravery! Yeah, she's the bravest one of all and this puny little country doesn't know the first thing about it. Heck, she even was brave enough one time to wear white shoes with a black dress!

Alicia Keys: U.S. 'Cannot Claim to Be the Home of the Brave' Until Gun Control is Passed

It would have been a beautiful thing if that Priest had a mini sub machine gun under that robe, pulled it out and said "Get ready for your 72 raisins, you worthless mother..." Tap, Tap, Tap, Tap, Tap............

'Horror': Nun Speaks Out After Attackers Viciously Slit Throat of 86-Year-Old Priest in Normandy

It's well known that Horny Billy has a bent drive shaft. Now, when you combine that with Crooked Hillary, you have imagine how difficult the contortions had to be when it came to sexy time.

Bill Clinton Details His Love Story With Hillary Clinton, Leaves Out a Key Part

I love the fact that Mr. Trump is campaigning right through the middle of their convention...Those are the kinds of balls reserved for guys like Patton! We have lost the last two elections because our candidate rendered so, so much respect to our opponent that it almost seemed that they were supporting the other side. Not Trump HAHAHAHAHAA Hey, we used unconventional warfare to win the Revolutionary War!

These people are so tricky. You see, most people think that what the DNC is doing is holding a convention when actually what they are holding is the World Lying Championship. Each one coming out and outdo each other for a supposed gold trophy but when they bring the prize out at the end, they present the winner with just a stick. When the winner looks surprised the presenter shrugs her shoulders and goes "We lied, here's your F-ing stick"

Mr. Trump, if you win, this HAS to stop. It would be an insurmountable task in this age to rebuild our military from the ground up again if it does finally get pushed off of the cliff.

This administration is doing everything it can to destroy the Military, including all the kinky homosexual crap, to weaken us to a point where we are unable to defend ourselves 1. and no. 2, the Military is being populated with people who will easily turn on us. I don't mean to be overly dramatic but our Military is ultimately the last defense against the Liberal nation living within our borders. I mean that! The old Military like back in the 80's and 90's and before would have never turned on us. The Military the Barak is making and Hillary wants to continue with....WILL.

Report: Navy to Name Ship After Iconic Gay Rights Advocate Harvey Milk

Jul 30, 2016 6:28 am

I hear some folks complain that Mr. Trump got and gets so much free media coverage. To that I say...be relevant if you're going to run.

The most confounding element for the establishment to understand is why people are embracing reality vs. the plastic BSer. People had become so conditioned in a way, including myself, to judge candidates by how well they can deliver a message...as though every election was really just a speech giving competition and we chose a winner. This election, either the Americans are going to come home from a fantasy space voyage of political idealism and let mechanics do what mechanics do and fix a heartless, goofy, immature, wasteful, power hungry, paid for Government.

The effort in my mind is that by the time Mr. Trump gets finished, there won't be much of that Golden Calf left to worship...perhaps leaving some room for the Lord.

Jul 30, 2016 6:49 am

After the perp. was bailed out of jail he made his way to the local bar to spend his nightly fun with the boys. "Hey, I'm out now so let's have a beer!" Silence... except for one guy at the bar who mutters "Yeah" under his breath. The sound of the cracking of pool balls and shuffling feet on the creaking planks of the floor was finally overcome by someone in the back. "Wussy!"

Bikini-Clad Police Officer Takes Down Suspect, Posts Photo of the Aftermath

Jul 30, 2016 7:15 am

If a person can't pledge allegiance to our flag, they should be promptly ushered to the border and kicked out with citizenship revoked until they can prove otherwise. This country is not just a convenient place to crap all over for your personal self-interest. It is not within the definition of liberty to be used by those who want to take the same.

Jul 31, 2016 5:38 am

For me growing up in the 60's & 70's a thug was like a robber, a guy that robbed you on the street with a gun or something like that. And then I think that movies portrayed mob guys that way. Whatever, I've never pictured a black guy as a thug. What did the media do, steal the term so that they have another way to point fingers?

CHAPTER 8

AUGUST 2016

Aug 3, 2016 6:16 am

In graphic arts "Layers" are exactly like transparencies that they used to use with overhead projectors. Most electronic graphic arts consist of at least 5 or 6 and up to 30 or more. I happen to be a self-taught fairly good graphic artist using Photoshop and Illustrator.

When the Hussein released his birth certificate he said it was a photo copy that the hospital in Hawaii made. The PDF that was sent out, when opened in my Illustrator, had about 12 layers if I remember right...a bunch. The base was a raster (pixels) image like a standard photocopier would make. The multiple layers on top of the base were vector images. You need a program like Illustrator to make vector images. Vector images are produced not with pixels but by coordinances...x-y etc...The vector images are in the areas of the birth certificate that show details like names, dates etc...the pertinent stuff.

Now, why on earth would a hospital have a photocopier, which is the least sophisticated thing needed in a hospital, that does such complex tasks as making vector layers and is so sophisticated that only a graphic artist or the FBI might own one? NASA wouldn't even have a need for one like that.

Watch Panel's Reaction to Ex-Trump Campaign Manager Corey Lewandowski's Birther Moment on Live TV

Aug 3, 2016 6:51 am

What really freaks the establishment out is that if Mr. Trump wins, there will come a deluge of intelligent ordinary people running for Republican seats as opposed to these types of phonies. It's supposed to be that way. Never did the Founding Fathers even hint at power belonging to "smart" elites...we had just got done defeating that very thing after the Revolution. Why do people like Ryan, Krauthammer, and whoever else, think that it's now necessary?

Trump Strikes Blow to GOP 'Unity' by Withholding Endorsement From House Speaker Ryan

Aug 4, 2016 7:07 am

To the reporters who wrote this article,, I'm walking around on the moon right now. Yes, I am...I said so. From now on you have to call me an astronaut. That's not what you're up to?

Oh, the feminista's effort at conquering America is what you're up to! If that's a boy, let's see her gadget and rocks. Let's see her pee into a urinal from one foot away. What moron's.

Supreme Court Sides With Virginia School in Transgender Bathroom Case — For Now

Aug 5, 2016 5:39 am

Oh boy, Obama's getting tough! My goodness, he's gonna tear a whole sheet of paper in half and make everyone run for their lives! Some people just don't understand how scary that is!

Obama Addresses Rumors of Trump Leaking 'Top Secret' Information From Classified Briefing

Aug 5, 2016 6:12 am

Oh golly, can it be true? Is it possible to replace that big hairy and scary ape Trump? Does that mean that maybe we can replace him with a pleasant BS artist that we are so used to? Oh, that I dream that we can all stand up and cheer for the plastic UN Representative that loves us...we have to be loved by candidates again! If they don't love us, who will? Oh please, please...we just need to be loved and rocked to sleep again! If we can only get rid of that brute Trump then maybe the soft fury animals that he murders will come up and rub their pink noses on our tear soaked cheeks. What Happens if a Major Party Needs to Replace a Presidential Candidate?

This election IS THE most important one in the history of this Country without comparison. It will take only one second for her Supreme Court to determine that "Militia means, and is, the National Guard...only! For those of you who haven't the stomach for Mr. Trump might well develop a stomach for a violent life for the 2nd Civil War will then begin.

How a Clinton Administration Could Have a Major Impact on Second Amendment

While these types of reminders are good, I noticed that some poll results are showing something huge missing in the public perception of Mr. Trump and that is in the category of temperament or Presidential temperament. It would do well for the Trump campaign (or for those on behalf) to run a solid series of long format ads displaying Mr. Trump at work in critical situations solving problems. Dave Thomas called this "Shirt sleeve problem solving" rolling up the sleeves and fixing things. This is the thing that the public needs to see and it's something common people can relate to.

While everyone was at work and not paying close attention, we suddenly realize that the worst of our Country somehow now occupies many political positions. How about someone with dirty finger nails for a change instead of someone with a dirty heart.

1 Timothy 4:1-2 But the Spirit explicitly says that in later times some will fall away from the faith, paying attention to deceitful spirits and doctrines of demons, by means of the hypocrisy of liars seared in their own conscience as with a branding iron,.

There is only one reason Clinton could get elected and that is because a plurality of Americans are in the state described above. There is another verse that states that people will "Love lies" Some people think "Oh gee, Trump isn't doing that BS thing that politicians need to do...he's not cunning enough" or "he's not ACTING Presidential" The key word here being "Acting" When the debates come and Mr. Trump gives his opening statement, he ought to just start out by saying something like I'm not here to lie to you, I'm not here to be a fake...I'm not an actor, I'm real.

All our lives we hear everyone complaining that there aren't ordinary people in office, if Hillary gets elected she will just be another crooked politician among the many...the big problem for the Country is, she would be in the most powerful position that we have.

Aug 11, 2016 6:26 am

Meanwhile, at an auto glass center somewhere in Virginia:

"Hey, anyone seen the grippers? I can't even find one...they were all right here last night!"

"No, but has anyone seen that dumb kid they hired last week? He didn't even sweep the shop at closing time last night!"

"Dudes! Get in here! Look at the news, the Moron is a third of the way up the Trump Tower in New York!"

Man Spotted Scaling Trump Tower in Manhattan Using Suction Cups

Aug 12, 2016 7:14 am

So, go ahead and keep snubbing your fancy and way smarter nose at Mr. Trump. Maybe you fakes can lose the House as well.

Mitch McConnell Says GOP's Chances of Keeping Senate Majority Are 'Very Dicey'

Aug 12, 2016 7:21 am

If there are people refraining from watching the movie "Hillary's America" it's because they are too engrossed in watching the live episodes happening every day.

Seems like there are a lot of people wanting Mr. Trump to stick to a litany of issues but think about this: Let's say that you are in a small meeting of 10 people and you're gathered to solve some really serious issues but everyone else is just gabbing and making jokes the whole time.

Well, it's the same thing that Mr. Trump faces. It's completely unreal that Hillary is even a candidate and immune to bald face crimes, the media is just a cheap carnival full of freaks and the "Never Trump" monkeys are running around knocking everyone's peanut dishes over. Mr. Trump owns a multi-billion dollar family owned company that develops beautiful places for people to enjoy, works his butt off, has sober, straight productive kids and now look at the stupid environment he finds himself in now.

It just has to be really difficult for him to just not throw his hands up in the air and say "Whatever"

I wonder what this guy does all day. Have you ever thought about that? I know, I know...but after that, what's he do? What do you do when your whole life is a scam? What, does he just sit in a Victorian chair and play with a peanut shell all day? He can't possibly have any friends besides Carville. But even in that case, what would you talk about? Scamming more?

Crawling like a dehydrated lizard across the desert floor to the grave...gotta scam, gotta lie...just one more time....just one......more...........lie........

Bill Clinton: Email Controversy Is the 'Biggest Load of Bull'

Now, here we have a school that must be run by intelligent people. By teaching problem solving you are cultivating intelligence verses memorizing which only makes you smart. If we want to have any kind of future in this Country, it should be mandatory that males have 4 years of shop class. Wood working, welding, fabrication, engine rebuilding etc...Not so much that it makes a fella industrious, which definitely greatly enhances his self-esteem but that it creates a mindset that thinks...solves problems.

A thoughtful and productive mind has absolutely no room to entertain foolishness when it comes to fixing things.

Arkansas High School Teaches 'Problem-Solving' in a Way Its Students Probably Won't Enjoy

Aug 13, 2016 7:20 am

If I were to win a gold medal at the Olympics, I would come out wearing my shirt on the bottom and the pants on top just to see how quiet the crowd would get. What are they gonna do, yank the medal of your neck in frustration or something?

Aug 13, 2016 7:29 am

And Bobby from Massachusetts and Jeffrey from North Dakota and Billy and Mary (they just got married, God bless them) from Topeka and Frank! good ol' Frank don't like that big hairy brute neither. And Sally sifting cinders in the garden and Thomas, not the skinny one, the big fat one from the machine shop on Friction Street.

And Tammy, she don't like that meanie, she likes her puppy. And Nick and Sam don't like Trump either...they smash their cigarettes out real hard every time you mention his name... that's how mad they are!

More Than 100 'High-Profile' Republicans Refuse to Support Trump — So Far

Well now that's odd. A Christian out making every Christians life more miserable. Hmmmm....boy, how long do we have to think about that one?

Dem. VP Pick Tim Kaine to Christian Leaders: Clinton's Faith is the 'Root of Everything She Does'

Crimes or no crimes, black communities do feel more economical pressures when the economy is terrible...naturally. This is Barak Oboma's economy, maybe that's why he never has anything to say.

Riiiiinnnggg, riiiinnnnnggg..."Hello?"

"Do you have Prince Edward in the can?"

"Oh you! I think I'm gonna hang up now"

"No! Wait!...I'm watching you right now...mmm, getting undressed"

"Really?...but how?"

"I'm in the closet"

"But I'm in the closet too"

"Yeah, that's me sitting across from you...wow, you're kinda dumb aint ya?"

Pelosi Reportedly Receiving 'Obscene and Sick Calls' Since Hacker Released Dem. Phone Numbers

The speech Mr. Trump gave last night was FABULOUS!!!!!! This will definitely change the course of this election season. I just kept thinking that if Mr. Trump keeps this up, he will be the President...no question. Speaking of inner cities, I often wonder about the feasibility of creating enterprise zones at or in inner city area's that gives companies that might otherwise leave the incentives to locate there. If we can lift the lives of black folks in these area's it would render a death blow to Liberal powers for a long time.

Trump Accuses Clinton of 'Bigotry,' Says She Is 'Pandering to Communities of Color'

Aug 17, 2016 5:21 am

Hey Hillary, don't blame everyone else because you're looking like a ward out tabaccy pouch, they isn't the only one that's noticed the obvious.

Aug 17, 2016 5:32 am

In Hal Lindsey's book "Satan is alive and well on planet earth" he has a chapter called "The guilt trip" In it, he describes the tactics and persuasions that Satan uses to try and defeat people. Interesting that this is the CHIEF weapon that Liberals/ Democrats use. Putting Kahn out there was supposed to have the same effect as when they had Christopher Reed come out at a previous convention. They are purposely trying to lay on a guilt trip if you don't go along and agree with the unfortunate speaker. Tricky isn't it? But just think about how demented one has to be to intentionally do this...ordinary and real people just don't that.

Aug 18, 2016 5:17 am

Hi, my name is Hillary Clinton. When my husband was President of the United States his semen was prominently featured on a blue dress that a White House intern was wearing and the whole world saw the picture of it.

Aug 18, 2016 5:52 am

There is something about these times, this election, that's really bringing out the true heart in people. Knowing the permanent damage Hillary would do, any Republican or Conservative that doesn't or won't back Trump is, by all angles of thinking, in full blown allegiance to the enemies of this Country. And all that talk of Saul Alinsky...now his kiss is sweet.

What Former Breitbart Editor Ben Shapiro Says You 'Need to Know' About Trump's New Campaign CEO

Aug 19, 2016 5:54 am

What good is that going to do when the dirty money has already been donated and the favors are already on the dock to be done?

If there are enough people in our Country, all from particular cities, that get Hillary elected despite the absolute ruin that she is, we're gonna have to release those cities from our Country somehow. Make them self-ruled territories, sell them to Canada, just kick them out and let them figure it out...something.

The vast, vast majority of counties that comprise the United States simply will not live under their rule. I can sort of understand un-smart people voting for Obama but think of this, it would be exactly like being ruled by 12 year old juvenile delinquents that just escaped a Corrections Facility.

Aug 19, 2016 6:24 am

No, exorcising religious freedom is not to be "within boundaries" The 1st natural liberty expressed in the Constitution states that "or prohibiting the free exercise thereof" That means shall not...anywhere, anytime, for any reason, period.

Aug 20, 2016 6:10 am

Wisdom is acquired throughout life when as one makes mistakes is able to admit them, learns from them and then is able to find solutions to avoid those mistakes in the future. Hillary has pride, which is the opposite of wisdom. Churchill had wisdom. Donald Trump has wisdom.

It really wasn't a mask, the cops just made him take some Geritols. The prisoner was seen in the jail common area dancing around and singing "And now I feel so young!"

Massachusetts Police Are Not Fooled by This Fugitive's Elaborate Disguise

After the civil war, black folks boarded trains by the thousands and headed north, getting the heck out of the South understandably.

They found themselves to be disenfranchised in a society that was very industrious and moving right along. The immediate result was the huddling together and finding low level jobs in order to survive in this new kind of jungle. Nobody in the North sought to lift them or could even help them because life was tough for most folks and they were too busy trying to keep their own heads above water.

In general, black folks are faced with two main things. One, they are greatly outnumbered. The second is the expectation to "act white" in order to be acceptable to Liberals.

I'm not even going to reflect on this mess Hillary anymore. On the ranch growing up, like many farms and ranches, we had a ball of haywire. Yes, haywire is a real thing for those unfamiliar...it's the pile of discarded wire from hay bales. When you looked at a ball of haywire, there was no way of finding any use for it, making any sense of it and then dreading the day you have to do something about it.

Every ball of haywire eventually grew to some particular size and you had to, by any various means, take it to your dump. It was the object in the dump that other things bounced off of when you threw them in. It almost became the game every time you went to the dump and threw objects in that you would throw it on the haywire ball just to conquer it...not much damage.

What did conquer the haywire was water and time...rust. After a couple of years, you find yourself throwing an old tractor tire in on the haywire again but this time, poof!, it's flattened! Hillary is like the haywire.

It's all coming from our schools...they don't teach a youngster intelligence, they teach compliance, non-thought and accepting obvious untruths as reality.

Mike Judge Says It's 'Scary' How Quickly His Movie 'Idiocracy' Is Becoming Reality, Offers Examples

Man, these guys are weirdos. Throughout all mankind men have been manly. Good at management, manifest destiny's, and helping to save manatee's....yes, even manatee's. Big hairy, scary, sweaty, cussing, spitting men. Boy, oh boy...they're just flat out mean and ugly men to us little princesses!

Princeton University Wants Staff to Avoid Using the Word 'Man'

I have often wondered why don't the packing plants and furniture makers just set up factories right on the border with Mexico and from the employee entrance, build a bridge across the Rio Grande? If we change wage minimums for foreign workers it will offset the additional shipping required. How come I'm the only one doing the thinking around here? :)

Here's why today's youth are dumber and it's Satan's greatest trick of all. Make kids doubt their OWN sense of truth and reality.

Here's an example, and pay particular attention to the fact that it's most prominent in schools: One day you see a guy, and every kid knows what that is all about, but the next day, after having some fake

97

taters installed and is now wearing a dress, kids are compelled by the use of guilt and punishment to now accept that he's a woman.

This defies every ounce of a kids OWN logic thus preventing him/her from reasoning in the future...there are consequences for being truthful and honest and real.

Next example, again prominent in schools, mind you. People are somehow able to go to a magical thermostat and adjust the temperature of the Earth!... WOW! But there are mean people that are preventing us from getting to the room where the thermostat is.

This defies all reason and again it fortifies to the young mind "What you know is real, isn't" So what happens after the Devil's hand maidens have done their dirty jobs? A young person grows up turning away from any truth that they themselves may have and replacing it with the most fanciful of lies told to them.

Aug 23, 2016 5:40 am

There are stories out that Mr. Trump is going to amend his immigration stances...if so, it would be a death blow to the campaign. The record turnout in the Primary's, the great increase in Republican voter registration is based on the expectation that Mr. Trump will halt and clean out all of the foreign invaders...we are horrified by the full blown assault on our Country especially since Hillary and Obama are facilitating it.

Aug 24, 2016 3:54 am

Here's the most important aspect of all regarding illegals that might be upstanding and that is to never let them be able to vote. Our huge problem is a vast influx of people who are either from a Third World or Socialist country. The Globalist order would be totally happy with one big union of countries like EU and they want the US part of it...NOT GONNA HAPPEN.

I truly believe that he has been ahead ever since the Republican convention. If I recall correctly Mr. Trump was 5-8 points ahead afterword's and then they say Hillary went ahead by 10 after the Democrat convention that few people saw...really, a 15 point swing based on nothing being different? Mr. Trump is looking great and Hillary is just becoming a bigger mess every day. Mr. Trump is ahead right now...I'm just tell'n ya.

To the degree that a Country believes in salvation through faith alone in Jesus Christ is the degree to which it is prosperous. And I'm not talking about money alone.

I wonder if it even occurred to him while he was there that anything that he says or does didn't, or will, make any difference in those people's lives. Everything up to this point was done despite him and everything will eventually get back to normal without him. He is insignificant to the prosperity of American's but he is significant to their demise if possible.

While Touring Louisiana Flood Damage, Obama Meets With Families of Police Shooting Victims

Mr. Trump should keep courting the black vote from time to time...maybe even hold an event or town hall. I hate to use an already over used word but think of black folks' impressions when Republicans won't even talk to them or ask for their vote as if they don't matter...being snubbed is insulting, maybe even more so than being racist.

Custome: "Welp, here's your car back"

Salesman: "But...ahhh...It's on its side!. Ruined!"

Customer: "Hey, are those donuts over there?"

Salesman: "Ahh, yeah...help yourself. Did you get the chance to see how well it handles?" following her.

Customer: "Nope"

Salesman: "How did you...how did you do that, put the car on its side like that?"

Customer: "Not sure. How about the red one over there...you got the keys for it?"

Woman Test Driving $60K Mercedes-Benz Somehow Manages to Flip Luxury Vehicle in Parking Lot

OK, so if we have these illegals who have been here for years and don't cause any trouble then here should be the compromise if at all. A new law that flatly states "Any person of any age that enters the United States illegally shall be banned for life from Citizenship, without the right to ever vote" Any illegal alien who is here that hasn't ever caused trouble, pay back taxes and be taxed from here on or get deported.

HEY! The perfect solution! Since us bad, bad, terrible, meanie Conservatives have damaged the Earth to a point that it's virtually inhabitable, the Liberals can start making rocket ships and head off to the "New Utopia" Just think Libs, if it's a planet all to yourselves, it'll be paradise...no God, no heaven, cool stuff like that! And when you leave in your rocket ships, use crude oil as the fuel just to give the meanies one last fart of disapproval and help finish us off! HURRY!

Scientists Discover New Earth-Like Planet

Can you ever, ever imagine that Marine outside of Air Force One saluting this pile of slop Hillary? God forbid...God forbid.......

You see, if I were President and could throw around power like Obangladesh does, I'd make a mandate that they have to teach this as a lesson to all students before getting funding...a little more important than where a horny little drag queen poops.

Mississippi Islamic State Recruit Gets Eight Years in Prison

I always feel really embarrassed for Hillary when I see her try to laugh it all off. She doesn't realize how like Elaine Bettis on Seinfeld doing that funky dance, how absurd she is.

Former Obama Strategist David Axelrod: Clinton 'Should Not Joke' About Her Emails

What in the Dickens is all this stupid drag queen crap come from? I ain't seen a drag queen since I was at boogy street in Singapore but somehow we all got instantly invaded by what, Tranny's from Mars or something? Should we expect to find them hiding in our garden sheds, climbing on our roofs and scratching at our windows now?

'Do You Prefer Ma'am or Sir?': New DOJ Video Shows Cops How to Treat Transgender People

There are three primary absolutes that have to be maintained, bad ones out immediately, the wall, and a lifetime ban on anyone who has entered the Country illegally from ever getting citizenship and voting...either previously in the past and in the future.

It was funny how careful she was trying not to sound like Fred Flintstones' Mother in law. Just so everyone knows, this is going to be her debate style. She's gonna try to come off as the mature, measured and 'reasonable' candidate because when you are a sociopath and you really need to take cover, this method is the last ditch trick to keep your face from turning bright red.

I'd love to see one get close to a Carrier and get vaporized by a Phalanx.

Report: Navy Fires 3 Warning Shots After Iranian Ship Sails Too Close in Persian Gulf

All this stupid knit picking by so called Republicans and so called Conservatives is getting ill. Mr. Trump is way, way closer to what we want. Mr. Trump stomped in the Primary's because he was the furthest from the establishment and now these establishment Republicans are still out proving the point we made in voting for him...period. Notice the trick here, they are trying to force him into an establishment mold so his followers will lose enthusiasm. Ain't it ridiculous though, the establishment types are trying to badly paint Mr. Trump as being what THEY ARE! odd.

It wasn't a joke...that was an embarrassingly stupid campaign stunt and they got caught. Just about as bad as Hillary's bizarre, spooky, Valium induced speech that Mr. Trump is part f the KKK. Yes Hillary, there are mysterious villains in black robes roaming around the internet secretly making black people float across the rooms to vote for Trump and it....must.....be....stopp.....ssssllllleeeeeeeeepp.

'It's a Can-spiracy': Jimmy Kimmel Responds to Alex Jones' 'Pickle Can' Conspiracy Theory

Not only is Hillary a gimped up slaughterhouse cow she is also psychotic. Her KKK speech was really freaky and made me think she was up all night listening to Coast to Coast radio. Putting it bluntly, my short diagnosis of Hillary is that she suffers from Bovine Spongiform Encephalopathy (Mad Cow Disease)...sorry, politics is a rough business:)

Isn't calling a person a "bully" bullying?

What are we going to be doing for the next 4 years? Are we going to be sitting there watching Hillary use her power of the Presidency to get rich? A daily dose of depressing revelations about an astounding example of everything we hate about politics as Hillary plows her Bridezilla agenda on the people? Or are we going to do something about the shabyness of the Country that we now deal with?

What if we did something great. What if instead of watching a mess, actually changed things for the better...for the future of our country...the future of our youth. What if once again the history books could record a milestone moment in civilization whereby freedom and brotherhood superseded the awful ones...the killers, the greedy and those who seek to suppress the humble?

It's a pretty simple proposition and we have proven that before...we are not at all obligated to live our lives at the expense of the abhorrent, the Godless, the violent. What if for a change we the people and not professional politicians banded together, under God, under a united purpose and made things better...the way WE want it?

What if we could look past backgrounds, race and all the other things that make us all unique? What if...we made the grand old example of "We the people" be real again? What if...WE made America great again!?

PolitiFact: Clinton's Claim About 'Trump Effect' on Bullying Is 'Mostly True'

It just makes you so proud of our Third World government doesn't it? And Hillary just keeps showing so much poise through all these reckless inquiry's... I'm sure that it takes every ounce of her strength to keep from crapping her pants and start throwing poop at everyone like the zoo monkeys...just makes ya well up inside.

I remember a while ago reading an article called "The browning of America" The article was pointing out that while there was a growing population of people of various colors, the interracial relationships are producing a growing number of just plain "Brown People" and ostensibly America would turn into just one big race made up of lots of nationalities. Obama is a racist like non other. A large part of my thinking says that these open southern borders and bringing in as many Syrians as possible is just his effort to "Brown" America. "Breed out the white folk, them bastards!"

I truly think that Mr. trump will win and win big. The way to determine this is simply asking anyone "What do you LIKE about this candidate?" If it's very little or none, that candidate will not be the President

Here is an example of being fair and getting along and crossing the aisle. This is a political contest not etiquette school. It does not help at all to lump Mr. Trump's comments into the character of Hillary. They will come after the Republicans every time with race allegations, you have to hit back just as hard or harder!

It's a good move I think...it looks Presidential. There's no way Mr. Trump is going to talk about any future arrangements because Mexico is such a tangled mess. I like to frequently put myself into a condition of mind like a casual observer of politics...like I'm judging mathematicians (I don't like and I'm no good at math) When I get in this mind I just sort of shut off my thinking and just sort of react to stimuli...whatever is out there. Folks, I can tell you that in all reality, Mr. Trump is way ahead.

How about you idiots at the EPA just worry about the job at hand? Unless them having sex is part of the work day. It's unreal that they actually sit there and think about peoples' sex lives when they get home. Do they also have to submit a self-recorded sex scene as part of their job application? Unreal.

EPA to Start Collecting Employee Data on Sexual Orientation, Gender Identity

I think it's very possible that the FBI/State Department are covering their butts here. Meaning, after the upcoming document dump from wikileaks, people are going to be asking if these showed up at wikileaks why couldn't the FBI or State Department find them...were the FBI and State Department hiding them? So they need to get them out now before wikileaks dumps the same. It's a possibility here.

FBI Uncovers Benghazi Emails Involving Clinton, State Department Says

CHAPTER 9

SEPTEMBER 2016

Sep 1, 2016 5:03 am

Working at home today I was able to catch everything there was to see in the news and the contrast could not possibly be more dramatic!

So, the first thing we see is what looked like someone had put a garden hose in one gopher hole and Hillary came out the other one...she looks sick! I had the volume off because I just can't take her negative, broken machinery sound...being half German, it's an annoying sound.

But just watching that I was thinking what a bitter, sour, tired soul that is! Next is Mr. Trump standing with the President of Mexico. Here in Nebraska, we have a pretty good work ethic like much of the Country. The State Department said earlier that Mr. Trump shouldn't be going to Mexico and Hillary said "That's not how it's done" and I thought BULLHORNS...that is how you do it! You don't sit around and have meeting after meeting and then lunch and then come back and see how much you still can't do!

I loved how Mr. Trump's presence in Mexico was showing these current No Loads how adults go about getting things done...the RIGHT things! Next, Phoenix. Previously was Hillary with a stale blue background and from what they were saying on the network, the crowd only uttered a few murmurs but in Phoenix was a rousting, excited, enthusiastic, sign waving, happy crowd!! Mr. Trump bypassed all of the stupid speculations that were swirling about and dispersed with a strong, thoughtful, comprehensive speech.

A speech that reflects the exact sentiment of what everybody in America, except the ones that hate us, are thinking and feeling regarding illegal immigration! We are tired...done!...with every destructive element that is at war within our own borders attacking us on a daily basis! It's our Country! We are not a giant day care facility that is supposed to do nothing all day but cater to the needs of a bunch of snot nosed, ungrateful, shin kicking brats! Folks, if for whatever Global, Elitist reason Mr Trump doesn't win in November we truly, truly have a very serious problem...a problem that no one can imagine. A problem that no one wants to imagine!

It's really time we come home from solving everyone else's problems in the world. Since WW2 we have found ourselves putting out brush fires for everyone else while in our own Country, we have neglected the tangled undergrowth of fodder that is now catching fire. First here and then there. A big one here a bigger one over there...at an increasing rate. Obama and Hillary and the like are the ones protecting the existence of the fodder as well as often actually stoking the fires. We gotta get Mr. Trump in office...we have got to grow up, we have got to get real!

Oh, OK Josh. Well when you make it to High School you might be surprised that things have changed a little bit... you can even drink your milk without a straw!

Josh Earnest Lectures Journalists to Report That the Obama Administration Is Transparent

Now really, if you were to walk up to Hillary and ask her what's the best way to dig a hole for a fence post, could she answer it? If you were to ask her "what current is used in automobiles, AC or DC", could she answer that? While I don't expect everyone to know everything, I personally don't take advice or supposed wisdom from people who have only a scant realization and awareness of the real world around them. Think of that! Really, the only thing she really knows how to do is gather money in various nefarious ways.

Clinton Blasts Trump on 'American Exceptionalism,' Fails to Mention Where Obama Once Stood on the Issue

Sep 2, 2016 5:04 am

The NFL better grip on this crap before it becomes a political battleground and loses all legitimacy. What's next, burning cars on the 20 yard line?

Kaepernick Does Not Stand During National Anthem Before Game Against San Diego

Sep 2, 2016 6:05 am

Here's why coastal Californians are the way they are. I lived in San Diego for about 10 years during and after the Navy. First, every hippie from everywhere else that could, moved there. Second, lack of winter. For the vast majority of the days, the weather is basically the same beautiful day...and hardly ever, ever any wind. Because every day is a beautiful day they have no sense that things can, or will turn into wholesale misery. To them, you can just live any ol' way you want, vote any ol' way you want because no matter what, tomorrow will just be another beautiful day. They just don't have a sense that there are consequences for things. Basically, they are spoiled brats.:)

California Lawmakers Deliver for Liberals on Climate, Wages

Sep 2, 2016 6:27 am

Boy! Ain't nothing like a real good explosion every once in a while! I bet there was a lot of "Whooooa doggy!" going on in the control room after that one.

SpaceX Rocket Explodes at Cape Canaveral, Destroying Facebook's Internet Satellite

Isn't it something else? Here, someone is running for the United States President and if she ever did have a press conference there wouldn't be any questions on policy, they would all be about her crimes...that's astonishing when you really start to think about it. Let me put that in perspective, if it were possible, it's the exact same scenario that would occur if Al Capone were in her current position.

CBS Hosts Grill Kaine Over Claim That Clinton 'Talks to the Press All the Time'

The more this comes out, the more those who hate the Lord go blind.

Report: Bill Clinton Used Taxpayer Money for Foundation, Private Email Server

You can't blame him, I've always wondered what would happen too. Like pull one, you get a Pez, pull another, you get a Jolly Rancher...sometimes you pull a good one, you get a nickel.

Iowa Cop Disciplined After Yanking Suspect's Dreadlocks

I watched Mr. Trump's visit to that Church and it was a beautiful event to behold. It would be earth shattering if he were a politician, but he isn't. He's just a guy. He doesn't have a political ax to grind, a dollar to be made or fame to be garnered...he's just a good guy.

I live smack dab in the most Conservative of Conservative places in America. I don't know if we still have this status but a couple of years ago it was pointed out that we were the 2nd most prosperous, by scale, county in the United States.

My neighbor downstairs came from the most opposite area of the US, South Chicago...and I mean, SOUTH CHICAGO. I can't hardly understand him on a cell phone. I have lived here since '94 and he's lived here for about 9-10 years...he and I are dang good friends. We have commonality, we have brotherhood, we have love for one another and help each other...we are Christians. We have the same Father.

Angry Protesters Ready for Trump Ahead of Visit to Black Detroit Church

Sep 4, 2016 8:16 am

I guarantee you this, if that were Mr. Trump on that plane he would have had them taxi back out to the runway and fly off. And yes, you might have heard an utterance of profanity.

Obama's Arrival in China Is Met With Tense Confrontations Between U.S., Chinese Officials

Sep 6, 2016 6:20 am

"I get allergic when I think of Trump"? What, did she hire a 7th grade drama class to come up with her jokes?

Clinton Suffers Another Coughing Episode During Speech — and Shares Crowd-Pleasing Diagnosis

Sep 6, 2016 6:42 am

Well Mr. Zeid Ra'ad al-Hussei, here is some more bullying for ya.

You might mean something to yourselves, you might mean something to Establishment American politicians but to red blooded American citizens, we view the UN as a threat to our Liberty. Oh, I know that you have a lovely Nirvana in mind of a borderless, socialist world. A world populated with defeated souls, rampant immorality and a complete lack of prosperity except for those who manage to wiggle their way up through the pond scum. You sweet darlings...NOPE!

'We Will Not Be Bullied': Trump, Populists Slammed by United Nations Human Rights Chief

Notice this new thing, these people are not protesting this particular group or that that hinders them in their thoughts, the protest the whole dad blane Country! The whole thing...right down to the Constitution! This is a new thing that because they don't perfectly get everything they want, screw the whole Country.

So here is this goofy President that gets embarrassed in China, completely disrespected in the Philippines by the President, no less, and he has to reveal once again that he is nothing more than just another 2 bit community organizer and take a big public stand on really immature football player. Sometimes I wake up and feel like I'm living in the middle of the Cuckoo's Nest...I'm looking around for Jack Nicholson to get an autograph.

Obama Responds to 49ers QB Colin Kaepernick's National Anthem Protest

When asked of Jackie Gleason, what makes great acting, he said great acting is great lying. When you think about it, that is an absolutely true statement. Only the soundest of mind's in Hollywood are able to separate their occupation of performing "lies" from the realities of the real world. But Hillary, her entire public, and probably most of her private life is an entire lie...just plain ol' acting.

This guy just looks devious or demented. You certainly wouldn't want him to be the face a sales team to garner a new contract or order. Being a good liar is deadly in business, being a good liar in politics is lethal...to us, that is.

ABC Anchor Absolutely Grills Clinton's VP on New Email Scandal Revelations

In the past when Conservatives have speculated or warned that the Hillary/Obama agenda was to bring the United States to ruin we always got "Vast right wing cooks" or some such accusation. Now we see the reality of their intentions... and we were absolutely correct! let me remind you who intend to not vote, vote for Hillary or go and hide in a toy box and vote for Johnson. This is their direct and purposeful goal. Not only will Hillary have the Supreme Court Judges but many, many others down the chain. It's an odd trick they are using. They are hoping to just look stupid choosing "Sharia Capable" people to Judicial positions in order to be politically correct but the fact is they know in their hearts that these people will act as agents of war against our Country. Imagine a Supreme Court Consisting of Muslims and Radical Liberals...our Constitution will be vacated inside two years. And yes, this IS what they are after!

Obama Nominates First Muslim American to Be a Federal Judge

Some hallmarks of an intelligent person is the ability to set aside emotions, pride and self-pity in the course of pursuing a positive, effectual outcome.

Mr. levin, and it's not really a surprise, has retained his status as one of the great intellectuals that are so valuable to the political discussion.

If you were swimming around in the bottom of a well that you accidentally fell into, are you intelligent enough to grab the only rope hanging in front of you even though it's not made with a color that you like?

'I'm Gonna Vote For Donald Trump': Mark Levin Abruptly Changes Course

In their hearts, minds, hands and schools. In some of the most notable tenants of their verses lies the reality of their soul that is anti-Christ and anti-Jewish.

Think about it- lots of religions in the world and not a single one has hatred for Christians and Jews let alone wanting to kill them except for one...Muslims. The Radical Liberals keep trying to brain wash people into thinking that it's a Religion of peace and I'm asking why? Why are they trying so hard to make people believe that they are a Religion of peace (Love) when there isn't any proof of it.

I'd like to offer to Muslims that are seeking a peaceful and loving soul, proof of the source of the answer hung on a Cross more than two thousand years ago.

Sep 7, 2016 7:27 am

Well and good Mr. Watson and I would like to add something additional to think about regarding racism. The Government that is perceived to be the answer for every societal ill is the only entity in this Country that categorizes people by race...and that is the definition of racism.

Sep 7, 2016 8:13 am

That's great news! I love Humpback fillets!

Feds Remove Humpback Whales From Endangered Species List

Sep 7, 2016 8:17 am

And in other news today, for some weird reason, all of the local fast food restaurants have reported that they have sold out of bacon double cheeseburgers.

Tractor-Trailer Carrying Bacon, Ribs Catches Fire on Interstate. Let the One-Liners Begin.

Sep 7, 2016 8:23 am

Folks, she really has something seriously wrong with her. I mean, when you just listen to the audio of Hillary coughing by itself, it sounds like a terrible death is happening behind a curtain in a hospital somewhere.

OK, let's see here...how'd they say how to shoot your own foot? Oh, Ok then, here we go...ready? BANG Yep, that hurts!...that hurts! Yep, that really, really hurts. Damn, that was stupid. That was dumb!...man that hurts!

Reliably Republican-Backing Dallas Morning News Won't Support Trump: 'Not Qualified to Serve as President'

Historically when countries have been taken over by Dictators or political regimes there have always been immediate and shocking indicators that told the population "You no longer have any power" If a day where to come that a Marine, with all his valor and honor, is standing at the foot of Air Force One saluting someone as vile and undeserving as Hillary it will be an oft reminder "America, you no longer have any power, you've lost your soul...the horrible is in charge now"

Well they aren't playing games, they have and are demonstrating an outright protection of Hillary...obviously to everyone that they are unabashed about it. But don't be so fooled, it's the Obama/Hillary/Globalist machine doing this...Comey is just trying to stay alive.

'We Don't Play Games': FBI's Comey Defends Decision to Release Clinton Notes Ahead of Holiday Weekend

Oh dear, doesn't it just give you so much comfort to be able to lean on such a solid rock of integrity as Hillary...it just makes me want to bake her a freaking blueberry pie!

Clinton Promises No More 'Ground Troops' in Iraq 'Ever Again'

At some point she has to run out of material...but the again we might see something like this in the future:

Matt:" The word judgment has been used a lot around you, Secretary Clinton, over the last year and a half,"

Hillary: "Matt, I feel your pain but everyone knows that Jim isn't always as responsible as he should have been when we were trying so hard as the transparently header thing."

Matt: "What?...who's Jim?"

Hillary: "Oh, well, he's the one that did it."

Matt: "Did what exactly?"

Hillary: "You brought it up, Matt! My email thing. Everyone knows at this point that a vast Republican conspiracy is trying to turn attention away from the fact that a header with a transparency issue of servers was not the FBI's idea of truth gobbling chickens by a pond...excuse me, cough, cough, cough...oh, my. Cough, cough, cough, hack, hack, gurgle...oh, uh...cough, cough, excuse me, cough."

Matt: "Sorry, I'm not even going to ask if you're ok...I think we better go to a commercial right now."

Hillary: "Cough!"

'Why Wasn't It Disqualifying?': Matt Lauer Intensely Questions Clinton on Email Scandal

I joined the Navy early in Reagan's time as our respectable Commander in Chief (I'm so glad that I can say that) The guy's that had been in for a while talked about Russian Migs and Bears doing fly-by's of our Carrier. I was like, "We've been out for 3 months...I haven't seen any and I'm on the Flight Deck all day" They would then answer "Oh, they don't do it any more...not Since Reagan got elected" These other aggressive countries are just pushing this phony, community organizer around by doing all this. Believe me, it's as demoralizing to the troops as the prospect of having to salute a Drag Queen.

Russian Fighter Jet Comes Within 10 Feet of U.S. Navy Plane

Sep 8, 2016 6:41 am

It's just amazing that even after 7 ½ years as President, he is still bowing to foreign leaders. He is really more of a "World guy" than an "American guy" but he is one of the bitches that gets teased by the others who have way more grit than he does. "We are the world, we are the world" the crowd sings. But Obama has to stand in the back, licking a lollipop because he ain't as cool as the people at the front.

Sep 9, 2016 5:46 am

Putin has seen both sides of the coin. He knows the economic effects of Communism/ Socialism and he has seen what happens when you have Liberty. Putin purposefully chooses Socialism because that model affords him personal power and riches. I'm sure he laughs at Obama for actually believing that aspects of Socialism are a viable economic solution. Putin uses Socialism to bitch slap those who believe in it...and Obama is just one of the slapee's.

Sep 9, 2016 6:19 am

It's dog food made of dead alligators...who doesn't know these things?

Libertarian Candidate Gary Johnson Stuns MSNBC Panel: 'What Is Aleppo?'

My goodness, doesn't she look like a big important person like Mr. Trump speaking in front of her new shiny plane...she's a grown up now. And for Pete's sake, she really slammed those hard questions right back at those rough and tough reporters. Later, they are all getting Graham Crackers and milk and get to watch Power Rangers on the plane!

Clinton Does First Press Conference in 278 Days, Gets Zero Questions About Email Scandal

Hillary Clinton does two things every day, and only two things: Make excuses for her crimes and bash Mr. Trump. A rabid dog on a chain has few friends.

Clinton Slams Trump's 'Unpatriotic' Praise of Vladimir Putin

And yet another player from the Bronco's does a kneeling. The NFL is going to quickly become a joke. Whatever happened to "Blood, sweat & tears"? The whole thing, including most of the reporters, has become just a big liberal stage act depicting football games. Homosexuality, pink shoes, Black Lives Matter protesters...I miss the good ol' days when the players got arrested for DUI's and bar fights.

You know what, even if she is never indicted, why is it that she has to always be dragging down the progress in this Country with her constant troubles? How come we have to pay for all her crap? The first time the Clinton's were in office it was the same thing, we have to put up with all their scandals! They must love the hell out of, but were pretty sick of it. It's like having to constantly watch your wayward son getting arrested all the time. At some point her depressing effects on this Country has to stop. She's her own private Dust Bowl Years. It's unreal that there are people who are actually wanting 4 more years of depression.

Sep 10, 2016 5:16 am

Ain't that cute coming from a lying sack of slop that's infested with fetid, rotting fish guts and the puss that was squeezed out of her rotting brain. Ain't that just deplorable?

Clinton: Half of Trump's Supporters Are in 'Basket of Deplorables'

Sep 10, 2016 6:05 am

Mr. Trump is absolutely correct. If Hillary wins, a person with a multitude of legal troubles and zero positive attributes, it will be absolute proof that the Global Establishment in conjunction with our elected officials have a complete fix on our elections.

We will have officially obtained the title "Oppressed People" Consider what the other Western Countries are seeing. Because they really don't have any skin in the game, they are able to see things "As is" in our election. On one hand they see this old bat who is in a constant struggle to stay out of legal trouble, has very little people attending her rallies, and is having these very troubling coughing fits.

On the other hand they see a non-Politician who obviously has the skills to manage a lot of complex issues, is robust and healthy, honest, real, and has crowds at his rallies like NO Politician has ever seen before...they see this huge fervor for Mr. Trump! Now, if she wins, they will be just as perplexed as we will be. They'll be looking at each other going WTF? and then the next realization that they'll have is "Oh, oh...we are all really screwed, America was the last hope of Liberty and now that's gone too"

Trump: The U.S. Will Become 'Another Venezuela' if Clinton Wins in November

Larry King is still out there? He's been 85 years old for 30 years now...weird!

Just think of that, she wants to be President and despises tens of millions of Americans. Donald Trump is right, she is a hateful bigot and thinks that she is somehow the entitled queen. She hates Americans like ISIS does.

Hillary, welcome to your final blow...that was you're Howard Dean scream. You just lost the election...the Bible say's "Be sure, you're sins will find you out"

Clinton: Half of Trump's Supporters Are in 'Basket of Deplorables'

We were having such a nice day until we heard that Hillary hates us Americans, now I have to explain this to my children....

Clinton: Half of Trump's Supporters Are in 'Basket of Deplorables'

We were just getting ready to sit down and have chili dogs and Lay's potato chips and now my kids are crying...thanks Hillary. Now they think that you're gonna kill them or something.

Clinton: Half of Trump's Supporters Are in 'Basket of Deplorables'

Hillary you need to just stop hurting all of us with your criminal stuff, you're husband's sperm flying everywhere and all of your insults...delete yourself....please!

Clinton: Half of Trump's Supporters Are in 'Basket of Deplorables'

Sep 12, 2016 6:16 am

Well, that was the moment that I could see coming. I think the Clinton campaign need to start getting a lot more serious about her health...she could very well die as a result of over driving someone who obviously can't take it. This is like college kids watching one of their overly drunk friends trying to walk across a street and laughing.

Video Shows Clinton Suffering 'Medical Episode' as She Stumbles, Leaves 9/11 Memorial Early

Sep 12, 2016 6:20 am

That has to be embarrassing for the NFL...Pee Wee football players display more maturity during the National Anthem.

See the New Way Some NFL Players Are Now Protesting During National Anthem

Sep 12, 2016 6:23 am

Her candidacy is just really, really looking weird...it's like they are rolling Andy Warhol around in a wheel chair in his last bazaar days.

Clinton Diagnosed With Pneumonia Days Before Attending 9/11 Ceremony, Doctor Says

No, you can't take that back, she meant it. This is exactly why Mr. Trump is where he is...the Liberals, the Establishment, they absolutely feel this way.

Clinton Expresses 'Regret' for Saying Half of Trump's Supporters Are 'Deplorables'

It's a very odd contrast that we are witnessing this election...if not surreal. On one hand we have Donald Trump, canvassing the Country with overflowing events like a Top Fuel dragster. On the other, we have Hillary Clinton who is like a battered '54 Ford that was the sole survivor of last years' demolition derby with four wobbling wheels and the ever presence of steam barreling out of the hood and running on only 3 cylinders...accented with the constant barrage of back-fires, shocking the crowd.

Ex-Secret Service Agent Who Protected Clinton Shares 'Nonpartisan' Rundown of Why Her Fainting Video 'Really Scares' Him

I often wonder, how can it be possible for a person to live out every day, the whole day, telling lies, covering up previous lies and scandal with other looming bombshells yet to drop. I think what we are witnessing is the fact that you can fool yourself, you can fool the people, but it's impossible to fool your body. And I wonder, what could possibly be on her mind in the last minute before she goes to sleep every night.

Without any doubt, they would insert Joe Biden. They have already prepared for this scenario. In the meantime, the weirdest of weirds, and I believe to be a first in the world's history, her husband will be campaigning for her as she is lying in a bed with a frilly bed cover and ten pillows...throwing Kleenex's on the floor and screaming at the staff.   What Would Happen if Clinton Dropped Out of the Race for President?

Ok, that's very unfortunate and all that stuff but why are we having to be dragged along with her problems...everybody has enough of their own to worry about. The freaky notion put forth by the Democrats regarding Hillary's problems is that WE have to be the one's doing the hard work of enduring them.

There is so much weirdness to that whole event. I imagine that after a little bit Hillary is desperate to escape the apartment, regardless of anything. Chelsea finally gives up on preventing her from leaving and is last seen sitting on the couch filing her nails saying "Fine, leave...suit yourself then" Hillary then goes outside, oblivious that she is a Presidential Candidate, but for some reason is walking down the street looking for her Secret Service detail.

Twitter Erupts With Clinton Body-Double Conspiracy Theories Following Health Scare

I ask myself why? It's freaking basketball. The NCAA has no obligation on earth to say a thing about these social drama's but chooses instead to insert themselves. if you are over, say 45, just think back to the 70's & 80's and contrast that with today. it's like you see a Bulldozer enter a car wash but out the other end emerges a pink convertible VW Beetle

ACC to Pull Championship Games From North Carolina Over Controversial 'Bathroom Law' Days After NCAA Does the Same

No, both sides are not just yelling at each other. You have one side attacking America and the other side defending itself. The core problem that we now live with is a fairly large population of people that live in abject reproach of reality, deferring to their own preferences and fantasy's as a suitable state of mind.

Here's a little lesson, really for everyone. You can teach this in your Corporations in executive and sales training. You can teach this in your counseling and most importantly, teach it to children.

When you come across someone who has the kind of glowing self confidence that you can almost feel, you should know that the greatest reason why is that they are someone who is honest with themselves first and then honest to everyone else as an automatic extension.

The false replacement for being honest with one's self is pride, arrogance and a self-constructed sense of superiority based on fantasy. So here's why self-confident people vs. arrogant people are way more successful in life...and I'm not just talking about money.

Lying to yourself will automatically impose self-guilt and the more guilt, the more cover up is needed. The more cover that is needed, the more weight you add to your life. The more guilt and cover up you have and the constant maintenance thereof, the less ability you have to tackle the important necessities of life.

People who are honest with themselves and others develop a sort of absolution from condemnation from others, it sets them apart as special and down inside, they know it...thus the self-confidence. Honest people are the ones that are well loved and have a lot of friends. So the question is, how is it that Donald Trump beat all those experienced politicians and why do so many people show up at his rallies? Honesty.

Trump Campaign Manager Challenges CNN Anchor When Asked if Candidate Will Release 'Proof' of IRS Audit

So, this little kid who has never lifted more than 20 pounds in his life, spends any time he can golfing instead of working, has no real tangible accomplishments except for one book that nobody read, has got some kind of authority to describe those who are industrious?

It's a lovely thing to see and it's really the first time that we are seeing it. Hillary's only campaign strategy is to smear Mr. Trump and that's all because they thought that if Obama got elected twice then surely the dumbing of everyone has official been achieved. Now they are finding out that it's not so and desperation has gotten to such a point that they need to interrupt the election season to re-guilt the citizens.

I think that what's really bugging the Establishment and the media is that all the support for Mr. Trump is a shocking realization that the people aren't obeying them. That people are being rebellious and not regarding THEMSELVES as the hierarchy. Mr. Trump's popularity is a slap in the face of the conceited elite with an extra kick to the shin because he's richer than them...and that makes us smile!

Check Out an Incredulous Obama Needling 'Working People' Who Support Trump

I'm sure, a State Senator who is assumed to have some level of maturity beyond 7th grade, now join's the drama queen contest. When the football season is over, Colin Niknak is going to invite all of his new found friends over for some cake and cookies so they can praise him in person and giggle at the big scary Americans.

State Senator Refuses to Stand During Pledge of Allegiance in 'Solidarity' With Colin Kaepernick

Now, how in the Sam Hill ("Who was a real person, by the way"-Rush Limbaugh) can you expect Bill Clinton to remember all of the lies when the Hillary people are always changing the excuses? Man a living, he's got the girlie's to entertain, he ain't got time for all of this BS!

Bill Clinton Says Hillary Has 'the Flu,' but His Spokesman Immediately Walks That Back

That's nice but...what's Aleppo?

Gary Johnson's Campaign Announces It Has Gained Ballot Access in All 50 States

The fake Conservatives are really getting flushed out of the underbrush this year. Oh, but for the love of vanity, they stand to lose it all.

There is no other plausible reason for this than a directive from Obama...thus the lack of reason being posited. Yep, Obama really likes them girlie boys, I tell ya..

Chelsea Manning to Receive Taxpayer-Funded Gender Transition Surgery After Announcing Hunger Strike

We are a sovereign nation, there is absolutely nothing that obligates us to act as the world's dump.

When I was in the Navy my Chief was Stoney Burke, who is now regarded as the top ABE of the Navy. He used to always say "Proper Prior Planning Prevents Possible Piss-Poor Performance"

At this point, you have to have a pretty dark heart to not like Donald Trump. It's a strange phenomenon, but there are people who are actually scared by a politician who doesn't put on that fake stage act to make themselves appear flawless. It's as if these never-Trump people have a craving to be fooled. Mr. Trump is real.

This problem we are having with people in this Country being offended by America will be addressed shortly by the next President.

School Officials Apologize After Complaints of Trump, Betsy Ross Flags at Football Game

Ronald Reagan was the first President that I was old enough to vote for. My high school years were such a dreary time in America and Reagan was so badly needed and then he won.

No longer the need for a constant vigilance against a hostile enemy, the Government. No longer the assault, no longer a sense of doom. A quietness for a change as the dust settles and the sun comes to light.

Wouldn't it be nice to go about the day knowing that the President is doing that job now, the job of battling oppression? It's the job equal to a General and his Lieutenants and the troops doing the fighting for us now. No longer the need to stock up on ammo and survival supplies, desperately. No longer the worry that the next day will be worse than the last.

But first, you will have to sacrifice. You'll have to sacrifice only one hour of your day on November 8 and vote. Your liberty lies in your heart of priorities and that hour will be the one that determines your destiny. Vote.

Mr. Donald Trump is not in this race because he needs the fame or the money. He doesn't need the opulence and posh formalities of the White House, he really does just want to make this Country the great Country that once was. Give not only we the reason to sing "Happy days are here again" but also the skeptics.

Trump Pledges No Taxes for Low-Income Americans, Lays Out Plans for Growth in Economic Speech

Sep 18, 2016 6:09 am

And just so as not leave a hanging chad, I'll explain why Mr. Trump, while not an Idealog, is by this time very, very close to Conservative one.

While Mr. Trump looks at our Country's problems as badly in need of repair and not being an Idealog, he surrounds himself with nothing but! Have you noticed? Not one mediocre Conservative is on his team that I have seen, anyway. What we will find with Mr. Trump is that Conservative principles are played out in policy while he gets to get his hands dirty fixing things. There are not a bunch of philosophical problems regarding all these bureau's there are a lot of tangible one's as an example. And for goodness sake, he's the only one on the Republican list that will ACTUALLY build that freaking wall!

Sep 19, 2016 10:40 pm

Mr. Trump, I'd like to say something to you in the closing months of this election...thank you. Thank you for caring enough to forego a life of ease to dare to go into an environment of idiots and try to make sense. Thank you sir, that you spent your own money to vanquish the stupid politics of people running for important positions of political power and undue the same crap that we are so tired of.

Thank you for being real...and honest. Thank you for being the next President...we have long needed the hammer and nails, the ax and log, the pole and fish, the prairie and wagon...and the truth.

If Hillary were to win, by the end of her first term it would mean that out of the last 28 years, 20 of those years were occupied by either a Bush or a Clinton...what are we, Zambia?

I think that in a lot of ways Mr. Trump has changed the public perception of typical politicians and what they expect. It's so undeniable that Mr. Trump is honest and says what he thinks and when people contrast to the typical B-Ser politician, it's laughable...and this is what really, really pisses off the Establishment the most.

And after David Simon said this, he and the two other little girls that he was with turned and ran away, giggling and clutching their Raggity Ann dolls while licking their lollipops. But later on, he was spotted sitting on a park bench crying and being consoled by his Mom...one of his little yellow shoes was missing.

Hannity in Twitter battle with television producer over Trump

First of all, "The World" didn't come up with the idea of America, a bunch of patriotic people pissed off at the way of the world did and rejected it. Support for Mr. Trump now is the direct result of the exact same sentiment. So no, Bono, you don't get to redefine America...you big, tough, and rebellious rocker.

U2's Bono: 'I think Trump is trying to hijack the idea of America'

The way to understand Obama is to look at what he does. He want's terrorists here. He loves these attacks on America because to him, these American, Christian honky's are getting their come up'ns. Yes, it is that plain and simple.

Krauthammer: Obama admin's 'reluctance and denial' to ID terrorism 'hovers between the inexplicable and the delusional'

When Mr. Trump gets elected, there will need to be a lot of house cleaning to be done at the Pentagon as well as the subsequent reversal of the homosexual and drag queen crap in the Military. What Hillary and Obama people are doing is trying to load up our Military with people who will turn our weapons of war on us because they know that the Red Blooded servicemen won't...period!

Navy to require all sailors to undergo transgender education training by 2017

That's neat, bye, bye.

Obama reflects on time in the Oval Office: 'I curse more than I should'

Gee wiz, the guy is just a living Hustler cartoon series, name and all.

Anthony Weiner's latest alleged sexting scandal involves 15-year-old girl

If we can make tranquilizer darts that drop large animals then we can make them for people like this. It would be a good, safe and non-lethal way of subduing these types of characters.

Trump on Terence Crutcher, killed by police in Tulsa: 'He did everything you're supposed to do'

There are two basic mindsets that black folks have, both are justified but only one gives them liberty, empowerment and peace.

The most prevailing mindset resides with those in poor area's or Ghetto's. To put it simply, it's that sense of being outnumbered, and maybe even trapped in hopeless living conditions, by white people. While it's not true today, for decades and decades, black folks were elbowed out of the way of the burgeoning American Experience. Most importantly, it's the "us vs. them" mentality and that they are vastly outnumbered and therefore powerless.

The second mentality is the "Screw That!" mentality, referring to a refusal to just stay in the Ghetto. This mentality only comes to be for those who personally embrace some very special words in the Declaration of Independence that establishes that the existence of the United States is the Providence of God or that it is HIS purpose and then, of course, that includes African Americans. So, no matter how we all got here or how rough it has been in the past or even how rough it might be now, this Country belongs to you because it's God's place.

Panthers QB Cam Newton warns Charlotte rioters: 'You can't be a hypocrite'

Of all the things that I thought I'd ever say, this stunt by Johnson combined with Hillary's spasm and her video asking why she isn't 50 points ahead, really has me wondering if aliens and body snatchers aren't real...either that or just simple demon possession. Mr. Trump is so much more sober and real and sensible compared to these really odd freaks. This election is really something of an American idiot survey. If you know of anyone voting for Hillary or Johnson, you will now know to stay far, far away from that person...unreal.

'He really did that?': Gary Johnson's sudden antics during interview leave MSNBC panel dumbfounded

Sep 25, 2016 7:52 am

"And you might be asking yourself why I'm not 50 points ahead at this point, which at this point, what does it really matter? And why is Donald Trump killing all of the African American children while my assistant is out back in the alley hammering away on my cell phones, you might ask. Well, I'll tell you this, I'm gonna go and kill everyone's dog that isn't 8" tall...right in front of there...cough, cough,cough...uuugghhh cough....ewww cough, cough, hack, flim.

You can all go to hell if you don't vote for me!"

Sep 25, 2016 8:30 am

I think you have to go for the jugular here. An add juxtaposing Hillary's denials on the emails with Trey Gowdy and Comey exchange and a montage of Hillary falling in the airplane, coughing, the 911 memorial seizure etc...saying she is not healthy enough while expressing sympathy that someday she will get well again. Most of all, the 50 points ahead thing mixed with all of the other clips that show her scary bitch side...which is who she really is. The 50 points ahead thing is the killer...it's the killer!

Trump campaign plans $140 million ad buy that would outpace Clinton's ad reservations through Election Day

Sep 26, 2016 7:03 am

Mr. Trump is going to do just fine in the debate. He's been in many close discussions with way more important people than Hillary. She just better hope that she doesn't burn out a circuit board at some point.

Mr. Trump won that debate. If you are trying to judge the debate by the rules established in your high school debate class then you will miss the results that are important. Hillary was full of political blah, blah, blah Mr. Trump came out with new answers and really came out strong with business and the economy and that's what most people are concerned with. Mr. Trump came out as the one who had the real world grasp on trade, business and the economy.. Hillary could say nothing.

It's the same every election. All the analysts go on TV with all of the most sophisticated paradigms possible but the fact is that every election is won based on only two things, Independents which act as the quality control department and the other is turn out for a candidate. Mr. Trump has the Independents and most certainly, MEGA turn out...big league! :)

As a guy who has only did labor in my life, I can't help but look at solving problems by putting my hands to it. Most people can relate to that in other ways in their life as well even if they are more the office worker type. From mowing the lawn, grocery shopping, changing a tire, starting a campfire etc...people are familiar with the fact that many problems take a physical effort. Mr. Trump will win this election based on that factor...that's his greatest relatability. He's a doer, she's a blabberer.

If anyone is perplexed by Evangelicals' support of Mr. Trump it's because we already have our Lord...we don't look at Government as our "religion" We don't look at Government as a problem solver, a comforter or anything else other than build some roads, protect our Country and borders, pay the light bills and then shut the heck up! An election, and this one in particular, is about the public hiring a qualified technician and not some fairy priest floating around to the sound of violins, showering your feelings with flower petals.

Folk's, there are two more debates. Like a well thought out boxing match, the knock out is coming!

I have a good friend that is an old time style Democrat but pays no attention to politics but still had no love loss for Mr. Trump all year. I asked him last evening if he saw the debate and he surprised me by piping up with enthusiasm for Trump saying that he's voting for him. His first thoughts were that he thought Mr. Trump is a smart (expletive...in a good way) The second thing he liked is when Clinton brought up bankruptcies, Trump said something like "That's good business" He loved the unabashed candor. Folk's, I really do think that the polls that came out after the debate reflects the fact that many people are just now getting to get to know Mr. Trump and that his candor and genuine character will win the day. I see that Hillary is trying this big smiling thing now, she doesn't know that it just makes her look even more fake...it matches her empty words that everyone forgets 4 seconds later.

Few actors in history have found that certain place down in themselves that recreates the kind of mania that Howard Dean displayed in his scream speech. He looked like he could have chewed the head off of a rabid opossum while it was still alive.

Howard Dean stands by suggestion that Trump might be a 'coke user'

So, that's why Hillary was smiling all day! I think I see a little honeymoon in Mexico on the horizon after the election. Vicente Fox is sitting there thinking "Nobody else in America is in love with her...maybe I get her" Wouldn't it be charming, Vicente and Hillary retiring in a little stucco bungalow in some small town in Mexico? She could throw a lamp at him from time to time... as often as he slaps her for not sweeping the floor.

Sep 28, 2016 6:15 am

Mr. Trump is correct but it's a really convenient excuse for many, many causes... primarily for human control but also in trade battles. Global Warming is an abstract and intangible notion to which no one can either prove or refute...it is the séance of the corrupted and greedy soul.

Sep 28, 2016 6:21 am

Miss Universe is a contest after all. If Mike Tyson would have showed up to a boxing match weighing only 150 lbs., wouldn't that be a problem? Or if Farrah Fawcet Majors would have showed up on a set for a toothpaste commercial with 3 missing front teeth?

Sep 28, 2016 10:18 am

I guess the Arizona Republic just came out with an endorsement for Hillary, a Democrat for the first time. If I were in the Trump campaign, I would start making a notable point that Mr. Trump steadfastly refuses to buy newspapers' editorial boards off...this is obviously the effort of the Hillary campaign and is obviously what they're are doing.

Can you just imagine the peace in our Country when this dolt is gone and Mr. Trump is President?

I see that the Clinton campaign has bought yet another editorial staff at a newspaper. Breaking news: USA Hookers Today allows Clinton's campaign staff write their editorial page, news at 11:00.

USA Today breaks tradition in brutal editorial, warns Trump is 'unfit for the presidency'

Good luck Tappy Pants, the Trump campaign knows that it would be a self-contrived distraction to bring up Bill's peener problems...there's way too much current, relevant and juicy material that Hillary is entrenched in NOW that is way more useful. Just a montage, by a third party, of her falling down, coughing fits and bobbing around in a catatonic fit before being thrown into the limo like a sack of potatoes is quite enough.

CNN's Jake Tapper tells Trump supporter the GOP nominee is 'surrounded by a philanderers club'

If they can rule that a trademark is offensive, which is against the 1st amendment, then they can easily rule that any business is offensive...thus the road to Fascism.

Supreme Court to hear case over government refusing to register trademarks deemed offensive

CHAPTER 10

OCTOBER 2016

Here's what I find confounding by a factor of 10, why in the Sam Dickens is there an existing expectation that Mr. Trump be flawless every step of the way, how come he can't have a few rough edges and why does he have to be absolutely pristine in light of the fact that Hillary is so obviously beyond faults, but rather a down right model of everything possibly wrong with a human being?

This judge took it seriously when Jesus said "Pick up your cross and follow me" I'd rather have the future of this judges soul than the souls of them on the Supreme Court who allowed this abstract and evil notion of extra horny dudes that do yucky poop sex getting married.

Alabama judge removed from office for defying gay marriage law

If Hillary is such the clear strong candidate, then why do they have to pay off the editorial boards? Here's why it's a waste of money though, how many stupid people that would be easily swayed by an editorial, read editorials?

136

In past years when polls showed Obama leading McCain or Romney they were believable, but I absolutely do not believe these polls this year because this election has so much to do about whether or not we are still America. Let me ask the real smart political pundits and professors, when was the last time that a candidate had this much of enthusiastic and overflowing crowds at events and still lost?

Some news entities are tricked into thinking that it's a close race by the polls, some news entities trick the public into thinking it's a close race for the sake of viewership...but then there is the street. All the media say's it's a close race all the while ignoring the masses. It's funny to see the dumb look on these newspapers' faces when they say "Gee, we didn't know that so many people are for Mr. Trump"

The extra smart people who wrote this article wrote "The hotel attempted to cover the graffiti with wooden boards" What do you mean they "attempted" as if something prevented them from doing something so simple. Maybe there was a piece of gum on the wall and when they went to put the plywood up they stopped and said "Oh, nope...we can't cover up the graffiti, there's gum on this elevation, but we attempted to" Or maybe this reporter thinks that the spray paint was so thick and viscous that it bled through 3/4" AC...but they attempted. It ought to be mandatory that all males take 4 years of shop class in High School.

Donald Trump's hotel in D.C. vandalized with 'Black Lives Matter' graffiti

Not according to Megyn Kelly. Good grief, she tore into Mr. Trump last night with hell in her eyes and a tightly wrapped face. That was before I had to change channels...like always. Dr. Toni Grant, who was the predecessor of Laura Schlesinger that always used to ask women "Do you want to be respected or do you want to be loved?"

People would do back flips when she would ask this, they didn't understand that by a woman being lovable she will also be automatically respected. The troubling element for feminist women trying to get ahead or respected like a man is that they resort to angry bitching...but I don't know of any guy that is a jerk (bitching) and is still respected. People don't respect bitches...they never have, never will.

Oct 4, 2016 6:02 am

They are building a data base on gun owners, just waiting for the moment the Supreme Court goes left and the First Amendment is determined to mean that "Militia" means the National Guard and confiscation can begin...which will also be the start of Civil War 2. Is that the peace and understanding that you Liberals were looking for?

Oct 5, 2016 4:44 am

Kaine looks and acts like some kind of toilet paper Rep that pinches girls butts on the way into a buyers office.

Oct 5, 2016 5:27 am

Mr. Trump himself wrote about the loss in his book "The art of the comeback" So what was Mr. Trump supposed to do after suffering a huge loss like that, give whatever money he had left to the Government for them to waste, fire thousands of employees and then go out of business? Here's a personal way of looking at this. If the company that you work for suffered a loss, would you want them to fire you and close the doors...or take the legal, freaking loss on their taxes and stay in business?

Mike Pence: Trump 'used the tax code just the way it's supposed to be used'

There's no question that Mr. Pence mopped the floor with Kaine. He was so much more the adult in the room and he did really well with his composure regarding the little, yipping Chihuahua constantly biting at his ankles....smart guy...smart guy!

Kaine prosecutes Trump, Pence touts conservatism in VP debate

Recently some Republican (?) members of Congress said that they could work with Hillary if she were elected. Here's a hint for those Republicans who are scratching their sweaty heads over the fact that Donald Trump is now the Presidential Candidate. The masses of Republicans and Conservatives have absolutely had it with supposed members, on our side, playing Patty Cakes with Democrats and this obsession with policies that only line their own pockets with money all while the fundamental strengths and structures of our Country are pushed off to the side.

Only the strength and viability of our Military is what determines whether we are a country or not. And whether we are a sitting duck in a world full of countries dying to conquer America or not. Hillary will do nothing but continue and exacerbate the full blown decline of our Military's capabilities, morale and the reversing of it's true role by turning it into a High School diversity experiment. Think of this, if we came under a full blown conventional or nuclear attack by a united group of hostile countries, where could we look for help?...at that point, it's too late.

But why wouldn't you trust him? Is it because he will select Conservative judges? Or that he will protect Religious Liberty? That he will disconnect America from Globalism and Crony Capitalism? There's an old adage that goes back centuries, Don't stick your arm into a wood chipper if you still plan on being able to get that little end of the rubber hose of a grease gun onto the grease zerks of a combine while pumping the handle at the same time.

All of the sudden, Tea Party. And then all of the sudden, Donald Trump. Some say that these two phenomenon's are perplexing to the Establishment Republicans...they are not. They know exactly what's going on...the jig is up!

These two movements are the DIRECT result of the fact that those on the right side finally got tired of people running for office as Conservatives and then being nothing more than Democrats when in office PERIOD! Donald Trump's historical support is not rebellion. It's not a message to the politicians...it's in spite of them, or what they say or what they think.

They shouldn't flatter themselves...we are not even thinking of them. Donald Trump, as it happens to be, has a quality few politicians possess, good ol' fashioned freaking honesty! REAL honesty! Now, this year is having a profound effect on several people that have been considered to ostensibly be on the right, or have professed that they are. The stage curtain is being slowly pulled open and revealing the phony act behind. Oh, there are the "Noble" excuses! Trump isn't sophisticated, He don't like the Constitution, Trump is brash, and in Megyn Kelly's case, he's mean to chicks!

Media elites were doing just fine playing along with the game. The politicians gave them fake premises and they obliged by doing there bidding for the gain of popularity...a mutual affair, shall we say. But this year, there is a serious problem, in fact, a horrible one...Donald Trump don't do dat!

Libertarians are like a one eyed rabbit, they see things clearly on the Right, but to the Left they can't see the hovering hawk.

For you women out there that are satisfied with this evil storm of turning all the boys into girls or sissy's, are you prepared then to endure the grueling and horrible job of defending this Country upon an attack, caused by this disability?

Connecticut football coach fired for making kid run laps after he allegedly bullied fellow teammate

And you might be wondering why she's not 50 points ahead by now!!

Clinton campaign reverses decision to air campaign ads on Weather Channel ahead of Matthew (UPDATED)

My goodness!, offended?...OFFENDED!? YOU FREAKING HYPOCRITES! When every morning on talk shows, in sitcoms, news etc... people talk about the act of a fat hairy man sticking his willy in the place where you poop as if it's the same as eating a bowl of cereal? You're offended??????? When TV people sit there and slowly stroke their gonads as they talk glowingly about drag queens and bathrooms...YOU'RE OFFENDED??? REALLY??? When you sit there and watch strippers on a half time show of a Super Bowl and think it's nothing, you're offended????? In front of kids? And you're offended??? WELCOME TO THE HYPOCRITE DOME

RNC chairman addresses Trump's 2005 comments about women

What's that?

A fly.

Are you sure?

Yeah...it's a fly, just a freaking fly!

Oh, I thought it was something else.

You're an idiot, toss me a beer, ya dink.

Trump in 1989 on controversial 'Central Park Five' ad: 'Maybe hate is what we need'

Mr. Trump, just slough this off. This matter will only be lasting as long as you spend time with it. Apology said...it's done. Move on. Trust me, trust me, trust me...the liberals do it all the time. The media who will try and keep it going will only look like they always do, hyper. Forgiven...keep moving.

Republican leaders condemn Trump for lewd comments about groping women

Ahhhh...hasn't Russia been influencing you freaking Democrats' THINKING for the last 50 years?

Obama administration "confident" that Russia is trying to influence 2016 election via hacking

"I never talk like that."

"You don't?"

"Nope, never have."

"What happened to you, ya got yer junk ripped off by a PTO drive or something?"

"I like Batman."

Leaked hot-mic audio catches Trump's explicit 'locker room banter' in 2005

Oh, by gum, we really, really trust these internet outfits that freaking openly support commie Libs...Boy oh boy, they're the mostest honestest of ever!

Here are the issues Americans are Googling before the next presidential debate

Well, if they are so proud of abortion, why don't they also show the glorious picture of an undeveloped baby hanging off of the end of a pair of forceps?

Planned Parenthood targets Trump in seven-figure ad buy

Wait a minute, aren't we always told that if we think guys talk dirty that you ought to hear what girls say when they get together?

Ryan: Trump will no longer be attending campaign event in Wisconsin

Darling, should we have the sex tonight?

Yeah, we better, everyone else is doing it.

OK but let's be careful not to do it in a disgusting way.

Right.

OK so, open that little part in your pajamas.

Done.

Ok, so you're going to feel a little pressure so don't be alarmed.

OK.

Are you pregnant yet?

No.

OK, so I'll keep going…don't look.

I can't, I'm reading Women's Day.

OK, I'll let you know when I'm done. Yeah. I'm done.

That sucked.

Republican leaders condemn Trump for lewd comments about groping women

NOPE! Every squirrely politician can imagine for themselves their own insult here...THIS IS THE PEOPLES ELECTION.....STAND BACK!

'Your conduct, sir, is the distraction': Sen. Mike Lee calls on Donald Trump to step down

You can do what you want RNC...we the People will be holding a huge collective BBQ! Get out of the way. YOU STUPID ASSES! Oh you're really offended like dainty little snowflakes when absolute proof of YOUR freaking Global Establishment CRAP is revealed in Hillary's Podesta emails and YOU THINK THAT'S FINE?! Go ahead and release more of this crap WE WILL ONLY GET MORE AND MORE WIZZED!!

RNC halts production of 'Victory projects' aimed at electing Donald Trump

You freaks are forgetting something huge...Donald Trump is US!! We know him, we knew him a long time ago. Reality, reality, reality....SEIZE IT!

The list of Republicans urging Trump to step down as GOP nominee continues to swell

Mike , please hold on...this won't last long. Mike, have you ever heard any of the plumbers you have hired? Or contractors? Have you ever heard what those highway workers that Indiana hired say while on the job? Hold on!

Report: Mike Pence will also not be attending campaign event in Wisconsin with Paul Ryan

That ain't true because Donald Trump was with me that day snowboarding down the dirt slopes of a plateau in Utah at the time. What...you don't believe me? How dare you insult my dedicates!

CNN host claims Trump popped a Tic-Tac and tried to kiss her friend

The locker room talk left the building. Anybody still wanting to drag it up again will only look as hapless as Hillary did last night.

The jail comment is the one that won the night and will be remembered for a long time.

Trump says he'll appoint 'special prosecutor' to look into Clinton's emails

Before summarizing the last debate, I wanted for Monday to pass...it's interesting, the ghosts and goblins that get scared up when you walk through a graveyard.

Drudge had a headline the other day "Trump Vs. the world" If you only watch TV for news and information, you might just think that. If it weren't for the tens of millions of Trump supporters, pitchforks in hands, Mr. Trump would be alone. If it weren't for Rush Limbaugh and Sean Hannity etc..., no one would know. This election is this Nation's 240'th year integrity test...are we still who we are?

A more stark contrast in candidates has never been. A more contrast between reality and the dark world of morbid government has ever been displayed. Not since the days of our Nation's founding has there ever been such a sober decision to be made. At first I was skittish about how rough Mr. Trump should get in the debate but after he started rolling, I loved it.

It was the boldness of reality that got him there in the first place...he can't let up. Since Hillary has tried to pull Mr. Trump and Americans into the gutter, then grab her by a thatch of her scraggly hair and pull her out of the gutter for everyone to see...we can't let up! Hillary Clinton is THE poster child of the hideous hierarchy, the anonymous demons and the dark underworld that the upper chambers of government are. Here's the test: Are you more concerned with your lusts or are you concerned more about your liberty...You don't get both in elections.

Oct 11, 2016 6:00 am

The little girls who are grabbing up their dresses and running away screaming from the hit piece on Mr. Trump were only looking for that excuse. When you start to think that's it's equally possible that the GOP could be behind it and is acting in conjunction with the media, the picture becomes very, very clear.

These goofballs that are abandoning Mr. Trump could have just said nothing but they chose to take the occasion to run away. They had to open their mouths and let the Establishment know that they are still with THEM. Just think of how immature it is that locker room talk between two guys 12 years ago is somehow more awful than a Clinton Presidency. Thank you Mr. Cruz. Only the bold get to ride the biggest and most noble horses.

Cruz stands by Trump following release of offensive comments about women

Oct 11, 2016 6:22 am

Isn't it odd that the younger folks today on the internet immediately become fascinated by anything that is slightly more different than a square chunk of tofu.

Oct 11, 2016 6:39 am

Of all the election year polls, I don't believe them this year. Really CNN? You really expect anyone to believe that that Hillary won that? It's supposed to be a poll but instead, it's just all out propaganda. It's the year of the push polls...period. They just don't match ANYTHING that we are seeing and hearing...nothing!

CNN/ORC post-debate poll has good news for both candidates

OH, so it is OK to say Blue Jays? What a hypocrite, doesn't he realize how hurtful to blue jays that is? Plus now, every time people see a blue jay, they are gonna start shooting them...great! Dead blue jays laying all over peoples yards just because this guy, Jerry Howarth, chose to disparage them by daring to utter the words "Blue Jays" Thanks for saving the planet, you climate denier!

Blue Jays announcer promises not to use 'Indians' name during ALCS broadcast — here's why

Yeah but,but,but,but,but I'm offended by all the guys talking bad...where's my Teddy Bear?

Emails raise further questions over possible Clinton pay-to-play tactics

When you think about election maps showing the vast, vast majority of counties that are red and the fact that we are the very population with all the guns and the food, it's going to be a long, long day for the Establishment. All we have to start with is just the simple refusal to deliver all food stuffs to blue counties until every Establishment politician steps down...including Hillary, if she wins.

The media has become THE PR firm of the Democratic party...the anchors being miniature spokesman. Miniature, dutiful Privates. Isn't it cute, the media lost its marbles but they have been given the little jobs of licking the boots of Hillary.

NBC News 'mass hunt underway' for more damaging Trump comments

I LOVE THIS AD! Remember the speech that Josey Wales gave to the crew right before they were to battle the Union soldiers? "You gotta get mean, and I mean mad-dog mean!" Josey Wales won.

New Trump ad paints Clinton as too sick to lead country

Slap a 5 hundred million dollar libel lawsuit on 'em...topped with a gag order. Gawker them.

Two women claim Trump touched them inappropriately: 'It was an assault'

Mr. Trump's events in Florida yesterday were great! back to the good ol' style...gigantic crowds!

Team Trump: 'We're gonna go buck wild' on Bill Clinton

Trump is back! He had a huge event in Ocala Florida Wednesday and he was imitating Hillary when she lost her hydraulic pressure...really funny!

I'd like to point something out that is so obvious but of course missing in the Media of Hillary. So, I'm watching TV and all of the sudden, I see a couple of seconds of video that occurred just as Mr. Trump and Bush got off that bus and met the girl that was kind of part of that locker room talk.

Well, he very politely shook her hand and dipped his upper body in respect and was nothing but sweet to her. Now, because of the "Male banter" and the media take on all this, aren't we supposed to see him attack her? It's obvious right on video that he was joshing with "The

148

boys" on one hand and acted completely differently in an actual circumstance.

Another thing. We know for an ABSOLUTE FACT that the media coordinates DIRECTLY with the Democrats...no question! Right when Cooper was interrogating Mr. Trump in the last debate about the bus video, Cooper kept going "You say that you have never actually done these things? Are you saying that? Are you saying that? Are you saying that? You are saying that you actually never actually done these things?" I thought to myself "There's a trap here. Why is he so focused and why is that one little part so important to him?" Answer: Because in complete cooperation with the Clinton campaign and the NYT and whoever else (Probably the whole establishment), they had already lined up these false victims to compliment the Access Hollywood tape. The whole freaking made up drama is completely false...what else would you expect from Hillary?

Liberty University student president defends Falwell, Jr.: 'Majority of students' will vote Trump

"Oh, ew, oh my golly, that sign really scrinched up my panties with a sweaty creaking sound!...yes, I'll take whipped cream on my latte"

Here's the 'downright scary' sign CNN's Jim Acosta found at a Trump rally press table

One thing is for certain, this election IS the "War of The People"!!! (I added quotes for emphasis) Let's just take an honest look at what's happening here.

The Establishment hates Mr. Trump. Media hates Mr. Trump. Godless people who have to serve the two former, because they have no place else to go, hate Mr. Trump. And then there is Mr. Trump...AND THE OVERFLOWING THRONGS OF THE AMERICAN PEOPLE! It's not easy for me to get emotional but lately since Mr. Trump has gone Buck Wild and when I see the symbiosis of Mr. Trump and the uproarious, passionate crowds, I sometimes do.

My Lord, I say to myself, My Lord...the people are fighting back! For the first time in my life THE PEOPLE ARE FIGHTING BACK!!!! and look at who's fighting us! Mr. Trump, THANK YOU!

Oct 14, 2016 6:49 am

Oh dear, did he insult your little Snick for a husband? Did you have to wrap him up in a blanket and rock him to sleep? Goodness sake, just promise him an ice cream cone the next time you go out to fill your large butt with greasy cheeseburgers and he'll be alright.

Michelle Obama: Calling Trump's comments 'locker-room talk' is an 'insult to decent men'

Oct 15, 2016 7:19 am

To Hillary and her goons, the Bunker media, and to the actresses that tried to pull off the great "Molestation Show" Nice try!

Trump takes apart his teleprompter during North Carolina rally — literally

Oct 15, 2016 8:27 am

NO, no, noooooo Stop saying that the Molestation Show ain't working! Hillary will have another seizure!

New Emerson College swing-state poll shows the changing dynamics of the presidential race

Oct 16, 2016 4:58 am

Let me say this. When you see the huge passionate crowds at Trump rally's, they are only a small representation of the masses of millions of Americans that are TICKED!. Note to Establishment: You will not like it if things turn physical...you are messing with AMERICANS after all!

Paul Ryan pushes back against Trump's claims that the election is 'rigged'

Oct 16, 2016 5:56 am

Every criminal has only two things on their mind while in the midst of committing a crime, "I'm gonna get or do this thing" and "I'm gonna get away with it" and they are blind to everything else.

Now, the Media and the Establishment, like the criminal, is blind to something blatant in their pursuit of getting Hillary elected...there's NOTHING to vote for regarding Hillary. In the polls, how can Hillary get 47% when she isn't even around? Isn't it obvious? Why would anyone be voting FOR someone who is missing? And has not one outstanding issue to vote FOR? And where in the world is Tim Kaine?

It's the most bizarre thing you ever saw!!! And if it wasn't so ridiculous enough, anchors in the news sit there and talk about a close race but there is only one guy out there working his butt off every day against...what? and they act like it's nothing! Yeah, it's normal that the winner of a campaign doesn't have issues and is hardly ever in the public eye?? And They think there's something wrong with Donald Trump??

Oct 16, 2016 6:33 am

Well she's on something...she keeps walking around with that big Joker smile. There is a condition called Creutzfeldt–Jakob disease, it's the human variant of Mad Cow Disease and is fairly prevalent in tribal communities in South America where they practice cannibalism. One of the effects is that it causes those who have it to develop a "perma-grin" That could also be Hillary's issue.

Trump suggests Hillary Clinton is on drugs, calls for drug testing prior to final debate

Sympathy is always good publicity...may have just strongly tipped NC for Trump.

Republican field office in North Carolina 'firebombed,' police say

Well, it will be the most confounding thing ever in politics that someone who has rally's that are 20 times bigger than the opponent who hardly ever campaigns, loses. That would be unreal.

Mike Pence says GOP ticket will 'absolutely' accept Election Day outcome

While I don't think we should be saying that the election is fixed at several polling sites publicly because that could cause a lack of people on our side to go out and vote, I'm starting to think that this Molestation Show is a ruse to use as an excuse if in fact, they have rigged enough polls. They need an explanation for how it could possibly be that the candidate that is vastly more popular, and who's main issues match the public's top concerns loses to someone like Hillary that is very unpopular, has little crowds attending her rally's and is up to her pulsating eyeballs in crime and dirty politics. People might be saying that it's so odd that Mr. Trump is where he is at, but if Hillary wins, it would be an absolute "miracle" and defy everything known about American election history. DO NOT STAY AT HOME! OVERCOME THE FIX!

It's hard for people to actually grasp just how wicked the Clinton's/Media are to go after decent American's like the Trumps. She can't be seen in public, her annoying voice can't be heard in public...so, the Media does her campaigning for her. It's absolutely laughable how easily the Liberal media allows itself to be played like fools!

Never before have I seen someone characterize the way they look in public by imitating an animal...and so accurately to boot!

Elizabeth Warren clucks like a chicken while mocking Trump on his tax returns

Think of this. If everyone were to take 100 steps back from the election and just sort of make a quick summery of each candidate, the only adjective that could possibly be attributed to Hillary is corruption or scandal. To be fair, to look at Mr. Trump you might think rich Playboy. We have had two "Playboy" Presidents...we have never had a President whose only identity is scandal, in fact she is The Queen of Scandal. Scandal or crime or corruption have ALWAYS been THE political killer. Sex a long time ago didn't hurt Bill Clinton one little bit.

As you might remember from the "Spaghetti Westerns"

"Wanted in 14 counties of this state, the condemned is found guilty of the crimes of murder; armed robbery of citizens, state banks and post offices; the theft of sacred objects; arson in a state prison; perjury; bigamy; deserting her wife and children; inciting prostitution; kidnapping; extortion; receiving stolen goods; selling stolen goods; passing counterfeit money through her foundation; and contrary to the laws of this state the condemned is guilty of using marked ballots ... Therefore, according to the powers vested in us we sentence the accused here before us Hillary Rodem Clinton, and any other aliases she might have, to hang by the neck until politically dead. May God have mercy on her soul. Proceed."

Another poll shows Clinton leading Trump in a traditional Republican state

They ask "How dare you have a conspiracy theory about the election?" Well, it's easy once you realize that the whole entirety of the Democrat party is one big conspiracy...that's all it is.

Good! This is a war between good and evil and there is no place for "Fair And Balanced" in that conflict.

People who know, know Hillary has bad BO.

Here is where wisdom comes into play. Mr. Trump was very, very smart to say that he will wait for results. It's a shot across the bow that we will look into any fishy results and we will look into any areas of possible fraud thoroughly first. They will be scrutinized.

Here's how Trump responded when asked if he'll accept election results

Hardly ever before...has the dust of the boots of the American Pioneer been more prevalent than in that of Donald Trump's daily walk in this election.

These goofs who come out with "Moral outrage" towards Mr. Trump are going to find themselves struggling not with the Establishment, who they eat fancy cookies with, but with the people who pay for those fancy cookies.

Poll: Ryan's favorability plummets, Republicans see Pence as future of the party

Oct 21, 2016 6:02 am

Has anyone ever given thought to just how exactly BORING politics would be if Hillary wins? Wouldn't we all really miss him? Now, for something interesting to the poll watchers. Just from a marketing perspective, I was curious and fired off a question in an email to the people who make Chia's...response below.

Hi Greg, Thank you for contacting us regarding the Freedom of Choice Chia Pet. Good question. We actually sell more Chia Trumps than Chia Clintons. If you go to our website, chia.com, we actually show a comparison graph: As of the beginning of this month it was 79% Trump and 21% Clinton. But as of mid-October, it changed to 84% Trump and 16% Clinton. Any other questions or comments please let me know. Have a wonderful day! Enmanuel De Jesus M. Customer Service Joseph Enterprises, Inc. 425 California St., Ste. 300 San Francisco, CA 94104 (415) 397-6992 (800) 557-5856

Oct 22, 2016 6:11 am

The only reason that 2nd and 3rd World countries are always run by absolute tyrants is because the politics had become so corrupt, and in so many ways, that the people had to give up trying to keep track of all of it and then just gave up and concluded "That's just the way it is" It is their precise and purposeful desire that we just put our hands up and quit. The only point that we lose the country is the moment we give up. Fight!

Smooth move: Clinton's lawyer may have exposed entire email server to China

Oct 22, 2016 6:56 am

Wanna know what it's like to be a soldier? Vote! Sacrifice your time on that day...GO VOTE! November 8th.

That's peculiar, coming out of obscurity just long enough to fall back into it again.

Former RNC Chairman Michael Steele won't vote for Trump

Peggy, Trump does have the ability to be a fake politician if he tried really, really hard. He's not bothering with that though. Consider whether or not you have been hypnotized by all the fakey politicians of the past and whether or not you are addicted to being fooled. Mr. Trump is reality...no nuttier than you or I. It could be that you have spending way too much time hanging around phony and dishonest people.

WSJ Columnist Peggy Noonan: If Trump wasn't a 'nut,' he'd beat Clinton in a 'landslide'

The principle issue of whatever millions of undocumented illegal aliens residing in our country really is just this one thing: The Democrats are on the war path to make them legal voting entities because if they were to be able to be legal voters, say by-by to Republicans and Conservatives from ever controlling anything, probably forever. From a practical standpoint, the wall and kicking out the worst will be the priority and will take some time and doing because the well payed off Republicans & Democrats will want to thwart the effort. There is the overall picture as a guide though.

Yeah! If it weren't for the Republicans of the Establishment trying to defeat Mr. Trump! As I try to distill and simplify this election, a certain striking reality has hit me. The sheer weirdness and surreal nature of the election is that it turns out that what we are looking at is the Global Establishment is at war with the People.

Frank Luntz: This election should have been a "slam dunk" for Republicans

Well, of course, if we want to get that wall built and do it quickly, we will initially have to put up the funds. The Mexicans will eventually pay for it with import taxes etc...

Seems to me if so called "Self-Identified Conservatives or Liberals" are voting for the other side that it might benefit them if they were to meet at the fence and realize that they have been living in each other's houses all this time. And after that embarrassing realization, they might want to see a doctor about the possibility of having Alzheimer's.

New poll: Many self-identified conservatives plan to vote for Hillary Clinton

And she say's "He touched my arm and brushed my breast" with tears in her eye's hahahahahahaha SHE'S A PORNO ACTRESS....TEARS????

Trump hits back at latest accuser: She's probably 'been grabbed before'

Now, you have this situation, two of the filthiest Gynocockarea smelling witches in one place having a circular saw cutting through tin roofing competition, and promising to come after you. Women, who knows, but any dude voting for that is a dude that should just be put to sleep like young male deer that got his nuts torn off on a barbed wire fence and is bleeding to death.

Elizabeth Warren has a scathing three-word message for Trump: 'Nasty women vote'

Why? Why investigate what happened? Truth discovery is such an arduous undertaking, apparently. People are gullible so don't even bother with all the trouble, just say that the Russians left a nickel on the Interstate and it caused the crash...take the rest of the day off.

NTSB to investigate bus crash that left 13 dead, 31 injured

Hey, the Establishment abandoned Mr. Trump long ago so, it's called winning baby. I've only worked in a couple of environments with several other people and it was always frustrating to have to drag along low performers...so I understand that Mr. Trump has to be experiencing that same frustration with the Republican Leadership. It's funny, the Republican leadership is just sitting there wondering how Mr. Trump is barn storming through the election, 10's of thousands of people at events while they are sitting in the trees scratching their butts, wondering which of the other monkey's likes them or not.

Report: Trump abandons high-dollar fundraisers, leaving the GOP in the lurch

As I saw that video of Biden saying that. Biden came across to me like some dumb 10 year old kid with his underwear pulled out the back of his pants, telling his friends what he's gonna do if he ever meet's that High School Senior in a dark alley.

'I'd love that': Trump hits back at 'Mr. Tough Guy' Biden

That's a very fine gesture on Mr. Hannity's behalf! Think about it Barak...you really could go and be a REAL Third World Dictator!! Your dream!!

Oct 27, 2016 5:54 am

These pollsters better be getting very accurate if they expect to have even one dangling chad of legitimacy left.

Trump cuts Clinton's national lead in half in new poll

Oct 27, 2016 6:10 am

Well of course, the Lefty's always do come out with violence...that's why us Red Neck's carry us some whomp'n a big pistols!

Poll: Majority of voters express concern over possible Election Day violence

Oct 27, 2016 6:15 am

I don't think that would have been a good idea, him and Bush slow dancing on stage during the Republican primaries...I don't think we need any of that out here.

Mitt Romney admits he sometimes wonders why he didn't run for president in 2016

Oct 27, 2016 6:17 am

There's gonna be a lot of shock-a-roo's come election day.

Trump beats out Clinton in Maine's mock student election

Oct 27, 2016 6:24 am

People in this country are exhausted with putting up with the lies and corruption in both parties. How about some reality for a change? Wouldn't it be relaxing for a change...to not be having to grip your arm chair in frustration while watching the news every night? Aaaaaaah.....Trump. Peaceful reality.

"Bill...Bill! You're up now, to give the speech!"

"OK, wait a minute"

"Get off that Ho and get out here!...crowd's waiting"

"There's a crowd WATCHING?"

"No, they want to hear a speech"

"How come they don't wanna watch me do this here fine looking broad?"

Silence

"OK, I'm ready...gimme the microphone"

"You ain't taking that out there...the bottle of Jim Beam. Give it here"

Bill Clinton makes glaring error while reciting wife's two-word campaign slogan

Oct 27, 2016 7:12 am

Hmmmm...I wonder if she has the "Bobbing Seizure Hustle" in mind?

Clinton wants to have a 'big national dance' to bring the country together after the election

Oct 27, 2016 7:16 am

Goodness sake's, Carter's a big boy now! Taking time out of his busy day making Drag Queen's out of service men to address an issue with all of the grown up's. Doing something important for once.

Pentagon chief says U.S. should honor commitment to service members by not requiring payback of bonuses promised years ago

But, I like Bigly better...it's charming.

Is it 'bigly' or 'big league?' Donald Trump finally settles the debate

Just one of those tongue-in-cheek comment's that makes Mr. Trump so much more human than that....that.... What would you even call her? The world hasn't even seen this before and no adjective has been created yet.

Trump suggests U.S. 'cancel' election and 'give it' to him

I think it would have been funny if afterword's he walked back to the press and told them that they almost ran off the edge of the planet but everything seems fine now.

Pence plane skids off runway at New York City's LaGuardia Airport; No injuries reported

Putin is Putin. He looks across to the United States and see's all these little, immature, mindless sycophants and fans of communism, trying stupidly to emulate it because of a fantasy of creating a Nirvana. But he's the Grand Pooba (Of Flinstones fame) and he rolls his eyes as he watches these rank amateurs like Hillary and Obama, stumbling around like idiots, trying to copy him. He knows that communism is junk. He knows best how to make selfish enterprise out of it best. He knows how stupid the people must be to allow him to get away with it...and he gets away with it, he's the "Don" in that game. Being in such a vaunted, nefarious position, Putin looks down on America's Liberals and sigh's "Tysk, tysk...children!"

Putin taunts American intelligence agencies over claims of election influence: 'Is the U.S. a banana republic?'

Here's the cure for voter fraud: Only paper ballots. Every ballot has the same security measures used on paper currency. No, it's not cost prohibitive. They do this for millions and millions of 1's, 5's, 10's etc... A strict accounting of how many ballots each polling station receives is recorded and by the end of the election, there is another accounting to ensure that the same number exists. All ballots are stored in containers and are accessible to the public for review.

Rigged? Texas officials respond to Trump's 'vote flipping' charge

It is on purpose that Almighty God instructed us to not let women be spiritual leaders over men in the Church (the body of Christ on earth) If you don't like that, then you have an argument with God, not me.

Dear Christians, it doesn't matter how you feel. It matters what the Bible says.

Chapter 11

November 2016

Nov 4, 2016 5:29 am

When a gum filled brain decides in college to go for a journalism degree, it's an implicit desire to join the propaganda arm of the Democrat Party, the Liberal agenda and the war against Christianity.

It's an easy career to get paid to vent their frustrations of having a low self-opinion of self.

Nov 4, 2016 6:24 am

OK, here is my official prediction. It's the same one I made back in the Primary's last year to a Liberal friend of mine.

Donald J. Trump will win this election in a landslide.

Trump campaign makes play for Pennsylvania — a state that hasn't gone red since 1988

Hey, not gonna ask the whole world from Mr. Cruz, understandably. Thank you Mr. Cruz for what you are doing...it proves that indeed, you do love this country more than your selfish ambitions!

Cruz declines to mention Trump's name once as he campaigns for the GOP nominee

Hmmm. Injun seem simple, but Injun not like woman who crooked like snake.

Democratic elector pledges not to vote for Clinton

Whether it was staged or not, Obama was getting all mad because he was in the middle of hypnotizing them and they so quickly turned away from him.

OK, OK focus now, focus. Now the Honky's...hey, focus! Focus on da Honk....focus! The Honky gonna get you!

Obama defends Trump supporter's right to protest at Clinton rally

They had to do this for her so that as she spends her waning days, wasting away in bed amidst laced fringed pillows, she can recall the one and only single time that she had a huge crowd like Donald Trump had at every event.
Except for that sinking feeling that always creeps in...the fact that they weren't there to see her.

One of Satan's greatest weapons he uses to try to disable and paralyze Christians is to make them feel crummy about being in God's personal family...that they don't deserve it...the privilege.
I see now as we near the end times, Satan using willing hearts and minds that will channel the very same thing in socio/political ways to discourage the heart of American's.
Here's the effort: You should feel like thunder for being so 'lucky' so lay down your defenses and give us your country.

Beach Boys hit songs decried for 'straight-male privilege, white privilege' — even 'beach privilege'

This would be cute if it weren't for one outstanding element and that is the fact that there is not any moral equivalence between the two ideologies. One is focused on the destruction of the country while the other is for liberty and the building up of the country based on that freedom.
It's not like we are having a discussion on how to fund a portion of some interstate highway repairs.

Watch what brings Clinton, Trump supporters together to cast a 'vote for good'

I would place her in the same category as Laura Bush, who I thought was wonderful. Except that Malania with her room silencing elegance there will be a greater sense of Camelot much like Jakie Kennedy.
And Hillary being the toothless, crabby wench at work on the butter churn, screaming at the horses.

Where would Melania Trump rank among first ladies?

Nov 5, 2016 10:51 am

This is what it looks like when one Gladiator keeps his foot on the neck of the femme fatale...The Hyena Of The Barren Svelte.

Poll: Clinton's lead continues to shrink in run-up to Election Day

Nov 6, 2016 8:53 am

I bet that afterword's she went back to her people and demanded to know who allowed this rain to happen... as they insert another Ralgro in her ear and wheelchair her away.

Watch: Mother Nature literally rains on Hillary Clinton's parade

Nov 6, 2016 5:05 am

I hope that it was indication that God will spare us from judgment on this nation and prevent the hell of Hillary.

Watch: Mother Nature literally rains on Hillary Clinton's parade

Nov 6, 2016 5:26 am

Think of that, Hillary asks for strippers and rap artists to speak for her. Add to the mix, a teeny bopper rocky rolly kid that my friend from New Jersey beat up as a kid, and a folk singer who decided to get into acid way, way too late in life.

'I didn't have to bring J-Lo or Jay-Z': Trump mocks Clinton for campaigning with celebrities

What's the matter? Can't the Hillary people find anymore actresses that are willing to get sued for slander while Hillary laughs at them?

Woman who accused Trump of raping her as a teenager abruptly drops lawsuit

This election is way, way, way more different from any other in that there isn't even any arguments over policy...I mean in the Media.
Oh, there is Mr. Trump out there furiously fighting and laying out real solutions to real problems but then there is Hillary and her crowd out there with nothing but "never Trump" and that's it.
Ain't it weird, the Left and the Establishment doesn't even care at all who Mr. Trump's opponent is? Just someone they can prop up. And just to top it off, they put forth someone who is the complete opposite of ideal as a way to laugh at us, I guess?
I really hate to think in terms of conspiracy but this election is just freaking unreal...it doesn't match reality.
Except for this: All of the Red counties in this country will choose their President on Tuesday and all of the Blue counties will have their President chosen for them on Tuesday...that's reality!

Report: Clinton team thought email scandal was so bad, they wanted to focus on Benghazi instead

I hope that all other Republicans in Congress take note here, regarding Ryan. Here is a once VP candidate being taken to the woodshed...by the People!
It ain't funny, we ain't sleeping and we dang sure ain't tired of fighting!!!

House Speaker Paul Ryan campaigns with Pence in sign of GOP unity

For whatever reason, this year I have been monitoring the way Iowa goes because it has always shown it's fickleness in elections. Des Moines has a metropolitan, artsy bend to it and the Quad Cities has a huge Union population. This kind of lead spells bad news for Hillary in Michigan and Pennsylvania...trust me.

Poll: With only two days before Election Day, Trump is up by a huge margin in this swing-state

By just comparing the size and fervency of the Rally's we know that Mr. Trump will receive tons more votes than Hillary. If they say that she won, the Federal Government will have finally reached the peak in the chief argument in the Declaration of Independence regarding the King and that was simply the "Usurpation" of the Authority of the People.

Gingrich: FBI Director Comey 'caved' to political pressure by not charging Clinton

When Mr. Trump wins we will be Stronger-To-geT-Her.

And take note, there is no such thing as 'Fair and square' when it comes to Liberty.

Sarah Palin on why Trump will win Michigan: 'Polls are only good for strippers'

So, if you are planning to vote for Hillary, what does this say about your level of maturity...perhaps you've had it with being stupid and have decided to really go ultra-stupid by having a tattoo of Beyonce applied to your sagging butt, buy a sack of sour candy and then die like an unknown salamander in a South American jungle...while desperately crawling across the muddy ground....I am something....I am something............ oh, I hope I'm something.....

National high school mock election goes to Clinton — and 17 percent of votes go third-party

The greatest grass roots enthusiasm I ever saw was Obama...was. The grass roots enthusiasm for Donald Trump is about double with 5 times the fervency. They are going to have to stuff ballot boxes like mad for Hillary to get her close to winning.
Now, if they say Hillary got more votes, it will be nothing short of comedy to watch the media trying to explain how in the hell she mustered all that enthusiasm when so few people went to her rally's. And, if they report that Mr. Trumps vote totals are similar to Romney's, that too will require the most ridiculous of explanations. Either way, if they say Hillary won, it will be because of nothing short of wholesale fraud...from the top of the Establishment down. We are all going to have to get out and VOTE TRUMP...it's the only way to outpace the fraud!

New Yorkers celebrate Trump with parade, rally ahead of election

I think her staff finally remembered that things that flash cause Hillary to have seizures. So, when Mr. Trump wins, maybe everyone should flash their headlights all at once just so we can see one more freak out for good ol' time's sake.

Clinton campaign has reportedly canceled a key part of its election night victory party

It is hard to imagine anything more American than a bunch of colorful, rowdy, unconventional, God loving people actually voting for the same as President.
A LOT of people are going to want to be a part of that today!!
We are the Americans!!!!!!!! The very first Election Day results are in: Dixville Notch, N.H., votes

Nov 8, 2016 6:55 am

You know what would be really cool is instead of all the Washington inaugural balls, Mr. Trump just held a ginormous pork roast picnic, open to the people…that would really piss off the elites!

Clinton campaign has reportedly canceled a key part of its election night victory party

Nov 9, 2016 8:54 am

So anyway, as I was saying, there's these here dirty, rotten, rebellious Sons a Bucks with dirt on their boots and smoke in their pistols…

Overwhelming white evangelical support might have been what launched Trump to victory

Nov 9, 2016 6:39 am

We won! They ain't a gonna be liking those big rosy apples!

'Head home:' Clinton skips her concession speech

Nov 9, 2016 6:32 am

Anyone or everyone can bark about policy and hurt feelings…the only thing that I'm thinking of is FFFRRREEEEEEDDDOOOOOOOOOOOOOOM!!!!!

In victory speech, Trump promises to be 'president for all Americans'

Nov 9, 2016 8:54 am

So anyway, as I was saying, there's these here dirty, rotten, rebellious Sons a Bucks with dirt on their boots and smoke in their pistols…

Overwhelming white evangelical support might have been what launched Trump to victory

I'm happy...not for myself alone, I live on the high plains of Nebraska, we are free here. I'm happy for everyone else! I'm happy that people will now have to learn to be free again...to embrace it. I'm happy for all the young folk, you don't have to be perfect, just embrace the Lord and fight like a badger...trying hard, your efforts, are not in vain. And, love your brothers as yourself.

Trump stuns the swamp, wins the White House

Dear Fox & Friends, straight up Steve, the incredibly adorable and wise Ainsley and the smart and cleaver Brian...thank you for being a very nice and Godly place for us to wake up to, you gave us hope. Thank you!

In victory speech, Trump promises to be 'president for all Americans'

Dear Mr. Hannity, with dirt under your fingernails and the sort of tenacity that only a stout German could appreciate, you fought like the most lovable and ferocious dog on earth! Thank you Sean!...well done.

In victory speech, Trump promises to be 'president for all Americans'

Dear Mr. Limbaugh. I know that you are fond of borrowing the phrase that "You can read the stitches on a fast ball" And over the years you have proved that. I know from where "Crooked Hillary, Little Rubio and Lying Ted" came from...the same place as "Henry Nostrilitus Waxman" came from :) You could have thrown your hands up a long time ago, taken your money and be swinging on a hammock in the Caribbean breeze but you stayed and chose to fight it out. The seeming lone voice in all those early years...sir, thank you!

In victory speech, Trump promises to be 'president for all Americans'

Let's not take this God given breather recklessly. Love your fellow man...regardless. Be thankful to our Benevolent Father in Heaven. Know that your efforts are not in vain. Make the most of these days...Jesus loves you!

In victory speech, Trump promises to be 'president for all Americans'

So, Soros blew the last little bit of money he had in the protest fund...every participant got a free pack of gum too!

Growing protests against Trump's election victory have sprung up in various cities across America

That look on his face is the same one I make whenever I accidentally hit my thumb with a hammer.

Bernie Sanders issues statement on Trump

It is going to be so nice to not have the everyday anxiety of having to always be looking over your shoulder for whatever Obama had next up his sleeve.

Here's a list of potential Trump Cabinet members

This election was the most important one to me by far. Not only did I think that DT was the right man for the job but I was deeply concerned that a majority of the population had lost touch with truth and reality.

Mike Rowe weighs in on the results of the election, and offers a bit of sanity

An hour of that meeting was Mr. Trump and the Secret Servicemen trying to coax Obama out from under a wing chair where he was hiding.

Obama and Trump hold meeting to begin exchange of power

Good thing is wasn't Dr. Marten's in the controversy…good luck trying to destroy those boots!

People are burning their shoes because they thought New Balance endorsed Trump

Earth shattering! I'm so mad that I'm gonna go out and shoot me a deer and eat the whole thing right there on the spot!

George Zimmerman accused of using racial slur in Florida bar

Just think of how easy it would (will for some) be to freak out this younger generation just to profit from them. For instance, if you make window air conditioners and your sales are sluggish, just write across the box in big letters "Prevents Global Warming!" Plus a notation "Bully Proof Technology prevents President Trump from turning it down all the time!"
Maybe even a little promotional raffle offering a chance to win a "January in Siberia, relaxing getaway"

Media outlets are suggesting that Trump is coming to steal your birth control

I just really, really, really hope that we get a Defense Secretary that will return the manhood back to the military…return to don't ask don't tell, and the absolute separation of men & women in combat and on ships. Who cares if some women complain, just do it and

don't offer up a bunch of flowery explanations other than it's inappropriate.

Like my Chief in the Navy used to do when questioned…with a cigarette in one hand and a cup of coffee in the other he would run his thumb across the stencil on his greasy jersey that read "A/G CPO" and say "Because I'm the Chief!" Then smoke the cigarette down to the quick in one drag and then slam the whole cup of steaming hot coffee.

Nov 12, 2016 4:32 am

OK, have those two bargaining chips in putting a new set of laws together in Congress AFTER YOU REPEAL OBAMACARE!!!!! If you were elected to do it, DO IT!

A broad sweeping "Plan" for people's personal lives is a horrible intrusion on any notion of Liberty.

Government has this assumed eminence and habit of always getting in God's way when it comes to benevolence.

After promising a full repeal of Obamacare, Trump is shifting course on the health care bill

Nov 12, 2016 4:49 am

We so badly need honor restored to our Military!

Happy Veterans Day: See relics of Corporal Richard Manly from the Nuremberg Trials

Nov 12, 2016 5:04 am

I believe that the majority finally got fed up and voted for a change because they believed in Trump. I wonder if he knows just how important it will be that he follows through on all the things he was elected for because if not, it would permanently damage any possibility of any sense of reality in politics for the future.

There seems to be this stubborn notion that the United States is a commune in some way...left? Right? Center? but a commune. From a political standpoint, the expectation that WE all need to choose for ourselves a Chief Hippy of our nudist colony to bring us together, that would go about delivering cracks of a wet towel to the genitals of those who don't fall in line.

In Nations, the only tie that should be binding is times of war and the overall liberty of the citizens...government can only be effectual as a mechanic at best or a horrid murderer in the least.

Good job on the election Kellyanne!!!

Clinton didn't make history in 2016. Donald Trump's campaign manager did — here's why

Prov 22:15: "Foolishness is bound in the heart of a child; but the rod of correction shall drive it far from him."
Prov 23:13: "Withhold not correction from the child: for if thou beatest him with the rod, he shall not die."
Prov 23:14: "Thou shalt beat him with the rod, and shalt deliver his soul from hell."
Prov 29:15: "The rod and reproof give wisdom: but a child left to himself bringeth his mother to shame."

Now, when state makes it illegal to use corporal punishment, the result is obvious idiocy.

'Suck it up, buttercup!': Iowa lawmaker proposes bill punishing schools coddling anti-Trump students

I'm having a hard time finding the right words to describe the level of irony here...perhaps Satan is making fun of them?

So...

If your diapers ever get full and slide from your butts and begin to streak down your legs, just know that you don't need to quit,

we'll pin those britches right back up so that you may forever be full of sh*t.

See why Trump protesters are wearing safety pins after Donald Trump's big win

Obama doesn't care about "A legacy" His one and only purpose and goal was to destroy and dominate a Christian Nation.

Krauthammer: Now that Trump will be president, 'Obama's legacy is toast'

The simple definition of a Redneck is one who is down to earth, honest...the intelligent. The definition of the unintelligent is simply, those who defer to pride instead.

Our brains can only process so much information at any one time...the amount of mental maintenance required to keep this facade of pride in shape, takes up most of it, leaving very little space for intelligence.

You can be smart, you can be clever, you can steal, cheat, and even kill... but wisdom and intelligence will always be far from reaching with pride.

If being a 'redneck' means all this, I'll take it

I think we all knew he wouldn't take the salary.

President-elect Trump pledges to forgo his presidential salary during his time in the White House

That has to be the most embarrassing desert crawl back to the camp next to the watering hole that he pee'd in.

Sen. Ben Sasse in new op-ed: Rooting for Trump's failure is rooting for America's failure

Mr. Trump is not fooled by this Climate crap which is nothing more than global business socialism...trade fixing, if you will.

Report: President-elect Trump looking to pull out of global climate agreement

This is a very important topic that needs serious cutting in many areas. There are 3 main reason's; It creates the sort of Fascism that Mussolini had in mind because by the time a company has complied with all the government regulations, it's butt is owned by the government. It also takes a tremendous amount of money out of compound production...that is to say, once a company spends funds to comply, it's gone when it would otherwise keep producing. Three, it stifles development of small companies...plain...and...simple.

U.S. businesses spend more on regulatory compliance than Russia's GDP

If by law you can compel people to act in a manor inconsistent with their beliefs, then it's possible to make everyone buy and use a prayer rug.

Radical left Oregon official who fined Christian bakery into shutting down loses election

I think he's considering new job options as he really kicked a lot of dirt in Nebraskans faces being a NeverTrumper.

Student hails an Uber and discovers his driver is a U.S. Senator

What we are actually seeing here is very much the same as when the South resisted the freeing of slaves.

When you consider the fact that they have a population of low skilled, low payed people that you don't have to be accountable to, don't have to respect, and you can get rid of (deport) them at any time for whatever reason...illegal immigrants are effectively these peoples' slaves.

To top it off, the illegals don't dare leave the city (plantation) or they will get arrested...slaves.

Sanctuary cities vow to protect their illegal immigrants from Trump's immigration plan

Now that right there hurt my feelers a lot. I'm gonna start crying, smashing cars and burning buildings and then call an ambalance to bring me a puppy and some warm cocoa.

CBS analyst: There's no such thing as a good Trump voter

Wrong "C" word...condescending is the correct one.

Obama maintains conciliatory tone toward Trump

This is very much akin to bull banding. Ranchers who don't want to bother with manual castration defer to banding the scrotum above the two subjects and they eventually just fall off.

And eventually a coyote comes across them lying on the prairie and goes "Look, Charlie, I found one of those cool snacks again!"

South African man's sex accident has a certain 'ring' to it

I expect that we will see nothing but a continuing sobering of government throughout the next great years.

Just imagine, waking up day after day and being surprised by more good news instead of being shot at again.

Trump to prevent administration officials from lobbying for 5 years

One of the things that I anticipate with a President Trump (Man, that's fun to write!) will be a full blown attack, through the Attorney General's office, on this type of CRAP!

As well, a full blown attack and elimination of all this politically correct junk in schools that is the main reason why these frail buttercup snowflakes are formed...they are freaking scared of being themselves!...It's child abuse!

11-year-old suspended for violation of school's 'weapons policy' after sharing fruit with a friend

The Bill of Rights is the area of the Constitution that most limits the governments tyranny. A CC is desperately needed to expand these God given rights...everything from "Shall not compel one to except and act in a manor inconsistent with one's religious beliefs" to "Shall not regulate food consumption"

There are many suppression's, clothed in earnest goodness, that greatly diminish personal liberty that the Founding Fathers could have never imagined.

And really, how much opposition would there be…expanding personal liberty? Anyone would look like an absolute tyrant opposing the notion!

Justice Antonin Scalia's support for a convention of states comes to light

Nov 18, 2016 7:38 am

Now, that's the textbook definition of chutzpah.

It's funny, though, that he's over there with the other sissy's, licking each other's' wounds and helping each other rectify their wedgies.

Obama uses last overseas trip as president to blast fake news

Nov 18, 2016 7:42 am

Funny isn't it, how politicians and other institutions always manage to create division and acrimony between folks when everyone really only needs one thing from the government…the protection of Liberty.

LGBT gun rights group sees spike in interest since election, Orlando massacre

Nov 18, 2016 7:55 am

Oh heck, Obama, do it…you couldn't possibly make your reputation any worse anyway.

It's like hiring Obama to simply pull a baler across a hay field and when you go out to check on the progress, you find that the tractor is upside down and the dude you hired is now somehow wrapped up in a bale of hay.

Rev. Jesse Jackson: Obama should pardon Clinton

There should not be a single adjective that defines the whole of the American people other than free.

They imagined a New World Order and the United States was to be the corporate headquarters. Finding the squalled peoples of the earth and making mass production machines out of them seemed practical...after all, it's good for one to be busy about the day.

Wall Streets' biggest concern is Bird Flu...how many Chinese might it kill, we have deadlines you know. Mexicans, vote slaves. God? kick Him out of schools, He's getting in the way of our social grooming...His blessings forgotten.

Left behind were the millions of Americans not involved in that game. Godly folk, slow to anger. As the Japanese Admiral Isoroku Yamamoto said after the Pearl Harbor "I fear all we have done is to awaken a sleeping giant and fill him with a terrible resolve."

A lot can be said but suffice it be said...DO NOT MESS WITH US!!!

Ted Cruz breaks down this election brilliantly as "the revenge of flyover country"

If you have ever wondered what it would be like to be eaten alive by a giant grasshopper, get real close to the TV when Elizabeth Warren is giving a speech and have one of your friends slowly crunch a bag of potato chips for sound effect.

Senator Elizabeth Warren mocks Trump and Romney on social media

My guess is that he says "Praise the Lord" often and she knew that he was going to say that.

We absolutely have to stop this anti-Christ thing in schools...NOW!

Watch: Teacher pulls mic away from autistic child at Thanksgiving program

Isn't it weird that for some reason, "Racist" is the worst thing a person can be? Not a murderer, not a rapist, not a thief but a racist is the worst thing you can be.

The reason why is this, and it's very close associate is Global Warming...guilt. The most powerful tool that Satan has is the casting of guilt. The Bible says that "Satan stands before the Lord and accuses his followers day and night."

But in order to be a very clever guilt tripper, you have to pick something universally prevalent so that it's hard to dispute. Everyone is racist...everyone on earth. If you took some Bush tribe out of the African grasslands and put him in a Japanese temple, it would be absolutely impossible for them not to form a racial opinion base entirely off of what they were seeing...peoples are different.

So, here's the trick; Accuse someone of being racist, it's true because everyone is, in order to disable that person who now feels terrible. Trick part two, the accusers now become a new "god" with all the rules and they determine right and wrong...power.

Dogged by 'white nationalist' allegations, Bannon promises movement 'greater than Reagan revolution'

I suspect that Melania will be just fine without you tracking mud through her home...madam.

Fashion designer urges fellow stylists to boycott dressing Melania Trump

Why? Why play an NFL game in Mexico, they ain't going to know what the heck is going on. They'll just sit in the stands and wonder "They run into each other instead of throwing cactus's…that's weird. But they do have some awful shiny helmets!"

NFL warns Mexico-bound players to not drink water…or eat beef

It's a delicate walk for me to make a certain point of this and can easily be misunderstood.

Same universal mindsets leads to the best vulnerability of being ruled by a Dictator.

Government should not be in any way be a solution for a persons' identity…or a groups identity. It ought to just be the dry, functional, thrifty and well thought out organ by which we pass the hat and pay the electric bill, or the highway bill, or the Military bill…that's it.

The government has become an ultimate fighting promoter and has built a giant cage match for anyone wanting to participate. "In the ring tonight, EVERYONE has to accept homosexuality, fight, fight, fight," "In the ring tonight EVERYONE has to believe in global warming fight, fight, fight" And on and on. By the time it's all over and everyone is bloody and panting, the government has amassed all of the power and is now exalted as the boss because THEY are the moderator of morals when in reality they should be nothing more than a bunch of black-rimmed glasses wearing, problem solving, diligent people who does the job that they were hired for.

The beautiful thing about Mr. Donald J. Trump is that he doesn't look at government as source of moral discussions…he rightly leaves that for each to their own. He looks at government as more a machine, a badly broken one. It's kind of like that commercial for Blue Emu where the guy say's "You, I don't know what you're trying to do but I can tell that you aren't going about it right"

One thing about Germans that folks should know about, when we are

183

at work, we don't stop and chit-chat about our personal lives…we get the thing done and get it done right, period.

Kellyanne Conway urges Trump detractors to join 'Team America'

And a pack of gum, a teddy bear, some antibiotic wipes in a little tin foil package. A couple of sanitary napkins…for the boys, of course. Some hand cream and a kiss on the cheek from an old crusty wart hog named George Soros…who's breath smells like he just ate the last remaining bit of road kill that he fought some possums to get.

School asks profs to offer extra credit to 'encourage' student attendance at left-wing event

Well, now why wouldn't he when he had so much success the first time?

"I'm smart" (run into a wall again) "I'm smart (falling down the stairs) "I'm smart" (wondering what would happen if he stuck his hands into the sickle bars of swather while the machine is running)

Evan McMullin won't rule out another run for office

Folks, Politics is a rough a business.

This presidential candidate had the most retweeted tweet of the 2016 election

When the Red Baron, the notable German aviator, crash landed in a grassy field in France and was approached by opposing forces, he uttered his last words "Kaput."

You may want to jot that down as a reference for your political careers' obituary…your book titled "My, Me, My"

Obama: Trump's victory 'is not the apocalypse'

I would have just done the same thing. You got some little kids begging for those suckers that you get at a bank, just give one each so they shut the heck up.

Donald Trump tweets the reason he settled his Trump U lawsuit

Everyone knows that Democrats are just a bunch of racist homophobes...I'm getting sick of their bigotry!

Pro-Trump rapper Kanye West calls out Beyonce and Jay-Z before storming out of concert

One of the best things I learned growing up was a saying "It's not the whales in life that swallow you whole, it's all the little minnows that nibble you to death."

I sincerely hope that PE Trump is mindful of such incidents like this that occurs daily all across the nation...I strongly suspect he's going to be, though.

North Texas land owners fight back against federal land seizure

I'm absolutely sick of this. However it gets done, lets a least start with retrofitting police cars with bullet proof glass.

San Antonio police officer fatally shot while sitting in cruiser writing ticket

It's the point that I have been trying to make for years, cities have become this bubble. They have become so organized and efficient and nicely landscaped that it gives many only partially smart people the illusion of living in a state of nirvana.

People of Frisco might want to brace themselves. Almighty God is not surprised that we are compelled to sin but he most certainly hates the celebration of it. One more click in those tectonic plates and there's gonna be a whole lot of reality a goin' on thar.

Watch: 'SNL' skewers liberals in 'The Bubble' skit

Nov 22, 2016 8:21 am

This is one of the thousands of little everyday things that has been eating us, bit by bit.

Imagine the notion, an American being arrested by some dude that isn't even a citizen of OUR country.

Change this to; No one shall serve in a capacity of law enforcement not having been a citizen for ten years, period.

It's OUR country, we make the freaking rules!!!

Denver Sheriff's Department fined for not hiring non-citizens

Nov 22, 2016 5:21 am

Don't pay the fine. Two or so month's left.

Denver Sheriff's Department fined for not hiring non-citizens

Nov 22, 2016 8:26 am

May just as well try roasting some hot dogs on a stick while they are at it...why not?

NASA plans to set fires in space

My first thought was, wow, that's one huge Democrat voting block and that's precisely why the Dems protect them...they sure love to own people.

There are plenty of departments and bureaus that can be eliminated or phased out or sent back to the states.

Trump is about to make life hard for government workers

The Clinton people are still trying to find out how Trump votes outpaced their ballot stuffing operation. As well, voting machines are not connected to the internet so the Ruskies would have had to sneak into the premises and physically get into the machines.

Group seeks to overturn voting results in three states on the basis of unfounded Russian hacking claims

"The Fascist State lays claim to rule in the economic field no less than in others; it makes its action felt throughout the length and breadth of the country by means of its corporative, social, and educational institutions, and all the political, economic, and spiritual forces of the nation, organized in their respective associations, circulate within the State."

THE DOCTRINE OF FASCISM
BENITO MUSSOLINI (1932)

Citing 'equality,' Obama defends TPP as Donald Trump seeks a withdrawal

What a long, long, long national nightmare. This is what happens when people forget that the position of President really does matter.

I remember seeing an ad years ago where it was showing the strange cultural things that have happened in America like those big collar, polyester disco shirts etc...They then ask, as a rhetorical question to the viewer "Just what were we thinking?"

Nov 24, 2016 4:01 am

I remember a ways back the push to close insane asylums but they have now been replaced with colleges...mental institutions.

'Suck it up p***ies!' sticky note mocking anti-Trump students being investigated — as a hate crime

Nov 24, 2016 4:29 am

The strangest transformation (and I'm trying to think of when and how it started) is how a bunch of anti-establishment, anti-government control hippies, that were stringing beads in the parks, have somehow turned into sadomasochistic love slaves to the very thing they once despised.

It's kinda as if Johnny Rotten were singing and dancing to "Staying Alive" followed up by an emotional rendering of "Feelings"

Actor Robert De Niro bashed Trump before the election. Now he's reversing course.

Nov 24, 2016 4:39 am

If "You are what you eat" is true, that might explain why they have such factory processed minds.

Millennials put their own spin on dining

Nov 24, 2016 5:06 am

I love how Mr. Trump is already conducting his "Presidency" at this "White House", complete with "Oval Office addresses" and how it overshadows Obama.

It's odd, I have really been nostalgic lately...it feels like America again. Betsy DeVos tapped to be Trump's Secretary of Education

If there is such a word as "Alt-right" isn't even more appropriate then to say "Ctl-Alt-Delete" when referring to Liberals?

Politico editor resigns after publishing addresses, threatening alt-right leader on social media

The healthiest food, any food, that you can eat is that which you thank God for and ask him to bless...and I mean that literally!

Dr. Jorge provides healthy holiday tips, just in time for Thanksgiving

Ahhhh......and they were having so much fun at the restaurant only hours before.

Customer sues Chipotle for making him 'too full' — really

My guess is that she must have a terrible personality that isn't offset by good looks so she routinely buys a pizza before going out to the bars and has to bribe dudes with a slice in exchange for a drink. After still no offers to take her home, bar after bar, she finally used her last slice as a bribe to get in and give it one more try but it ended up in the gutter with bits of gravel embedded in it...the girl, I mean.

Police: Woman uses pizza slice as ID to enter college town bar, gets nasty when bouncer says no

To me, the high priority in the coming years ought to be America coming home and separating from the Globalist's political social standards...you can still have free trade without adopting the stupidity of other nations.

If that's what they call a Populist, then I'm one of them.

The rejection being The New World Order…no, we do not want to join it!!

Donald Trump's adviser tells GOP: You're no longer Ronald Reagan's party

Nov 25, 2016 5:43 am

Since Obama has made his effort to try and flood the electorate with Democrats, we should offer the world political asylum from the socialist persecution they suffer in their country.

If they can prove through various means that you are a bonafide Conservative and have a complete understanding and love for our Constitution why, come right on in…legal or illegal.
Flood the borders with future Conservative voters for a change…but boy, oh boy the howling on the Left to cease immigration!

Report: Brexit leader Nigel Farage moving to the United States

Nov 26, 2016 5:26 am

Breaking news from my news desk: Fidel Castro had died…Ha, I was first to announce!

Book: Obama called Clinton on election night and told her to concede to Trump

Nov 26, 2016 5:30 am

Believe me, what they are attempting here is to buy time and find a way to inject ballots or find boxes of newly discovered ballots.

Book: Obama called Clinton on election night and told her to concede to Trump

Nov 27, 2016 4:34 am

Boy, ol' Hillary has got herself one big a whomping case of Battered Politician Syndrome.

OK, I'm game…

Ain't nothing like sticking your arm in a wood chipper only to to reach in with the other one to find the one that just got shredded off.

Castro was laying there watching TV and had seen that Kappynicknack was a fan of his and with that yelled "Nurse! Pull all the wires and tubes…I'm outta here!"

Oh look, when we went to the home of the healthy young lady that committed suicide by chopping her own head off had ten boxes of ballots that she stole from the election office where she worked…just exactly enough to overturn the results!

"Genuine political discourse" is reserved only for people who don't know what they are talking about but dang sure want to sound important.

The intrusion on liberty is personal…rights are protection of your person from abuse by government. Laws are often just the stupid impulses of idiots but even more often by influential elements.

Should anyone think, for instance, that lawmakers in states really care about your head if you ride a bike and that laws that make you wear a helmet are a result their concern or are they the result of bags of money offered to politicians by insurance companies?

Jeb Bush asks new Republican administration to flex its muscles with a constitutional convention

Nov 30, 2016 4:08 am

We should only make citizens who are staunch Conservatives, how else can you take the oath to the Constitution without being one?

Latino American becomes a staunch conservative

Chapter 12

December 2016

One thing I'm sure of and that is that Mr. Trump is very patriotic and that fact combined with his fearlessness at defending himself or others will offer some delicious fruit in the near future.

Mike Rowe wonders why we give federal money to colleges who refuse to fly the American flag

Maybe instead of wasting his and our time, he might better be worth his paycheck by grabbing a broom and getting the floors swept.

Levi Strauss CEO doesn't want you bringing your gun into his stores

Waste is a terrible thing to mind.

California just passed a law regulating cow farts

No, Christians don't believe that homosexuality is a sin, they believe Almighty God who says that Homosexuality is a sin...big difference!

Yes, leftists, Christians believe the homosexual act is a sin. Get over it.

The entire dislike of the homosexual crowd is based entirely on this delusional effort that if they can get everyone to believe it's normal then somehow it will no longer be considered a sin, the problem with that annoyance is the simple fact that we don't have that power and ability...stop bugging us!

LGBT wants more than acceptance; they want to be endorsed

This lady is smarter and more loving than most people. She is so above us all that she released a meat eating critter that has decimated thousands of other animals back into the sea so he can keep doing it.

Vegan activist buys 23-pound lobster, and then does just what you would expect with it

Well OK, if these Muslims don't like our society, traditions and Christianity, they should now be acutely aware of the reason's that we are going to stop letting them in.

The day they put up Christmas trees in Yemen, will be the day we let a few back in.

Police blame Christmas party for San Bernardino Islamist attack

I absolutely love how Mr. Trump went to the crowds of people to announce that indeed, Mattis is his pick and bypassing the media speculation and "privilege" to announce it on his behalf.

The media better quickly understand that respect is a two way street with Mr. Trump…if they do, it will suddenly smack them up long side the helmet that for the first time, they are actually doing what their career title describes.

Report: Trump taps 'Mad Dog' Gen. James Mattis for defense secretary

Dec 2, 2016 5:36 am

If I were a parent of a student going to these schools, I would buy the books, let my kids read them and then make a T-shirt for them to wear at school saying that they read the books anyway.
You absolutely have to fight back, all of us together….have we not learned anything from Mr. Trump 's victory yet?

Virginia school system bans these two celebrated literary classics because of racial slurs

Dec 3, 2016 7:33 am

BO: Ahhh…welcome everyone to the Choom Radio Network, grip the arms of your chairs and get ready for an exciting look at the Russian influence that turned the election against Hillary. Speaking of Hillary, she's our first guest tonight…hi Hillary!

HRC: Oh, ah, hi.

BO: What's that crunching sound, are you eating some Pez or something?

HRC: Pills.

BO: Oh, well…moving on..

HRC: Lots of them…and vodka.

BO: Ahhhh, now the Russians, they really did a number on you didn't they?

HRC: Yeah, that part where I was bobbing around and they threw me in the SUV like a sack of cheap potatoes…well, the Russians had shot a poison dart at me…got me right in the middle of the back and it took me a while to reach back and get it out.

BO: I get what you're saying, they got me that way too a bunch of times...the Secret Service guys always just laughed at me.

(Indistinguishable sounds)

BO: What's that noise now?

HRC: Oh, I'm taking a crap.

Is President Obama really interested in launching his own media company?

Dec 3, 2016 8:13 am

The application of self-control and patience is a good thing.

Mr. Trump is an intelligent and tactical thinker...avail oneself to a documentary on the huntings of the Cuddlefish...as a good reference.

While the premise of what Sarah was talking about is correct, Mr. Trump is very cognizant of Corporate Fascism and wasn't engaged in it when he brokered a deal to keep the Carrier plant going.

Carrier is a mascot for what is to come...the overall environment and understanding that welcomes the proliferation of manufacturing being retained and developed within our own country. Plus, not good to ask Mr. Trump "How...how, how you gonna do that?"

Here is something for fancy folks to think about. Our country has a sizable population of people that really don't have self-ambitions in life other than their things at home. Going to a monotonous and mundane job is but a brief interruption in their pursuit of life...these are manufacturing jobs. There are millions of folks on the government dole that would be much happier with a job and we can either provide an acceptable field of endeavor for businesses to utilize fellow Americans' talents or just sit and do nothing which by default, there grows the Fascism because the lesser and dull environment, the more reason for corruption to gain an edge.
A good example is cities providing streets and sewers for developers because a big development adds to the wellbeing of ALL. If one is

wanting to sit in the woods and eat pine nuts instead, well, there's nothing wrong with that either.

Sarah Palin turns on Trump: Calls Carrier deal 'crony capitalism'

Dec 4, 2016 6:53 am

Mmmm, rat on a stick roasted over a trash fire with Shitatooey sauce!

In reply to the story PETA claims rats deserve our protection, just like dogs and cats

Dec 4, 2016 7:28 am

A factoid about the Constellation, although the Constitution was the first ship commissioned, the Constellation, being the second in the United States Navy, was the first to hit the water.

There have been I think 3 versions since then and I'm going to be making lots of noise about the next one being, again, named the Constellation…it's important.

Ronald Reagan named the U.S.S. Constellation "America's Flagship"…it needs to still be in our fleet!!!!!!!!!!!!!!!!!!!!!!!!!!

The Fort Worth Police Department just released the greatest recruitment video of all time

Dec 6, 2016 4:21 am

It's humorous to me to see all the condescension coming out of the White House aimed at Mr. Trump. Obama has been in office for almost 8 years and is still, himself, unqualified. Want proof? All you have to do is see that we are already leaping in several area's and Mr. Trump isn't even in office yet, exposing the vacuum of a nothing but damage Presidency that Obama has had.

Contagious post-election confidence booster expands national economy

I was told by a friend in L.A. last night that parents in the L.A. school district had sent out text's to parents' phones informing them that counseling and whatever else will be available to Grade-schoolers because of the election.
Schools in cities are nothing but factories pumping out weak, frail and unintelligent future adults that will be absolutely prepared to be conquered.

Watch: University basketball coach has some harsh words about our "participation trophy" culture

Think of what it would be like to be Obama and have no skill other than trickery. I guess he's a lawyer but he must be really bad at that because of all his lawlessness and the court battles he has lost.

The only occupation Obama will have is sitting in some basement with Van Jones smoking pot and planning riots.

Obama has begun to drop hints about what his future plans might hold

Well now settle down. We have seen nothing but technological advances, sometimes in leaps, since the fifties and people are still working. I remember in the 80's there was a lot of fear with computers replacing people but actually, the computer advances created millions of jobs.

Meet the new tech that might make millions of jobs obsolete

This is exactly the type of thing that I was anticipating since last summer, we finally have a President who is not going to allow the citizens to be ripped off, their money wasted or be pushed around by snot-nosed bureaucrats.

The kind of executive sobriety that spells success is exactly what we need and have needed for decades.

Trump goes after Boeing for 'ridiculous' Air Force One replacement costs

Dec 7, 2016 4:58 am

And just to add, are the Holier than thou Sioux going to hold a forgiveness ceremony and apologize to the Pawnee for Massacre Canyon that occurred near Trenton, Nebraska?

Watch: Veterans bow before Native elders to ask for forgiveness for past military actions

Dec 7, 2016 5:07 am

If it occurs that in winter, a feller breaths in cold air containing moisture, it warms in his lungs and is then exhaled as steam then why wouldn't one think that if an airplane is moving through cold, moist air, heats it and blows it out as rolling rows of steam isn't logical?

Dec 7, 2016 5:38 am

Now, what some folks don't realize is that oil & natural gas are the most natural, organic sources of energy on earth VS their land and beauty destroying windmill and solar farms?

Protesters succeed in temporarily halting the Dakota Pipeline

Dec 7, 2016 6:01 am

The notion and belief of manmade climate change is the result of two kinds of people: Those who had read Chicken Little while on LSD and the unintelligent people who fall victim to their delusional rhetoric concerning the sky.

In reply to the story The Weather Channel rains on Breitbart's anti-climate change parade

What Trumps decision to run for the Presidency exactly reminds me of what sometimes happens in farming where the owner steps away from the day to day management to let his capable son or sons run it and then goes and gets a position on some agricultural board for the purpose of benefiting farming in whole.

Except for some occasions of advice and consent, Mr. Trump doesn't NEED to run the Trump organization, his sons are more than capable!

I believe that Mr. Trump sincerely cares about the whole good of the United States. I'm a dang good judge of character and I don't I see one bit of misleading or devious intentions in Mr. Trump.

Addressing the promotional effort by the real estate company...I think there is a little tongue-in-cheek here, a little fun.

Agent selling Trump Tower apartment is promoting this hot 'new amenity' — and you're paying for it

Kick sand in someone's face and what do you expect, Christmas cards?

The nightly innuendos against Trump and the stupid women thing didn't go unnoticed.

Megyn Kelly accuses Trump aide of inciting online threats against her

Gee wiz, if they are triggered by the sight of bones then I suppose when Halloween comes around and they are walking home and see displays of skeletons that they start running, increasing in speed as they go past each sighting in peoples' yards until they collapse in an exhausted heap on their doorstep.

Glasgow archeology students advised to skip lectures if the sight of bones is triggering

When I was in the Navy, every night at Taps the Chaplain came over the loud speakers and said a prayer. We ought to return to that and completely ignore any opposition...what are they gonna do, sue the Navy?

Watch: The Naval Academy's Glee Club sings a beautiful tribute to the fallen of Pearl Harbor

My tactic, and it's just my nature, is to listen to opposition because I am genuinely interested why they think a certain way, but the best way to make a point is asking honest questions because it allows them to answer it themselves and form a solid, sticking conclusion.

I knew a girl that in her mid 20's was quite liberal. In the midst of a civil discussion, I simply asked her "What politically liberal policy or idea can implemented without any force?" Inside a year she became quite conservative.

Roy Williams models how you can defuse a contentious political argument through active listening

The bombs on Japan ended World Wars. A time of only about 20 years separated WW1 and WW2...there have been 3 of those 20 year time spans since and nothing close to another world war.

The part of the story of America's atomic attack on Japan you never heard in school

Jill Stein has become the old lady beating the dust out of her rugs with a straw broom and when anybody looks at her she yells "What are you looking at!?"

Jill Stein: 'We have a case of Jim Crow in Michigan'

And I just have to add some thought. Where would the people who now work in the computer spectrum work if the computer was not invented? Likely, in an office full of filing cabinets, full of papers, I'd think. Now, some folks would say "Well, at least there would be a lot of jobs"

There is a problem with that train of thought…competition. While a certain sector of business languishes without innovation, someone else is modernizing, becoming more efficient and gaining the competitive edge while drowning out the old, tired and cumbersome operating businesses who eventually will go out of business, thus…job loss.

Carrier plans to use the money from deal with Trump to purchase robots that will replace workers

OH MY BETSY! He also owns a line of neck ties! What in the danged ol' heck will we ever do????

OH! WILL WE EVER SURVIVE?? Where's my safe space?…..where oh, where is my safe space….

Trump will remain an executive producer of 'Celebrity Apprentice' as president

Here's the BIG difference with regard to Mr. Trump. For decades, the citizenry has gotten used to being duped by politicians…in fact they expect it because that's "normal" Mr. Trump represents a full frontal dose of reality and the implications of that have a rippling effect beyond politics.

If you would allow me to sound like I'm abandoning this particular subject, just think about how removed society has gotten from reality by observing something about music. The artistic lyrics, complex composition etc…from the 90's and before mostly are much more advanced than today.

These days you mostly get songs of loathing, self-aggrandizement...and of course sex...I don't know about you but I really don't want to hear about someone's sex life.

Many aspects of society has departed from reality to self. I remember one time, listening to Dr. Laura Schlesinger. She had a caller on the line trying to figure herself out. To paraphrase, Dr. Laura said "Stop trying to figure yourself out! There's nothing there! What you are is what you are to others" And I thought "Some beautiful reality for a change!"

To Summarize, Mr. Trump is an assault to self-absorption. It's even hard to believe that he's in the Presidency because he really does care about others and people are not used to that.

Glenn Reynolds: 'Trump is FDR with the fireside tweet'

Dec 9, 2016 5:48 am

It's weird watching so many people flopping around like minnows dying on a beach over the Carrier thing. There is absolutely no way that Mr. Trump is going to be on the phone with every business...it's physically impossible. People are visual as opposed to just hearing about something or some concept. Carrier is an example of the coming business environment, uniform and fair to all. Mr. Trump is saying that we are going to make your lives much more simpler, more feasible, more free.

'Make your point before I deck you!': Fox News debate flares up over Trump targeting companies

Dec 11, 2016 6:12 am

I consider myself pretty up to date on current happenings and fairly perceptive, but just what is all of this "Fake news"? What are they talking about? Are people just making up "The Onion" type news?

One thing I have been able to put together is this, Liberals are always in a constant state of accusing others of the very things that they are guilty of AND as bizarre as fake news is, it seems to match "Russian hacking"

"Russian Hacking" wasn't gaining much ground because everyone is scratching their heads wondering how, so the CIA has to come out and say there was Russian hacking. Does the CIA do forensic computer analysis? I thought that was the in the FBI's spectrum. My thinking is that the Obama administration wanted the CIA to make this "Fake News" to give "Russian Hacking" more weight because the FBI is law enforcement and it's more dangerous to corrupt it rather than the CIA which has its own unaccountable world...the CIA can say practically anything and who would question the sinister underworld.

Should the federal government strike down fake news sites?

Dec 11, 2016 6:53 am

Ain't gonna happen. It's funny, Harry Reid and one more stupid thing to do before he leaves office...as if Comey resigning in August or whenever would have changed anything in the election. These are the type of un-smart people that Mr. Trump is avoiding in his administration...the Democrats keep pondering, "What, Trump isn't hiring any idiots that we can relate to...how unsophisticated of him?!"

Harry Reid calls on FBI Director Comey to resign over CIA Russian hacking report

Dec 11, 2016 7:07 am

I'm trying to figure out why the Democrats are using Russia, an ideological match to their thinking, to blame for the election loss. the only thing that I can think of is that the Republicans are the ones that have always been strongly opposed to the tenants of Communism and Socialism and thus the Soviet Union and Russia...Liberals has never been bothered by Russia until now. So what they are trying to do is try to hang a dark cloud over Republicans (Remember, depressing God fearing Americans is their primary goal in life) by what they believe to be stupid, conspiracy theorists who are Russia hating hicks...they want red-blooded Americans to mistrust the Trump Presidency.

Top House Democrat scolds Trump: Shame on you for going after CIA

It just has to cause the Democrats to be in a fit of pique over Mr. Trump actually demonstrating thrift with a superior outcome.

To make a bigger point about Presidential elections, the differential in the amounts of money raised and spent between Clinton and Mr. Trump is precisely the amount of money coming from special interests that went to Hillary...payola.

Report: Clinton spent more money than any other presidential candidate in history — and still lost

That is just completely rude aside from just stupid. So, OK Portland, if you are going to unfairly tax CEO's and keeping consistent, you should also tax the head coach of the Portland Trailblazers so that you will never be able to hire future one's that are any good because they will refuse to go there...the Duck's head coach too, for the same reason.

Heck, while you're at it, tax the lumber industry out of existence so that you may spend all your coming days watching the Fall leaves magically drift around your breezy minds.

Portland city council passes law to raise taxes on CEOs to address 'income inequality'

If women are capable of combat or not is a question that is irrelevant.

The most relevant question is "Does including women in combat and on ships make a better, more effective outcome or does it make it worse?"

The answer is: It makes it worse...quite a bit worse.

And now, here's why: Camaraderie. Physical ability is second and I'm not talking about pull up's and jumping jacks, I'm talking about an ability to carry heavy loads... especially when that inability leads to the deaths of servicemen.

Think about this, if you were the enemy of the US and couldn't match the physical weaponry, how could you gain an edge in combat? The answer is this, disable the morale and create division among the troops because when you have disorder, you lose strength and when you lose strength, you lose capability.

Now, for real life. In '84 or '85 I was aboard the USS Constellation as part of catapults and Arresting Gear. It was announced that they were going to bring aboard a group of females that were land based. And although you have a ship full of guys that like women, there was a collective "NO!...Why!" The women came aboard, they sequestered off a whole aft section on the 03 level (just below the flight deck...machinery and berthing) and gave us stern warnings and consequences for fraternizing with them.

That one act alone created resentment and division in the critical combat environment...thus, a loss of camaraderie, cohesion, purpose, and a nonsensical effort of self-disablement. We thanked God that it was only a two week Work Up and then they were gone...our mindset was "Good! Glad that huge obstacle is over!"

When you consider that the Flight Deck is a very small version of an entire Naval air base condensed to the size of roughly 3 football fields, and when you consider that one snapped cable, more than likely you will have dead people. One failed launch, you will have the loss of a 50 million dollar aircraft and the possibility of losing pilots...never mind the extra expense and loss of time dedicated to blow up the plane at the bottom of the ocean. When you consider that nothing on the Flight Deck is irrelevant and just there for no purpose...not even a little speck of FOD (A small object on the Flight Deck that can be sucked into a jet intake) And when you consider that only the best of the best are there running a complex operation with zero room for error, the personnel performing the actions needed need to operate just as efficiently as any of the machinery or you will have dead people. You cannot have division, disorder, poor morale and the loss of camaraderie and drama, especially for absolutely no good reason at all...that's called stupidity. Same for

Special Forces and combat. And do I really have to say, there are elements of "Human Nature" that is also a big distraction.

In 2000, a group of 5 or 6 of us gathered together for a reunion in Coronado, Ca where the North Island Naval Air base is and Home Port to our boat. It was a spur of the moment thing and not everybody could make it, otherwise it would have been about 15 or so...brotherhood. We went aboard the Constellation again (We were allowed to freely roam, outside of the guided tours) and later that night went out to the Little Club out in town.

The Little Club is the watering hole where the Topside guys would go to whoop it up. Well, in 2000 it was still full of Topside guys but now it was different...they were different. There wasn't all the laughter, the back slapping and the raising of glasses of beer. They were somber and introspective and when it came to talking about flight operations at sea, they were oddly almost removed from it...it wasn't "Theirs". They didn't own it. Women had been assigned as regular personnel and when that discussion came up, the only animation they displayed was the discontent and troubles it caused...and there was a list.

These men where subject to people whose stupid decisions imposed on them a sense of self defeat, purpose and camaraderie. Today, when I reflect on the wars in Afghanistan, Iraq and our war with ISIS, I can assuredly tell you exactly why it has taken so long to win.

Report: Science says women aren't as capable as men in combat

Dec 12, 2016 6:34 am

I saw that interview and when it came to the part where the daily CIA briefings came up, Mr. Trump's answer put a big ol' smile on my face! "I don't need it...I don't need that." The most salient word in that statement is "need." It's fun to witness the everyday, working mindset of our President and that it's very good.

When a kick-butt worker shows up at the job site, the BS stops...the wastes of time are obstacles and it's time to get rugged and dirty.

There is a goal to be met, the day is only so long and there will be enough hindrances of their own to be inviting even more unnecessary one's.

This is foreign to Liberals, naturally.

Media omits key context from Trump saying he doesn't 'need' daily intel. Briefings

Dec 12, 2016 6:41 am

One of the wonderful things about Mr. trump being elected, maybe the most important thing is that the dark and ominous, nightmare cloud of lies that bore so much suppression over the people of America, will be shortly gone.

Dec 12, 2016 7:35 am

Well, you asked for it Democrats. We told you not to mess with Americans. Just what where you expecting, a little paper thank you sack filled with peanuts and various candies?

Joe Biden excoriates Donald Trump and his 'vicious' presidential campaign

Dec 13, 2016 6:07 am

I finally came across the last piece of the puzzle regarding all this Russia stuff. It all has to do with one word and one number.

A couple of "Thank You" tours ago, Mr. Trump said something that not many people were saying, "Landslide"

In marketing, $19.99 is perceived as cheaper than $20.00, everybody knows, but $99.99 is perceived as way cheaper than $100.00...the higher the number, the more significant. In the same manor, 232 looks way less than 306...kind of like the Electoral counts in this last election. That's the number, "300" When you hit the next numerical increment, there is an enhanced value perceived.

"Landslide" and "300". Losing the election was one thing, but when Mr. Trump claimed it was by a landslide, and they finally had time to think about it, I think it slapped the Democrats and the Establishment up alongside their helmets that it really was a landslide by comparison. As a side note, on his radio show a few days after the election, Sean Hannity was giving Mr. Trump a list of people who he should not trust. Among the list he said "Mitch McConnell, he's not your friend!"

I was sitting in a friends shop last night with an Elk head hanging over my left shoulder. ABC news was on and I see this segment about these 6 Democrat Electors who have been getting leaned on by the Democrats and others to challenge, now, the legitimacy of the election on guess what, "Russian Hacking"

Right there, I understood what this whole recent, nonsensical "Russian Hacking" thing is all about. The notion of the Russians having an influence on the election had been laying on the floor of the opposition, it's use as of a week ago was pretty much over with. BUT, when the word "Landslide" was uttered by Mr. Trump and when they thought of how that, along with Democrats losing many other seats across the country, now gave Mr. Trump another powerful and frightening word, "Mandate"

"Mandate" the third word in the triangle of death for Democrats and the Establishment too, somewhat. The plan was now put in motion "How do we remove this "Mandate perception that Mr. Trump has?" The first order of business is the recognition of the numbers 232 VS 306 and the fact that 239 VS 299 doesn't really look so bad. They know that they can't turn over the election so they are desperately wanting to remove the public perception that Mr. Trump enjoys a mandate of the people…that gives him too much ease in getting his way and it may perpetuate and even grow. Widespread public support and admiration of Mr. Trump is the only two things in the way of trying to finish off America and man, are they going bonkers over it.

In summary, the six Democrat Electors that are coming out and demanding a CIA briefing before they consider the election results valid, along with the goofball Republican Elector in Texas, they have their magical 7. That would hopefully be giving Mr. Trump the magical 299 electoral votes thus removing the public perception of one big ol', red striped ass, a whoop'n that the Democrats got. Oh, and about my side note above concerning Mitch McConnell and the Establishment…aren't they just falling right back to their same old habits with agreeing to a hearing on Russian hacking, they have a lot to lose too with a Trump mandate.

Watch: Buck Sexton faces a hostile CNN panel while discussing Russian involvement in the election

Dec 13, 2016 6:24 am

Boy oh boy, ain't that something? Joe Walsh got himself a big ol' Important Man job down at the Establishment sewage treatment plant

Major Trump backer calls Trump's response to alleged Russian election interference 'almost treasonous'

Dec 14, 2016 6:21 am

I don't know if it could be called a "Charity" unless there are charity's that exist for the purpose of destruction. I know that Mr. Trump is being mature and gracious for the good of the people but Obama is literally, in its modern connotation, stupid. It would be like a college hiring me to teach a Quantum Physics class because I would be going "OK, class 5/8 is .625, 1/8 is .125 etc…"

And after they fired me from that and moved me way down to an Algebra class teacher I would be going "OK, class 5/8 is .625, 1/8 is .125 etc…" I literally wouldn't know what do because that's all the math I know and, frankly, it's all I care to know…I don't waste hard drive space on my brain for things that don't interest me.
Well, Obama found himself in the same predicament, he had a specific job and was physically and mentally unable to do it because he never cared to learn about and never cared about it. So, one would ask "Well then, how did he get that job and why?"

How?, I would have had to lie on my Teacher application and Obama would have to lie on his case to be President. Why? We both would have had to have fraudulent and ulterior reasons. Me, money, Obama, Social Revenge.

Well, now we have a President that is highly qualified for the job and specifically for the purposes outlined in the Constitution. I was putting myself ahead in the future for a minute the other day thinking about what the political atmosphere will be like in half a year. I thought people are really going to have to get used to something quite different...the whole atmosphere of politics will just feel different.It is going be, and I hate use the word feel, but feel much different. And yeah, with Mr. Trump's cabinet pick's, Weakness, inability, stupidity, candy land lies and nonsense is over with...and that may take some getting used to.

America might stay afloat if we run the country like a business, not a fraudulent charity

Dec 14, 2016 6:49 am

I know Putin is a bad guy. He's the bully in "A Christmas story" there he is, you still have to go to school with him and you don't want to make a mess by beating him up again.

First of all, I don't think Mr. Tillerson "deserves a chance" he's already there! He already has a better relationship than the current administration has and for better reasons...what arrogance.

Putin is shunned by Obama and the Establishment and the Establishment in other countries because he doesn't play New World Order plain and simple. And yeah, he also flexes his muscles here and there, probably because of that shun. I would think that all these anti-war people from all the past decades would welcome an opportunity to form some relationship with Russia that brings about peace but the Obama administration has done nothing but have little tizzy slap fights with Russia. I think he actually enjoys poking and teasing the skinny little idiot, Obama...makes him laugh when he puts his feet up at night, having a vodka.

Aside from having a dominant defense, militarily, a solid trade relationship is the peacekeeper and I suspect that it will be at hand. When you have two entities that mutually benefit from a relationship, neither one really has any reason to blow it all up.

Trump's new Secretary of State nominee deserves a chance to form a positive relationship with Russia

And there are several other of these precincts across the country that have been in place for a long time. It's going to be like finding all the remnants of the Mob after it was brought down (most of it anyway) if we were to keep digging and it's also the very reason that Hillary was so confident. I think what wizzed her off the most wasn't so much losing but that they hadn't been successful enough in cheating…she was throwing the pots and pans at the people in charge of that, not her campaign staff.

Voting machines recorded too many votes in over one third of Detroit's precinct

Tucker is absolutely correct, if you think about it and why the Founding fathers put that first in the Constitution, free speech is the fundamental basis for a free society. The Human urge to express oneself is the only means to be able to be one's own self. You wouldn't have the likes of Mad Magazine, the Onion, ABC News etc…without it. Having the discernment to recognize it and thus being able to roll your eyes, we may unknowingly prevent falling prey to it ourselves.

Fox's Tucker Carlson: Silencing 'fake news' is 'purely authoritarian'

There was that little period of time a couple of years ago when Christian leaders were trying to be nice and curry favor with the people who do Homosexual things as a weird way of trying to bring them into the faith (they fiddled with Global Warming too) but I just wonder if the Boy Scout thing wasn't a part of that push and that he now regrets that…didn't work out so good.

Tony Perkins: Trump's secretary of state pick 'should be particularly alarming to conservatives'

IF they have their OWN combat units and ships, there's nothing wrong with it if that's really what they want. Register? Let them choose. Do they really want to march into that meat grinder?

Should women serve in combat roles and register for the draft?

Again, of course, they're not even trying to hide what they are obviously up to. The Liberals are like one of these really strangely dressed fat ladies that you see on a Wal-Mart camera, who has gotten so mad that she tosses every vestige of self-respect aside as she wildly wipes out displays and is spitting on everyone as she is eventually dragged out of the store by police, half of her dress tore off.

Obama's "Graciousness" now over with, there is a full bore effort to get as many Electors possible to turn their obligatory vote for Trump into a vote for Hillary. The Liberals, the Establishment and other particular agencies are absolutely desperate to remove the looming and power crushing mandate that Mr. Trump has.

They are desperately mad to get Mr. Trump's electoral vote tally to get at least 299 or lower to erase the mandate that is apparent by Mr. Trump being in the 300's and Hillary in the lower 200's…that simple.

Intelligence agencies refused House Intelligence Committee request for report on Russian hackers

I wonder if the Liberals understand that they deployed all of these weapons all during the election cycle and it had zero effect. It's as if they are programmed robots that have only one mission, limited input on tactics options and a nascent version of Artificial Intelligence Freeware that was down loaded a long time ago, back when Yahoo was the only place on the web to have your email.

Did Russia deploy the perfect weapon in the recent election?

You all realize that polls are kaput now, right? It's gonna take a long, long time before they are believed again.

Poll: Republican attitudes about Wikileaks, Putin have changed drastically

If I were to draw a political cartoon about all of this fake hacking and interfering with the election, I would have one frame with Mr. Trump standing outside the White House door that's partially open and Obama's hand is out and he's saying to Mr. Trump "Welcome to the White House!" The next frame would show Obama inside with his foot against the bottom and Hillary, Reid and McConnell with their backs to it desperately keeping it from opening too wide.
The only one's interfering with this election are the Democrats with the Establishment gleefully loving it all.

Obama vows to take action for Russian interference in election

I was at a friend's shop and he only has digital broadcast so ABC news was on. It was this huge, beautifully produced stage play about Russians hacking the election as if was War of The Worlds part II...it was almost as if we better hit the bomb shelters!

I get home, Hannity come's on and it's just regular sensibility again, reality. A meek feller being interviewed simply say's something like "NO, Russians didn't LEAK anything to us"

Thinking about the astonishing contrast between the two, I was reflecting on the Obama years and how America was in such a constant fog of unreality...it was like fighting a constant storm of May Flies.

Fortunately, the life span of a May Fly is but 24 hours...and it is evening.

Sean Hannity had Wikileaks founder Julian Assange on his program to discuss the source of the Podesta leak

I'm seeing the footage on TV of all those buildings totally blowed up and I'm sitting there imagining that on the edge of town there sits about 20 rusty bulldozers with guys sitting in the seats. When finally there is nothing left to bomb, the dust settles and it's so quiet that there aren't even the sound of insects, one driver looks over to the bulldozer next to him and say's "Well, we all ready to go in?" the guy agrees, takes one last bite out of his baloney sandwich and puts the rest back in a baggy...the engines roar to life.

Aleppo evacuates while John Kerry calls for ceasefire, Obama complains about media focus on Syria

Well, if all the honky's were racist in this election, then that must have been one doozy of an internal conflict for Obama. I'm surprised he can even manage to put one foot in front of the other and walk!

College president blames election outcome on 'racism' against Obama

Think about the word discrimination and how there has been this full blow effort to eliminate it. It's not so much about race, gender, religion it's about the word "Discriminate" or better said, "discern"

Here's the effort: It seems that every day we wake up and there is a new no-no to discriminate against. If we were to get busy and do what they want and not make any discernment's, even if it violates our hearts or minds, pretty soon you will have no internal defenses and will just simply comply or believe anything.

See how that works? Tricky ain't it? Your opinions are not any good unless they come from us...we will determine how you should think, don't discriminate OR ELSE!

Department of Justice sues Michigan town over refusal to permit Mosque construction

His and the other Democrats' goal is to flood this country with as many less-than-smart people as they can so that they can win elections in perpetuity. I think one of the main points of horror to them on election night was that all of their efforts were in vain and that a President Trump will greatly diminish those efforts even further and further.

This last election was about three things, the economy, Judges and these illegal aliens…they greatly lost on all three points, thank Almighty God!

Here's his trick: People are not buying the notion that the Russians influenced the election and are rolling their eyes at the Dem's. So to keep the debate alive and try to give it more texture, he pokes a personal fight to draw the Republicans in so as to give their excuse more possibility of being true…as long as the argument goes on, they have more time to repetitively lie until people believe them. Tricky Boy!

Obama on Republicans softening on Putin: 'Reagan would roll over in his grave'

It ain't complicated! We can write whatever law we want, have the House pass it, then the Senate and then the President about whatever we want all in one day.

We should repeal Obamacare in full immediately, period. That gives a full year for everyone to iron out the change.

Next, as a whole and separate effort, start over with just some simple, applicable laws. No need for some "Act" with a bunch of central planning details influenced by special interests, just simple "Traffic Laws"

See how easy that is? Now you're done!...you can now go back and have a romp with your intern at some seedy roadside Motel with half of the neon sign flickering.

Americans expect Trump to repeal Obamacare, but replacing it will be complicated

These safety people aren't any good at making people laugh. I think that they should just make multicolored, full body, inflatable suits so that when they wipe out it will give nearby folks a little something to laugh about.

British driver: (Clapping) "Oh dear, that wipe out had a particularly jolly, surprise element to it didn't it?"

American passenger: "You mean that part where the dump truck hit him and bounced him all the way back to where he started from and then he started rolling back down the hill again?"

New bike helmet deploys like an airbag during crash

That has to be so upsetting to be rejected by the head of a political ideology that you have so dearly embraced all these years. What was it Hillary? Oh, what could it have possibly been that you couldn't quite muster up to the Stalinist threshold of superiority?

Hillary Clinton says Putin has a 'personal beef' with her

Thus, the condensed version of everything socialist, "Without me in charge, you are nothing...with me in charge, I'm great!"

Michelle Obama: The nation is experiencing 'what not having hope feels like'

217

Funny how at one time the Obama's and the Clinton people were such upright "smart" and dignified people but how quickly they changed into toothless hicks gathered in an aqua trailer house on the edge of town, hatching an elaborate shoplifting scheme.

Eric Bolling pushes back against latest media narrative: 'Russia didn't elect Trump — America did'

Well, the reason the Clinton's holiday party seemed like a wake is because that's what it was. They didn't celebrate the birth of Christ, rather, they were lamenting their political death...and even more grim than that, their political debt!

Report: Hillary Clinton's holiday party was so somber it was like a funeral 'wake'

We ought to just outfit a self-destruct mechanism on our drones with an audible warning. When lifted out of the water it begins "Bwonk, bwonk, bwonk...This device will self destruct in 10...9...8..." That should solve any future problems.

As for the mispelling that the Lib's are trying to make hay of I'd just tell 'em get used to it, I'm not oerfect like they are. (Yes, I meant those typoh's)

Donald Trump accuses China of 'unprecedented act' over stolen U.S. Navy underwater drone

Obama's last days in office are the living out of his Doctoral Dissertation in the book study of "Rules for Radicals".

Several months ago I made reference to an article I read about 30 years ago titled "The Browning of America" Perhaps Obama also read it as well because the notion put forth in the article is one of Obama's chief motivations for office. When combined with "Rules for Radicals" you have what we see today in Obama's legacy and that is nothing but destruction of anything American.

Anxious for the "Browning", opening the flood gates of illegal immigrants is what he considers merit...he lives destroyed, the source of a sinister grin. The record number of pardons and commutations, his party animal friends.

Terrorist attacks to him, toe curling hope...yes, that's his hope. Michele lamented in an interview that they now fear that their certain type of "Hope" will be crushed under a Trump Presidency.

The current and snotty head of the EPA recently said that the Trump Administration won't be able to change her rules and now the snotty and childish Obama thinks that there is nothing we can do to stop his flood of future socialist voters.

Take note, these people are as stupid now as when Donald Trump came down the escalator that fateful day and as far as their "hope" goes, they are about to get a whole lot stupider.

Obama suggests that America is about to get 'browner'

Dec 20, 2016 5:46 am

It is going to be lots of fun to see for the very first time ever, a logical solution to problems. Yet to be seen will be whether or not the Republicans in congress will be smart adults or will the just continue to be the disreputable co-workers down at the scandal ridden day care facility that's run by that weird fat lady.

Dec 20, 2016 6:01 am

Oh, break out the Disney...break out "The Circle of Life"

Bill Clinton casts an electoral vote for his wife on the anniversary of his own impeachment

219

It's going to be very interesting to see how Mr. Trumps style effects future candidates running for office. He may have just created a full generation of winners who are real and the losers who approach the lectern like a day old platter of Lutefisk and bore their way into obscurity.

'Bunch of sissies': South Carolina senator offers blistering takedown of Democrats, Republicans

These people really are this removed from reality.

Sometimes when I'm driving down a street I'll see kids doing things, things that an adult would really be embarrassed to do in public. I think back to when I was a little kid and how it seemed like you lived out of view of adult eyes in many ways, with regard to shame...there existed a license to be goofy. As one gets older, you naturally become more cognizant of your actions and you leave that bubble.

As kids, it never occurred to us that there were adults in the cars that we rolled apples under as they drove by or even that they were able to stop in the middle of the street, get out and deliver a good crack to the butt...until it happened.

Obama warns Trump against using the executive order too much — for real

Mr. Trump didn't run for President so as to have a political job but to fix the things that politics have damaged. The daily fights will be whether or not the Congress will abandon influence and embrace common sense or sneak around with little bags of lobby money.

If Trump delivers on his promises, 'he will build a pragmatic governing coalition'

I often make comments about the power that guilt can imbue a person's thinking and therefore acting. The German people are similarly guilt plagued by Hitler as the Left in this country would like for American's to be guilt plagued by slavery.

Now, the consequences. No one in sane societies would have blamed the German's if they never took in a single refugee as the UN was wanting but to assuage any possible criticism, they invite the Devil in their midst. I do believe that when they find this guy that he will indeed be one of the refugees or any of the various other immigrants from Muslim countries. This is what we simply call "Stupid"

It's going to be vitally important that we stand behind Mr. Trump in preventing the same types of people from entering our country.

The ginormous fireworks fire in Mexico City didn't get started because they all went off at once...it only took a few to cause all that damage.

Angela Merkel says it would be 'hard for us all to bear' if Berlin attacker were a Syrian refugee

When you compel young boys and then young men by threat of guilt and punishment in schools to abandon the pursuit of manhood, embrace Homosexuality and to be no different than girls except for your little pencil eraser AND there is no masculine influence at home, you shall behold the wussy, pasty, brain-not-working-correctly, little snots that we call a Millennial male.

Interesting is this; over the past decades in the effort to create parity in the sexes, there has never been a push to develop typical male characteristics and thinking in girls, it's always the other way around...a war on masculinity, the very essential part of humanity that both keeps its strength and keeps it's sensibility.

Hey, smug millennial liberals — here are some New Year's resolutions for you

Oh, and as a remedy instead of just complaining, four years of mandatory shop class in high school for boys by the Department of Education would be a great start…and I'm talking about the real stuff, basic carpentry, elements in construction, small engine overhaul, welding, fabrication etc…This is the quickest most natural way to make men out of boys.

Hey, smug millennial liberals — here are some New Year's resolutions for you

My instinct is to really lay it on current Military leaders for these stupid social experiments that they have engaged in but I know where those orders all came from.

It is my confidence that has me waiting for what I expect to be the major correction of the Military by General Mattis. First order of business that I expect is the removal of women in combat and the mixing of sexes on ships. If the chicks want to be on a boat then give 'em one or two and man it top to bottom with females only.

Navy nixes plan to rename all positions with 'man' in their title

It may take a while for some people to actually wrap their minds around reality with regards to a President. Since the 70's all I have heard from people commenting on politics is "Why can't they ever just put a regular guy in office?!"

A lot of people have just come to expect lies, corruption and stupidity as a norm…almost an addiction to have something to blame and vent about.

Being this way myself, I can tell that Mr. Trump just really likes people. He likes meeting them, making friends and genuinely wants the best for them…people from all walks of life. I truly believe that his chief motivation for becoming President is because of that.

People are going to have to eventually get used to a diminishing role that government has in our lives and the growing reality that the people have now taken back the power and that the most important thing in our country is the American life, after all.

Trump might do things that could actually be good for America

I bet most people don't know that the Arctic's were once lush tropical environments, fossils prove that. We can only wish to have global warming! Cold and freezing weather is a murderer!

So, what would happen if the earth really did experience global warming? Well, it would turn back into the terrarium that it once was. The atmosphere would stabilize, deserts would become farmable and there would be so much usable land that everyone on earth could each own 200 acres for cheap and be able to easily produce their own meat and vegetables abundantly ALL YEAR LONG! There would be far less necessity for industry to exist because as we see in the tropics, when you live in paradise, a simple home is all that necessary…perhaps even bamboo. Lots of clothing isn't necessary… lots of things aren't necessary.

But we sinned, thus freezing came upon us. Every time I hear someone crying about global warming I just have to imagine the devil rolling on the floor laughing at people begging for more of it.

Snow falls in the Sahara desert for the first time in 37 years

"Trump proof" it is not the right expression, he's trying to burn the barn down after robbing the farmer. He is in the outwardly and deliberate act of sabotage against his perceived enemy, Christian America…period.

Here's a look at how Obama is trying to Trump-proof his legacy

Fat man in 15C(leaning towards his wife): "Honey, I keep hearing rustling noises and little squeals and stuff."

Wife (pointing): "Oh, look honey, Richard Marx is wrestling with that cute little Korean guy on the floor next to you!"

Fat man (looking down): "Hey, you little buggers, you both better settle down before I take my belt off and give you both something to squeal about!"

Former pop star helps subdue violent Korean Air passenger

Here's what happened. Whereas the DNC contained characters such as Tip O'Neil, John Glenn and even Kennedy, they allowed the "ISIS" faction of their party to take control and with Captain Radical Obama at the wheel, from here on out we can only expect a parade of freaks to populate it's sticky rooms and halls.

The problem for them is that these extreme alt-left freaks have an inseparable shared DNA called stupidity. Don't believe me? How else can you explain the lack of thought in putting forth a washed up, coughing, wild eyed, seizure riddled, brain stem tumor inflicted, obnoxious hag with no discernible idea's as their Presidential candidate?

I had no Idea that General Mattis was a celebrity. Are we then supposed to expect him to show up at the confirmation hearing wearing a blue sequenced jacket and shiny red shoes?

Here is a teachable moment and one source of moronaciousness (don't bother looking it up). When you have a person or a group of people more worried about their appearances and what other people think about them, you would have people choosing cabinet members that are stupid so as to avoid criticism.

But if you are Donald Trump, you chose the most capable persons no matter what any snot-nosed critic might think or say.

Trump transition team is enamored with celebrity status

Dec 23, 2016 5:40 am

One thing I know, Obama is only setting himself up for some awful grim slap-downs after Mr. Trump gets in office and reverses all of his sabotage.

It might come as a surprise to this person with delusions of grandeur that he really isn't the President forever as that sinking feeling overwhelms him while sitting in some cafe with fellow hippies planning another attack on America that his only weapon is a yellow pad and a cheap logo pen that he found on the floor backstage of the DNC Convention.

Obama admin makes final push to dismantle program used to track mostly Muslim men

Dec 23, 2016 5:47 am

People who have aspirations in political office ought to learn a lesson from Donald Trump that purposeful convictions and the drive and capability to carry them out is far more important than trying to buy

the minds of a perceived constituent of "dumb people" with relentless advertising.

Donald Trump won this election way, way back before he even raised one million dollars.

Paul Ryan shifts fundraising haul to support GOP agenda

Dec 23, 2016 6:00 am

Hahahahahahahahaha Switzer just pulled off a double reverse trick hand off to the fullback that proceeded through the gaping hole in the middle untouched for 80 yards to the end zone.

How a former NFL coach got the gullible media to publish 'fake news' about Trump

No, Obama, those are your underwear...that's your shart right there. You created the fictional character when you decided to never mature but instead dove head first into your butterflies and unicorns fantasy world of self-aggrandizement.

Obama: My approval rating tanked because of the 'fictional character' Fox, Limbaugh created

If you are going to write an article and you are wanting to be thought of as smart, you might want to take time with regards to the meaning of words that you use. "Gaslighting" is a term used by Psychologists that describes one of many particular behavior traits exhibited by emotional abusers whereby they compel their intended target to doubt their own sanity.

Now, if this dumb girl might indeed be doubting her sanity because Trump won the election it's not because Mr. Trump was gaslighting her, it's because she is, in fact, nuts.

Author of controversial 'Teen Vogue' article doubles down on her criticism of Trump

Golly, not only is that chick nuts but apparently she is still using the tampons that her ex-boyfriend filled with 3" lag bolts.

Watch: Tucker Carlson's argument with a Teen Vogue writer gets hilariously fiery

What a mess Obama is leaving.

I'm being honest, when Obama got elected I was bummed out bad. I knew his policies would be awful but the only consolation I had was that maybe he could lift the spirits of the inner city folk and give them some pride, but instead, he just made them more wizzed off and left them with zero to be proud of.

US abandons Israel as UN votes against Israeli settlements, and Trump responds

I realize that the West wasn't all fun and games for everyone, just look at the Donner Party who got stuck in the snow and had to eat barbecued Frank. There wasn't running water, streets weren't paved and from what I hear, the hookers left much to be desired. It's not beyond the pale to me that from time to time the boys went out and shot themselves up a buncha Injuns and took their land just fer fun.

Here's the 'extremely offensive' county fair slogan Native Americans protested. Yes, it got changed.

This is very entertaining to me, Putin schooling the immature and stupid Sycophants of Socialism in the US, the Democrats. Putin is what and who he is, but it is the fault of diminutive and neutered idiots that he can freely slap them around.

Putin: Democrats 'need to learn to lose with dignity'

If I were the robber and found myself in court, I would stand up and say "Your Honor, I move that this case be dismissed on the grounds that the whole incident was just another chapter in business competition. I don't consider selling a single candy cane for $12,000.00 anymore unfair than charging a $35.00 fee for a $2.00 overdraft".

Festive bank robber hands out Christmas treats during heist

I can't hardly think of anything more ridiculous than a producer talking two people into going on TV wearing pajamas and talking about nuclear proliferation as if this is what ordinary people do when they cozy up to a fireplace.

Animals in cages come up with the silliest notions of what it must be like to be free.

'Let it be an arms race': Trump stuns MSNBC hosts in their pajamas

Dec 24, 2016 6:08 am

Maltan police (holding a bullhorn): OK dudes, whatcha got going on up there? The whole world is gripping their armchairs!"

Hijacker: "Ahhh…hijack, we do hijack!"

Maltan police: "How come?"

Hijacker: "How come?"

Maltan police: "Well, yeah. How come you you hijacked the plane?"

Hijacker: "Cookies"

Maltan police: "Cookies? There's some in the back where the stewardesses come out of!"

(10 minute pause)

Hijacker: "We find them!"

Maltan police: "Grab a sandwich too, if you want!"

Hijacker (with a full mouth): "We did!"

Maltan police: "Well, let the other passengers go so that they don't take any cookies away from you!"

Hijacker: "Ya, OK"

(Plane deboarded)

Maltan police: "So you guys coming on out now?"

Hijacker: "In few minute"

Maltan police: "Why!?"

Hijacker: "Hibjibby take poop on fancy, stainless steel toilet!"

Maltan police (raising his head and bullhorn back up): "Alright, we'll wait...(geesh)"

Libyan plane hijacked, standoff at Malta airport

Mr. Trump is correct. The UN is long past any usefulness and something happened as the members and their Representatives slowly began to realize that, and it is the same thing that happens in every governmental body, they have to invent or hype their importance to continue funding and because they are useless really, and bored, when they show up to work, they occupy their time with creating the importance of their club and creating a multitude of rules and in the case of Israel, Drama...the opportunity to gang up.

The only reason to be a part of the UN can only be made by Liberals wanting to impose their philosophy...a nauseating and self-centered quest for a purpose.

The Americans that voted for Mr. Trump just ain't down on governmental pomp and Academy Awards style self-reward...they are focused solely on the work to be done.

Imagine holding a kegger and dance party before going in and starting the cleanup efforts in a tornado ravaged town...it's just not a priority.

Here's how Trump's expected inauguration crowd stacks up against Obama's

Well Obama, that would be Mr. Trump...you are nothing more than a school janitor lighting fires in the classrooms a month before retiring.

White House tells Trump, 'only one president at a time'

The main stream media better wise up. If they don't hear and exactly reflect what will be President Trump's public dialog, they will be gone around. He is going to get HIS word out to the public, one way or another...and just what the heck is so weird about that?

Watch: CNN host asks Lindsey Graham if he thinks Trump's foreign policy tweets will be a problem

Thomas Sowell, and there are many others, gives the perfect example of why racial snubbing is so sad. All of the great potential in our inner cities that have been kept in chains by the Democrats over the decades can rightly be called a national asset holocaust, and the blame resides squarely with the Democrats.

Conservative intellectual icon Thomas Sowell retires his pen

I don't think either side has any cause to apologize. The leaders in Japan who attacked Pearl Harbor are gone and how does this generation apologize for them? That would be like our generation apologizing for slavery. And we definitely don't need to apologize, they deserved it.

Kind of like a bar fight between friends. "Hey I'm sorry I started it and punched you first" "OK, I'm sorry I put you in the hospital" would seem weird...some things just don't need words.

Obama, Japanese prime minister tour Pearl Harbor memorial site

As usual, Reid is wrong again. The list of potential Democrat candidates looks more like the crowd in the Insane Asylum in "One flew over the cuckoo's nest".

Reid: Group of potential 2020 Democratic candidates looks like an 'old folks' home'

Recently, in one brave little second, Obama took the tip of a dampened pinky finger and sampled his legacy and legitimacy…it wasn't good. His last days are going to be one big tornado against anybody and everybody and every fact there is…a final raised middle finger as he departs the White House door screaming "FU, Infidels!".

Hope and change? Americans already more hopeful under a Trump presidency than under Obama

Donald trump has absolutely no intention of handing information over to the press and allow them to then warp it as they deliver it to the people. The President has absolutely no obligation to keep the

"Press" informed. He does have an obligation to keep the public informed so he's going to have these other formats and the press will be seated next to the People, and that way it keeps the press out of exclusivity of information…I think it's a great idea!

Trump spokesman hints that Trump might not hold regular press conferences

They better be able to demonstrate visually, step by step, the trail between the DNC and Russian operatives and not just generalized pictures of whatever. But then again, when it comes to providing documents of proof, the Obama administrations last attempt gave us a 13 layered PDF with each layer containing a mixture of Raster and Vector alterations.

FBI and DHS release joint report formally blaming Russia for the hacking

Chapter 13

January 2017

This IS the priority in confirmations of Cabinet Members and I'm not surprised to see that PE Trump makes it one....there is so much catching up to be done from enlistment & boot camp to ICBM's...the most important being a strong, cohesive and self-confident body of Soldiers, Sailors, Airman and Marines.

Report: Mattis confirmation hearing will come quickly and will address Trump's interest in Russia

Here you have an exciting adult coming on as President compared to a red-haired, freckled-face 8 year old brat throwing his birthday cake all over the walls

Watch: Obama has no plans to leave your life after he vacates the White House on Jan. 20

If you are someone who reacts to real events of significance with emotional self-indulgence, it will be very, very difficult to solve problems because of the lack of being anchored to something real to begin with.

While we know that Russia is a little bit of a brat and flexes their muscles from time to time and are busy maintaining what power and significance that they have left, it's important in dealing with them to stay away from the ease of moral judgment, for we cannot change Putin, or Russia's history.

It makes sense to me that we engage Putin with man-to-man respect, an openness for mutually agreeable partnerships and trade all with a very stern stance that we will not put up with any of their dogs pooping in our yard.

Why fight with them? With regard to Russia being a threat to the United States, may I share a tid-bit of wisdom that I was always reminded of when I was growing up "You take care of your little problems, the big problems will take care of themselves" —-Johnny Walker

Evan McMullin slams Donald Trump: He is siding with America's 'greatest adversary'

If the Republicans in Congress are preparing to "get along" or "Be fair" they may want to take care and afford themselves with some thoughtful reflection.

The fact that Donald Trump beat out all of the traditional candidates ought to have told the feeble, selfish and cloudy minded Republicans that the voters in this last election were and still are finished with the failed capitulation with Democrats.

Our canon's are still filled with shrapnel and we are still merciless...don't become visible.

Pres. Obama to meet with Democrats to try to save Obamacare from Donald Trump

Effective slug-lines and failed slug-lines are always a source of entertainment for me. Whereas there are those that last decades for the positive like "Go ahead, make my day!" there are always the one's, mostly generated by Democrats, that too last decades for the negative like "I did not have sex with that woman"

Here's your next fail, Democrats. "Russian Hacking" will very shortly become a joke response by everyday people to make an excuse when something goes wrong at work, and the Democrats will be the butt of it.

I wonder what he plans to do, hit the wrong notes on the piano once in a while as punishment?

Musician John Legend vows to oppose Donald Trump's presidency every step of the way

Nice job Obama that this gross and goofy topic is actually part of public discussion.

Federal judge in Texas blocks Pres. Obama's transgender mandate in the Lone Star State and elsewhere

I often wonder what women who are put in positions of Pastor in a church think when they run across the verses in the Bible that say's that they shouldn't have that position.

Christian leaders say Trump's inauguration preacher is a 'heretic' and 'charlatan'

Gee, that break up with Burt Reynolds really scorned Sally for a long time...she's still mad about it.

If you start to think back now all the way to the primary days, just think that if Trump never used twitter how easy it would have been for the media to both get away with characterizing him and being the chief editor of his words.

That's really something of a contrast to behold, isn't it?

And then to also think about how Republicans have never had an outlet to get their real words and thoughts directly across to the public without passing through the filter of the media while the Democrats have always had their own "twitter" in the mainstream media.

There are only 4 basic elements in production that have both built this nation and are necessary to future on-goings; Food, lumber, steel, oil. Without these, or a dramatic shortage of these, we would encounter a colossal catastrophe.

It seems like magic that relatively cheap food is so freely available...almost an entitlement. But few people realize that every year most farmers and ranchers live on the edge of going out of business and while people might continue to laugh and giggle at that thought and site "free enterprise" your stomach sure won't when the fit hits the shan.

It must be an absolute priority to the existence of this country to see to it that our farmers and ranchers are given every single resource to

continue to stay alive and be able to supply cheap, abundant food.

It's not a given that farmers exist and may I ask a question? If the American farmers and ranchers die out, how much time do you have and how much do you know about growing and raising your own food with nothing more than a back yard or a parking space in an apartment complex?

Or shall we just give the American ranchers and farmers an easier path to succeed?… reinstate COOL!

COOL Law repeal means your table could contain sketchy beef

Jan 4, 2017 4:47 am

In order to conquer a nation or dismantle a military, all you have to do is remove it's masculinity and there is a full-blown effort to do so in the US…the ones active in this effort are chosen and willing surrogates of the forces that want our demise.

Boys! reject every bit of suggestion and effort to take away your prize.

University program seeks to counter the troubling aspects of 'masculinity'

Jan 4, 2017 4:58 am

And just what were these squirrely little knot heads going to do, start throwing their stuffed therapy kittens, crayons and rainbow colored popcorn balls at everyone?

CNN host to those who want to stop Trump's inauguration: 'Get over it'

Jan 4, 2017 5:20 am

I hate to pile on, I really do, but the visual and absolute sober fact that Hillary will be sitting there as "wife of an ex-President" really erases many, many years of zaniness…it will be like they finally got her to take her med's and she is on furlough from the mental institute for a day.

George W. Bush, Bill and Hillary Clinton will attend Trump's inauguration

I'm sure, the Liberals' greatest fear is that the Republicans are now in charge of the Great Magical Thermostat in the little room at the top of the Empire State Building.

Gee, that Cohen is one mean hombre with the insults, he even stole the term that Conservatives have been using to describe Obama for the last 8 years because he couldn't think of one of his own!

This guy is a one man smart people making machine. Everyone he talks to ends up saying to themselves "Wow, I always thought I was stupid…now I feel like I must be pretty smart after talking to Cohen!"

Watch: Dem congressman compares Trump to third world dictator

Whanna rule the world girls? First try working cattle in ankle deep cow pucky and mud for 5 days in the freezing March cold only to go home to have your spouse yell at you for smelling like cows while they are browning hamburger and still have the strength to just shake your head, for a start. :)

Unlocking the true intentions and meaning of female empowerment

My goodness, Mr. Trump's twitter account really puts a couple of elusive nettle leaves in their underwear, doesn't it?

Media can't decide whether Trump is a powerful Twitter user or not

The notion of an autonomous population of cars on the current roads is a fantasy. Trains operate on the most controlled systems there is and even on their own tracks, wreck routinely. Just take the number of train wrecks a year and times it by 10 million.

Electric, autonomous car executive suffers 'big embarrassment' at world's largest technology show

How about that?! Just when you thought that there didn't exist any more material for uninteresting, drawn out story lines in the Shakespearean realm of storytelling.

Sweden's queen says her palace is haunted by 'friendly' ghosts

This here effort would actually demonstrate the most effectual remedy for corrupt politics. Just the simple fact that they don't possess an eternal political crown over the people will do much to shift focus to doing well by the will of the people.

The people coming from England just came from a government with religious authority which was atypical to the free exercise thereof AND also distorted the meanings in the Bible. Notice, the priority of preventing the government of establishing a religion in order to protect the Word of God from corruption!

The expectation that the will and providence of God would proliferate through the PEOPLE, not government, was paramount. Thus, a small, benign and little "Necessary Evil" was allowed to barely act in a functionary capacity for matters of national good.
The body of Godliness resides in the people, it cannot possibly reside in a heartless functionary body called "government"…stop expecting it!

Watch: Fireworks explode on Fox News when Krauthammer challenges O'Reilly over Trump inauguration

238

And just to add. When people ask "Why is government considered "evil" it's because the bigger and more looming it becomes the more a false God is created. It's the only reason there are people fall to their knee's bawling and decrying those who seek to diminish it's prominence...IT IS THEIR GOLDEN CALF!, THEIR GOD!

Tucker Carlson will be great replacement for Kelly...relief!

'You just made the claim!': Professor hilariously fails to name source of climate change assertion

A lot can be said for the past but I am encouraged to know that very positive and much needed changes are a coming in government, but there are many selfish interests behind the dark curtain and we are going to see a lot of kicking and screaming along the way.

And yes, to all of the press and to all of you politicians, we do very clearly see your collective minds and hearts as you work together to try and undermine Mr. Trump's power in the Presidency...it is duly noted.

Have fun, Establishment, for the moment...like walking through tall grass, you can see all the way through to the ground from where you stand, but if you just keep walking it only snaps back in place.

But that roaring sound you hear approaching? That's Donald Trump pushing a big mower and the millions of people walking in the newly mowed path.

A skirmish occurs in Ferguson and a criminal gets shot, there is a long way to go in race relations, a kidnapping and torture occurs in Chicago and everything is fine?

I remember starting back in the late 70's and on through the 80's there was an explosion of self-help books, most of them pertaining to improving ones' heart and mind...people were actively wanting to improve themselves. But now, these Obama people don't give one bit of crap about that...they are absolutely content and even committed to living in the thin pink haze of unreality.

Obama responds to Chicago torture video by saying race relations are not worsening

What Mr. Trump is going to hear today is this big drawn out description of the environment of international hacking ending with an educated guess that the Russians phished (they'll say "hacked") DNC e-mails.

They will not show one little bit of EVIDENCE of who did it...not even a simple little IP address of the one who uploaded the documents to wikileaks.

The intended purpose of something called "Russians hacking the election" might work on Hillary Koo Koo's but the rest of the country is rolling our eye's.

The Establishment might want to keep in mind, you all tried your HARDEST to stop Trump during the election and you all got a big ol', bloody snot blowing, a whomping instead!

US Intelligence community prepares to release declassified report on DNC hack

If the people in the Establishment are left scratching their patchy heads in frustration as to how Donald Trump won the election it is because we are smarter than you. Did you all ever think of that?

In every aspect of reality, Trump voters, it turns out, are the smart ones in the US…we knew way back that blaming the Russians for the election was just an effort at proving a deeper possession and degree of idiocy, ironically belonging to themselves.

Better get used to it. We ain't gonna be fooled for the sake of borderless World Order.

Here is the big effort; From emasculating boys, to shemale restrooms, to crying 20 year old men and yes, even all the way to trade is an imposed compulsion to self-destruct by embracing weakness in our model.

It's like if someone were able to compel the greatest NFL teams like the Steelers, 49ers and Patriots to fill their squads with giggling 16 year old girls in order to beat them but only a fool would go along with it…guilt trip of unfairness and all.

When they find the one who did it, they will find a sweet, thoughtful, fair, multi-cultural, loving, diverse person from the grandiose crowd of Liberaldom.

Police: Ohio State campus carry activist found shot dead

At the end, Biden's mic was still hot and caught him saying "God save the Queen" and I thought to myself 'How sweet of him to be so concerned about Obama's retirement!'

"It is over." Biden stops cold House Democrat attempts to keep Trump from office

To all the Liberals, Don't worry about insulting Christians…the devil has already been at it for a very long time, is way better at it than you and we just learn to slough it off as usual. Having said that, you would be performing ill thinking if you are motivated to get in the way of God's will on our behalf.

University gives Bible students trigger warnings — that they may see crucifixion images

All I can say is that it's very, very easy to say things when there isn't an inherent obligation to prove it's veracity.

Intel officials say Russian leaders celebrated 'what they did' after seeing Trump victory

Humor is a good thing. Anyone being offended by this should be strapped to a La-Z-Boy and forced to watch Jerry Lewis and Mel Brooks movies for a day.

You have to know that there was a resounding "NO!" when the FBI asked to look at the DNC server. That would be like a guy who's growing pot in his barn to invite the cops into it to find out who stole some plants.

DNC rejected FBI request to examine hacked email server, law enforcement official says

By its own nature, people with paranoia due to schizophrenia never confront the thing they are legitimately fearing.

BREAKING: FL shooter allegedly told FBI in November he was being forced to fight for ISIS

I think they should name the monkey "Frankie" so that when some New Yorkers visit the zoo and one of them yells "Hey, Frankie, look at this stupid monkey!" the monkey would hear that and not know what to do.

Cameron Park Zoo staff prepares to welcome baby orangutan

I have a friend that lives in Watts, L.A. and he frequently tells me about a new HUD housing project to rebuild a development called Jordan Downs. Although there will be a little commercial space available for retail, the whole thing is going to be nothing but a tax payer money hole.

I've always thought of the lost opportunity there is regarding the inner cities and why it is that we couldn't entice manufacturers with lots of incentives to develop on the edges of these blighted area's offering employment, empowerment and life.

The one thing to be mindful of though would be to have the community really get on board so as not to be accused of taking advantage of what the Liberals would call "Slave labor" because they have so much to gain on the backs of their current misery.

Fiat Chrysler announces huge U.S. investment, including thousands of new jobs

There gets to be a point of addressing the stupidity of Obama People for me that is like making overtly obvious medical diagnoses of a horn toad that just got run over on a hot asphalt road.

Kellyanne sure is a fighting trooper!

Watch: Kellyanne Conway eviscerates Joe Biden for telling Trump to 'grow up'

I don't buy it, this big ol' campaign to stop Trump from tweeting. The media is going bonkers because he will just be going around them when wanting to talk directly to the people…I love it!

Keep tweeting, Donald!…

Many of Trump's supporters are pleading with him to stop tweeting

You can even look back at Bill Clinton's Presidency and find a couple of notable accomplishments, although they were the direct result of smartly taking Dick Morris' advice but when you look back at Obama's years….crickets…literally, nothing there.

Historians 80 years from now will look back and try to hang some sort of legacy on Obama and the only thing they will be able to conclude is transvestites…The Tranny Presidency.

Think I'm just being funny? Really, you just try and think of anything of positive notation that you can attribute to Obama's complete waste of time in the White House.

Obama's legacy and what it means for a Trump presidency

They made a conscious decision to go way far to the left and that caused many traditional Democrats to back away…it's their own fault.

This last election really, really meant more to the future of this country than any other and thank God Almighty that it wasn't just another run-of-the-mill Establishment Republican that won.

Wilson and FDR started the wheels in motion but especially over the last 30-40 years the Left has been steadily making ground, Obama was the culmination of all of their hopes and dreams and was supposed to be the final kill…Conservatives even contemplated that it was so.

When we look back in 6 months or a year from now, I think that it will be sort of shocking to look back at just what exactly happened November 8th. The precipice that we felt ourselves being pushed to will look steeper, the consequences more dreadful.

We are ALL still trying to discover just what exactly happened here. The Conservatives are elated that Trump won but we still have a hard time picturing what the real results are going to look like...meaning it's going to take some adjusting to actually believe that we aren't living in a confusing whirl-wind anymore. It's been a long, long time since there wasn't some huge looming ideology that chased our daily lives.

For the Liberals, this last election was the end of many, many years of effort to in Obama's words "Fundamentally transform America" Hillary Clinton was an exhibit of every single flaw in Liberalism and she was soundly rejected.

Now, you Establishment Republicans better take note, a HUGE note, because this election, starting back in the Republican debates, also proved that the Republican party has also hollowed out itself. It turns out that big, bad, bold reality WINS. I just know that there are many, many common citizen Liberals that even privately love it when Mr. Trump is so brash and grounded...you gotta really be nut's not to enjoy it.

'Is that on you?': ABC's Stephanopoulos confronts Obama over 'hollowed out' Democratic Party

Jan 10, 2017 6:39 am

Oh, they could insult us for watching football and martial arts but they are already insulting us by making TV shows and movies that are nothing more than adolescent after-school programs...some with CGI!

'Let's insult people for watching football and mixed martial arts'

OH, NO, NO, NO!!!!! DON"T LET THAT HAPPEN!!!!!

Caitlyn Jenner reportedly planning nude photo shoot in 2017

It was about 9:00 pm central when I was on the phone with my brother and assured him that we won. When I saw the margin in Iowa and having Ohio and Pennsylvania, I knew it was over…I went to bed around 10:00 as usual, happy!

Kellyanne Conway details Clinton's election night concession call to Trump

I didn't watch the stupid show but I did notice that Meryl Streep looked like she fell down next to the wino's in the ally and still had broken glass stuck all over her dress….odd.

Trump burns 'Hillary flunky' Meryl Streep after Golden Globes speech

So, Obama leaves just like he came in, a lot of showy production, acting (tears) and yes, even the "god echo" all complete with nothing in between but an economic recession and a social depression. The Obama years did have something else of a moniker associated with it and that is the fact that his years where notable for seemingly weekly mass shootings of all sorts…to be fair, it might not be his fault but, historians will be keeping tabs to see if there is any correlation between the atmosphere he created and the steady accounts of public carnage.

But now Donald Trump enters the Presidential scene. Those who sat, slack jawed and drooling at Obama's "magic" make a comparison to their fantasy world by referring to Mr. Trump as "Brash, rude, crude, unsophisticated, unintelligent…."

One of the news shows guests last night (sorry, I don't know his name, I was only listening at the time) said it well by describing

Obama's legacy as "Donald Trump".

There is a chasm in this country between those who live in the wild blue yonder and those who's feet are firmly grounded on earth. I really do think that Obama got reelected solely because many people watching his poorly produced movie, still wanted to see how it ends, perhaps out of nothing more than shear boredom...it ended poorly and only added to the boredom.

Let me make some clear water out of all of this "Russia/Trump" stupidity.

The ONE thing, that ONE impenetrable wall that the Liberals face with regard to Donald Trump is the absolute connection that he has with the people...the loyalty. They know dad gum well that if he retains that loyalty, the next election will just be a repeat.

Oh, they tried! They tried like thunder all through the whole election cycle. They pulled out every old trick in the book, and a couple of new ones too, to get the faithful to abandon Trump...........nothing, absolutely nothing worked.

So, they had an idea. Hatched in the basement of an abandoned building with blue paint peeling off the interior walls, they came up with the "best" idea yet to get the people to leave Trump...in a weird irony, their "nuclear option", "Russians!"

Democrat Strategists: "Yeah...YES, OF COURSE! The red-blooded Americans hate the Russians, they have always really hated the Russians and Communism!!!! My Dear Screwtape, you're a genius!!!"

Democrat Strategists: "All we got to do is connect Russia to Trump and voila!, his faithful will be leaving in droves!!!!"

Democrat Strategists: "OK, OK, Ok let's start working on more and more ideas! Boy, oh boy, them Americans ain't seen nothing yet!!!....hahahahahaha"

Someone in the back of the room: "But what if they are too smart to

fall for it…again?"

Democrat Strategist: "Somebody shoot the person who said that"

U.S. intel chiefs say Trump camp exchanged info with Russian gov't during campaign

I remember one time when I was using a staple gun to upholster something or another, I accidentally shot a 1/2" staple into my thumb. One leg of the staple through the thumbnail, the other leg in the knuckle…only a little bit of the crown was standing out of my skin.

Knowing there was only one way to get it out, I went up to Jack, handed him a pair of diagonal pliers and said "Just get a good hold of it and yank it all out, in one quick action instead of just working at it, extending the pain"

That worked.

I think Mr. Trump might have a similar philosophy with regards to Obamacare, end it… do it quickly…it will be way less painful that way.

Trump: I want Obamacare repealed and replaced within 'weeks'

Can you just imagine being forced to attend an intimate 3 hour tea party with these two wizards? It would be like someone tamping a thin stainless steel rod all the way down your spine and in the words of Morrissey, the pain would be "enough to make a shy, bald, Buddhist reflect and plan a mass murder"…oh gee, after being such a fan all these years, now I'm gonna get sued by Morrissey.

Barbra Streisand backs Meryl Streep's criticism of Trump, rips his 'disgraceful' Twitter battles

Why wouldn't they need a warrant when it wasn't an issue of imminent danger? I'm not a lawyer but if anything smacks of 1984, this takes the cake.

I'm going to take the occasion here to say something that is remarkably missing in political discussions...Insurance companies and the rude and tawdry relationship between them and politicians and the consequences to us.

I like playing escape games. When thinking about insurance companies and their influence I think back a a series of flash games called "Dibbles: For the greater good" In this game you are allotted a certain number of Dibbles who are little people of the Kingdom and you task them with a series of timed events to make way for the King to get from one place to another...all working in a very structured and precise way.

This is the vision of society inherently desired for a company in the business of taking in mass amounts of money from mistake makers without having to give any money back to cover mistakes. In order to do that, you can't have the participants making mistakes...at all...at any cost...to the people.

When you stop for a single second and wonder which industry is it that advertises the most, it's obvious that it's insurance companies. It's everywhere, inescapable and has a seemingly sense of being the primary element to life. The premise is an easy one to proliferate:

"For the greater good".

Seat belts, helmets, healthcare and now keeping you from getting your own car stolen...for your own good and the greater good. After all, who can argue about that?

So how do they pull it off? I'll start first with human nature. For ever it seems, there has always been this commonly issued complaint by people saying "Hey! There ought to be a law against that!" It plays off of our selfish tendency to get our way at the expense of others.

So, the insurance companies want a law make, send lobbyists, politician grabs the dough, a law is created for the "Greater good" And every time it happens there are the ones who applaud and the ones who are grieved and burdened...only to have the process to come around again but this time, the applause is on the other side of the fence and you are now the victim.

Selfish endeavors at the expense of others always have a way of eventually wiping everyone out...eventually.

Michigan man fined $128 for leaving his car running in the driveway

Jan 12, 2017 4:32 am

To be honest, it's hard for me to assay whether the Iraq war was appropriate or not. On one hand we destabilized a region giving way for a long desired Caliphate to take root. On the other hand we removed a cruel dictator and are trying to encourage Democracy...one that we will always have to baby sit.

The one thing I do know is that the people in the Middle East are not inherently imbued with any desire for liberty for all and that little fact makes any attempt for reason unattainable.

Rand Paul finally got to ask Rex Tillerson if he agrees with Trump on the Iraq war being a mistake

Jan 12, 2017 4:44 am

If I recall correctly, isn't it Dan Rather that went the way of Nixon?

Donald Trump's press conference yesterday did do one thing for the main-stream media...it gave them notification that at the start of the football game between themselves and Donald Trump to begin January 20th, Donald Trump will already be 100 points ahead.

Dan Rather warns Trump to change his ways or he'll wind up like Nixon

The same core mindset that is what we now call, ironically, "Liberalism" is the very same core mindset of Communism and Fascism. It was that mindset that built the Berlin Wall…but that was built to keep people IN not out. Today in the US the "Wall", complete with the very same purpose, is the entanglement of Liberal government policies which make it very hard to escape it's grasp.

Since I was young I have pondered what it is to have that mindset and why some people are attracted to it…why people like Bob Menendez and Hollywood actors adopt a notion that in reality, if ever fully actualized would severely oppress them, love this notion.

Here's the answer: In their minds, if Liberalism were to ever be fully actualized, they don't picture themselves as being the oppressed, they picture themselves as having what they perceive as the LUXURY OF BEING THE OPPRESSOR ! ohhhh….but don't they just love you so much!

Dem. Senator compares Trump's border wall to the Berlin Wall at Tillerson confirmation

This is very, very, very dangerous business, jailing someone for "hate" alone based on one single premise; many people consider the actions of politicians allowing illegal aliens to roam free in our country to be an overt act of "hate" against Americans!

White woman jailed on hate crime charge after video rant against Latino woman: 'Spanish privileged'

So, why is it that "Racism" is considered the worst of things by Liberals?

Here's the answer: EVERYONE on earth has prejudices.

So, keeping that in mind, Liberals possess the nature of "The Accuser" and accusing is a very powerful and useful tool because it only takes one little issue in one's soul to cause it to be disabled by guilt. And, because everyone has some kind of opinion about certain aspects of other peoples races, it's an easy weapon of guilt infliction to use when wanting to get one's way.

Here's how it goes; one guy say's "Asian people are always eating rice" The supposed friend say's "You're a racist!...That's racism!" and now feels like he disabled the other guy and empowered himself...that he is now superior.

'Back of the bus?': Black congressman implies GOP is racist during Sessions confirmation

Jan 12, 2017 6:11 am

Being in business, serious business, Mr. Trump very well knows the importance of avenues of communication and their usefulness.

This puts Mr. Trump in a very enviable position with regards to the media...if you are not a useful avenue of communication for him you will be relegated to be the red faced kid in class that has to sit in the corner because he pooped on the floor.

TheBlaze hosts react to Trump shunning CNN's Jim Acosta

Jan 12, 2017 6:19 am

Speaking of phones, Jeb Bush appropriately demonstrates that his political instincts and strategies still have a cord attached to them.

Jeb Bush wants Melania to 'steal' Trump's phone so he'll stop tweeting

Jan 12, 2017 6:23 am

These politicians are going to have to get used to the fact that the Trump administration will be filled with people that are way, way more intelligent than they are!

Tillerson's response to Kaine's question prompts laughter in Senate hearing room

Reporter: "Mr. Trump, Mr. Trump, Mr. Trump..

Trump: "What?"

Reporter: "Do...do you...do like corn?"

Trump: "I guess, what's wrong with corn?"

Same Reporter: "Mr. Trump, Mr. Trump, Mr. Trump..

Trump: "Yeah, what?"

Same Reporter: " Are...are you gonna....are you gonna release you tax forms?"

Trump: "What are you, some kind of idiot or what?"

Trump still won't release tax returns, insists public doesn't care

With all of this silly ambiguity and confusion in our intelligence community, I have a feeling that when President, Mr. Trump is going to have a whole lot of house cleaning done there.

People might think I'm a little nuts by saying this but I have concluded that when people utter the words "Climate change" what they are siting is the under-girding mentality of "The New World Order", sometimes just simply referred to as "The Establishment"...I'm not quite ready to refer to it as "The Mark" yet but I have a hunch that that's what's going to become of it.

"Save the Planet", "Hands Across the Sea", "Save the Whales", "Save the Trees", "LGBT Rights", "Global Warming" etc...all have a similar component and that is that all of the sudden an urgent need pops up that EVERYONE is compelled, to one degree or another, to embrace.

But those were and are just work-ups...practice if you will. Humans are fairly stupid and selfish by comparison to utter reality so I don't believe that there are really smart and crafty people somewhere orchestrating all of this, but rather it's just a collective human nature in the business of being a God and surrounding itself with a religion.

Whereas in past decades there have been several different ways that this has fleshed itself out, the effort has now decided to create a Union, an umbrella that covers all efforts combined..."Climate Change". It should never surprise anyone that if you come across one of these movements that you will find a fierce defending of Climate Change as well.

And why "Climate Change"? Well, that's simple...it's UNIVERSAL and the fact that weather changes and shifts all the time, the simple notion of it is unarguable thus, if you don't join the thinking of it, you are stupid and EVIL.

So, when you see an incidence like Kamala Harris asking Mike Pompeo if he would embrace Climate Change, even though it has nothing to do with intelligence ironically, what she is really asking is "Are you one of us, one of the stupid, selfish people?"

Dem Senator grills Pompeo on climate change in confirmation hearing

Jan 14, 2017 6:13 am

Habib, did you know that you have desert sage growing out of the top of your head?

Yeah, I got shot last month by one of the infidels.

The military wants to make bullets that plant seeds after they're fired

Don't forget that the establishment is still there. There is no other reason that certain Republicans are going along with the "Russia" thing than the fact that they have something financial to gain out of it.
That might sound cynical, but this last year just made facts out of all of our previous cynicisms, didn't it?

BREAKING: Senate Intel committee reverses itself, will investigate Trump's Russia connections

I'm convinced that it was all a very sincere gesture offering people the opportunity to render thoughtful sediments on behalf of Obama's departure.

'Don's Johns' portable toilet co. angry at Trump inauguration cover up

If one were to honestly endeavor to discover the raw earth and fully distill Liberalism down to a single component and apply a word to describe it, the word would come out simply as "Anti"

Anti-God, Anti-Christ, Anti-Love, Anti-Anything well, Anti-Anything good…Anti. Even terms like "Liberal" and "Progressive" that are used to describe them have opposite meanings of what Liberalism is…quite a remarkable feat!

So, having that in mind, Liberals are seeing that Mr. Trump is having success with motivating the American economy, businesses and jobs…they aren't going to have any of that so out comes "Anti". Anti-business, Anti-jobs, Anti-American…anything to destroy anything well and good.
Linda Bean is very correct here and businesses better buck it up and prepare for the ongoing assault to be forthcoming and boldly stand firm and learn how to say nope!

L.L. Bean board member says anti-Trump boycotts are 'smokescreen' for something much bigger

OK, Cecile Richards, since this is such an important passion of yours why don't you offer up yourself as the first one to be retroactively aborted?

Cecile Richards wants the government to 'triple' Planned Parenthood's funding

So, this story is meant to admonish Mr. Trump for shutting up a reporter and cast an accusation of Trump being against free speech.

Intelligent people know that the Constitution does not entitle anyone to take the possessions of others nor is anyone obligated to offer them and that includes ones' thoughts...as in the case of wanting to ask Mr. Trump a question, you are not inherently owed an answer to satisfy something personal.

Giuliani champions Trump as free-press hero one day after CNN dustup

Wouldn't it be easier for the girl to just say "Excuse me for a minute, I have to go outside and fart...there are pretty bad today because it ate a burrito for breakfast" and then just call Uber.

'Angel Shot' helps women report bad dates without fuss

I think what he means is that they will make conditions in the Insurance industry so that they are able to operate cheaper and more freely and therefore, everyone will be able to afford health insurance if they want it.

Trump vows to provide 'insurance for everybody' in Republican health care replacement plan

First of all, we notice that a plan meant to save the public money regarding healthcare but it looks as if it is a tax collection mechanism that they are still either addicted to or they are trying find a way to retain it.

second, these bite size bills are the exact way to address remedies after Obamacare is repealed…not a freaking "Plan" "Plans" and "Act" are nothing but giant balls of confusion, pork and whatever manner of corruption because by its nature, the public cannot grasp it all and just look the other way allowing it to corrode society.

Congressional Republicans readying 'bite-size' bills to replace Obamacare

Since this story is a hit piece through innuendo, it would be nice and complete if the writer could have made case through innuendo, what possible negative effect it will cause to either the Presidency and anything in America.

I hope Trump keeps using twitter to provide a defense against what historically was a free pass by the press in deciding what is true and what isn't…the press was like is being on offense in a football game with only 3 people or less on defense.

Trump organization announces Scottish expansion plan, despite Trump's no new foreign deals promise

On the occasion of this day January 20th 2016, the subject of IQ might well say it all. I took an IQ test from a credible online outfit a few years ago out of curiosity and I also had to take an IQ test as part of applying for a job when I went to work for a corporation here in Nebraska, but when I took that one I took a little bit of time to analyze the test itself and note what actual components mattered as well as the tools they used to determine something that is often arguable.

I think a lot of people would be surprised to find that unlike college exams, the questions didn't contain math equations, spelling, history or any other typical one that are commonly used...those exams are really only testing memory. The test examines how well one listens to, reads or sees a problem (the humility it takes to realize it) and how to solve it. The structure of it might seem like the easy style of test's as it is multiple choice, but that is a very important part of it because that is precisely what we encounter all day, every day...problems and the options we are able to perceive to solve them. The ability to physically remedy them are another subject altogether. As I paused to just simply look at both test's it struck me that what they were really after was, in most part, common sense.

American's have always took pride in having common sense and laughed at those who don't have it. Aside from the blessings of God, it's really at the core of what made this country as exceptional as it is because what comes from it is fixing things and impressive innovation.

From the time of my childhood, it has always been hearkened when talking about politicians that someone would always eventually say "Why don't they ever put one of us in office...normal people!?" In essence, we were laughing at politicians because of how stupid they were/are. Odd isn't it, the common man with common sense are the ones that built this country and made it what it is, all the while the elite and so-called, humorously, "intellectuals" merely served as critics and self-exalting bores...doing nothing to chip in.

On this day we will have the Inauguration of Donald J. Trump as our 45th President. And may I say to all of us Americans that ever asked "Why can't they ever just put one of us in office?" well, here he is, a common man with common sense...actual intelligence. Cloaked by God, a problem solver, an innovator...one of us. The Elites are appalled and loudly protesting, but then again, isn't that the exact same thing that the first Americans faced when we told the world that we are now independent?

At this time in American history, seldom before has the perfect candidate been chosen at the right time like now. Government has grown into a ball of confusion and disrepair caused by so-called "Intellectuals" and Elites who lack both common sense and the ability to solve problems.

Well American's, here we are! Us, in essence by representation, Donald Trump, who embodies every good quality about America, will take the oath of office at high noon today!

God bless you, Sir! And thank you for what is truly a personal sacrifice in service to this country for OUR benefit for once!

Trump: My Cabinet has highest IQ of any Cabinet ever 'by far'

Jan 20, 2017 1:55 pm

Let's see here, tool box, shovels, right side of the truck. Better take the jack hammer...right there. Air hoses, miter saw, fasteners. You got your hundred foot tape? Take that. Water jug, laser level. You got your tool box too? Good.

Grab some pizza when we get fuel...let's go

It's official: Trump becomes 45th U.S. President

Jan 21, 2017 7:10 am

I heard a sound bite yesterday of some hammerhead saying that we are all Mexicans and we are all women and I thought, that ol' boy's been spending way too much time with the monkey while gazing at a velvet painting he bought while on field trip to Tijuana...I suspect that Chris Mathews has one too but one of his friends must have borrowed it and he's frustrated.

Chris Matthews called Trump's speech 'Hitlerian' over two words

Jan 21, 2017 7:18 am

It's an expectation that is inherent with being human that we are corrupt by nature compared to God, and we sin...it's the official stance that those sins are approved of and supersede God's love and are established by law by a Nation that stands in grave danger of a judgment that is as hard to avoid as an ant trying to escape the heel of a boot.

Report: Trump will sign executive order to defund International Planned Parenthood this weekend

Jan 21, 2017 7:29 am

I thought punk and Av ant-garde was cool. What happened to these guys who gave up on some sense of individuality and fizzled out like a wet firecracker on the edge of the sidewalk.

CNN's Jake Tapper: Trump's address was 'one of the most radical' inaugural speeches ever

Jan 21, 2017 7:33 am

And that is precisely what it's like to come home from a weekend getaway with a spouse and find out that the house is a mess and occupied by a bunch of puking idiots with wedge haircuts and Cheeto dust smeared across their faces.

Commentary: Obama leaving Trump with a massive debt crisis

Jan 22, 2017 6:33 am

Although we were aware that Obama was anti-American, it's really going to more obvious as time goes on that we were really under siege from the very top and how close we were to losing the country entirely. It's nice to see President Trump in that office!

President Trump has already reinstalled the bust of Winston Churchill in the Oval Office

Jan 22, 2017 6:40 am

I don't see any value in continuing to blast Hillary all the time...gone is gone.

Trump had some surprising words for Hillary Clinton during inaugural luncheon

Jan 22, 2017 6:45 am

That's odd since Hitler espoused the same political philosophy as Mathews and the entire Liberal media...that is really just how wicked

they are, wizzing on people's heads while telling them that it's
raining.

Chris Matthews called Trump's speech 'Hitlerian' over two words

For those who like to consider things from the psychological point, I
have always thought, going back to the eighties, that
communism/Liberalism is really the political form of a Godless
woman's way of thinking...and the Godless man follows it.

The #WomensMarch gets expertly trolled by a trending hashtag for the second time

I think that the very first priority considering the Department of
Education is going after all of this really evil propaganda in schools
because if we don't and these kids keep pouring out into the adult
world we will only just be repopulating this Nation with our own
worst enemy.

The more Governors that display the kind of courage that Greg Abbot
is displaying, the more Governors from other states will see that they
can indeed use their offices for more than just a comfy place to sit.

If we can make self-driving cars, virtual reality, heat-seeking missiles
and machines that make micro-chips (If you thought a tiny micro-
chip is amazing, just think of the precision of the machine making
it!) then we can make a simple machine that picks peaches...and
only the ripe one's as well.

We don't have to have a population of low-skilled workers in this day
and age.

Governor Greg Abbott hammers a Texas sheriff after she refuses to comply with
immigration laws

I think that the Trump administration is in full favor of positioning Drudge, Breitbart, TheBlaze etc... right alongside the traditional media! Who says that only the old networks are some kind of authority?

Having a large audience is press credential enough, I'd say.

In President Trump's first full day in office, mainstream media taking a back seat

The best remedy to combat PTSD begins in Basic Training.

When I was in boot camp, on the 5th day of the first week (1-5 day) we had a berthing inspection that all were likely to fail and were subject to "cycling" which amounted to a lot of mean yelling, exorcising and humiliation as punishment. The purpose of it resulted in a good handful of guys that couldn't take it and they were then were gone.

I have a notion that the military may have changed things to mimic a college campus instead of a bold fighting force of well-disciplined but rowdy, foul, cussing comrades.

How are these soldiers coming back feeling alone and weakened instead of empowered and having a band of brothers at their side?

Raising awareness of PTSD and suicide within the veteran community

Makes you wonder if the Democrats are just buying time for the Department to get a lot of things hidden.

Democrats working to delay vote for attorney general

On President Trumps first day he went about killing the Obamacare mandate that sought to punish millions of Americans by not having health insurance...that alone was a huge tax cut for many!

For those concerned about people without health insurance becoming a burden to society then shouldn't the government quit making low income people even poorer and unable to get a leg up?

Trump says he's about to cut taxes and regulations 'massively'

And for those who were perplexed as to how we are going to build the wall down the middle of the Rio Grande, again, who say's we have to?

All we do is set the wall back in from the river an 8th mile and use that as a patrol barrier.

BREAKING: Trump executive order will begin construction of border wall

Oh, that's got to be stopped even if we aren't going to do something with them.

We should be dead set against ANY path to citizenship for anyone entering the country illegally...if they are fully "Americanized" then give them permanent work visa's or something.

This is very, very serious because we really don't know how many there are and if we give these people the right to vote, Mr. Trumps accomplishments will be dismantled as quickly as Obama's after future elections...for a very long time!

Gov't still accepting applications for Obama 'DREAMer' amnesty under Trump

I think that we should put a hold on ALL immigration for a while...too many foreign minds flooding in!

BREAKING: Trump executive orders expected to restrict immigration from Muslim countries

We need to change laws that allow us to fire government workers, all up and down the pay scale.

The idiot who tweeted that should be fired and if he can't be fired right now then reassign him to some remote park in Alaska as a janitor.

National Park defies Trump social media ban, tweets climate warming facts

Now, doesn't that just beat all?! Here some guy goes to all that trouble to be a girl and just because he still has his equipment, he gets shunned!

And just to add to that, even if they do take a paper cutter and cut it off, the women will shun them for having whiskers.

And if they have their facial hair somehow permanently removed, they will be shunned yet again for not listening to them!

And if they start listening to them really good, they will ultimately discover that they just made one horrible, horrible mistake!

Trans community: Women's March protesters' focus on female genitalia was 'oppressive'

Come on, dude, you gotta know that if they were to set up merchandise tables the women would immediately stop marching and start shopping.

Haven't you ever seen the expression on a woman's face when they enter a store and grab a cart? They slow down and look around at paradise...it's like they are on the biggest high of their life! :)

Why was there no merchandise for sale at the Women's March?

That sinking feeling that we were turning into a 3rd World country over the past years...that was the lack of law and order in large part.

The importance of law and order in a society is that it creates an environment whereby people are much more likely to predict the outcomes in life...without it, why try?

Trump: 'We are going to restore the rule of law'

You know what, if passed a balanced budget amendment would do more to drain the swamp than anything else.

All that debt? That's all of the corruption.

GOP senators introduce balanced budget amendment

Anybody in America with their head screwed on tight would have to conclude that the fact that being a Democrat politician means being a law breaker...and that would also mean that the voting process in their strongholds is also just as corrupted.

Here is something very notable. My neighbor downstairs is from South Chicago, and I mean right in the middle of it. His slang and accent is so deep that I'm humorously always having to have him repeat himself...forget talking to him on a cell phone! Since we have become friends after he moved in here 9 years ago, he has always been a strictly Democrat supporter even though he has a very loose grasp of the issues. He was strongly in favor of Hillary.

I was totally taken back last night when he told me that black community is mad at one of the black people that visited Trump and then came out and something against him. Also, just by the way he talks, it's clear to me that President Trump is coming through to the black community in general.

Anyway, cleaning up corruption in the forgotten communities is going to be important for future elections because the Democrats are going to get wind of Trump support and they desperately don't want to lose that voting block…let alone, lose their chief weapon of the word "Racist".

Liberal media focused exclusively on illegal voter claim

Jan 26, 2017 5:37 am

I'm not putting women down by saying this, men and women think differently. I do not think that the female perspective with regard to problem-solving in the military has merit. The military is contrived exclusively of a male perspective and as such, the men should also be the custodians of it.
You want a remedy that would immediately end sexual whatever's in the military?… separate the men and women…period!

Senator suggests Air Force base implement 'buddy system' to curtail sex assault

Jan 26, 2017 5:55 am

Good! Until some sanity and order can be implemented, these agency's should not be afforded the opportunity to embarrass the President! He has no obligation whatsoever to be tainted by a remarkable lack of sensible thinking by a bunch of hammerheads.

Trump administration reportedly shutting down its own agencies' social media accounts

Jan 27, 2017 5:27 am

One of the most irritating things for me to have endured is being busy at work only to have a co-worker trying to gain my attention by talking about things going on in their life but that there might just be the reason that some people aren't good at what they do or don't care

266

about how well they do it.

It strikes me now with regard to Presidents going back awhile that most of them just simply didn't care about their job and therefore not good at it...how or why they got there is a different story.

Donald Trump is much different...he actually cares and is therefore good at what he does.

Trump declares victory as city revokes 'sanctuary city' policies

Jan 27, 2017 5:53 am

That really is the real reason that the Liberal media is poor at doing their job because listening would be the first part of understanding something whether or not you agree with it...the Press just simply skips that part and dives directly into propaganda, using this word or that spoken to bolster their argument.

Senior White House adviser Steve Bannon tells media to 'keep its mouth shut and just listen'

Jan 27, 2017 6:10 am

Just pick out one the chicks with a stump-shaped haircut out of the crowd at the women's march...that'll do.

MSNBC host wants to know if Democrats will 'get a leader some day'

Jan 27, 2017 6:35 am

The nomination and Senate approval of Betsy Devos will cause the greatest still among the Liberals because it's the public schools, and public schools alone, that serves to propagate their agenda...if they lose that, they lose all.

Online opposition to Betsy DeVos grows

President Trump isn't defending Obama, Obama and Manning are both idiots walking down the street unavoidingly knocking their heads together in an almost rhythmic and predictable tempo.

Trump defends Obama from Chelsea Manning's criticism

If Trump were to change who he is he would look and act as stupid as every other fake in politics…and that, my good fellow Americans, is exactly what the Establishment and the media desires most!

Officer: D/L and registration, insurance please.

Guy in drag: Here ya go..

Officer (now glaring at the driver): Say's here that you're a dude, whatcha got going on in there?

Driver: Nothing…but I'm a girl.

Officer: But your voice is deeper than mine!

Driver: Oh , well take it from me, I'm a chick, man.

Officer: Speaking of taking, we got a report of someone who grabbed a cage full of gerbils and bolted from a pet store…in a car that looks just like yours.

Driver: Isn't that awful? Seems like you just can't trust anyone anymore.

Officer: Um, hm…Say, that cage full of gerbils on the seat next to you, are they yours?

California Democrats seeking to add another gender to drivers licenses and birth certificates

Speaking of the ship named Harvey Milk, THEY GOTTA CHANGE THAT, PRONTO!

The Liberal media is now officially vexed by the two options that they face; Either they just start to honestly report like their job title describes or keep doing what they are doing and end up having as much validity and value as a comic book because Mr. Trump ain't gonna give up, I'll dang t ya that!

Trump vs. media: First week of new administration highlights bitter divide

This might be a good occasion to bring up the topic of Sublime Indoctrination. I don't believe in conspiracy's that are wholly organized by a small group of people to assert an agenda, as human beings are incapable of being that smart and disciplined, but here it goes:

It started in the 70's and it started, with all things, the irony of itself...Subliminalism. "Back-masking" in particular. The birth of broadly sweeping rumor, today we call a meme, back-masking was the notion that music artists would insert satanic messages into music backwards to subliminally insert thought into the minds of the listener without them knowing about it.

The second one was a candy called "Pop-Rocks" Little crispy chunks of hard sugar infused with carbon dioxide that would sizzle and pop as they dissolved on your tongue (early ones were so powerful that

they could actually inflict a sting to your tongue or a tooth) but out came the rumor that if you ate pop-rocks while drinking a coke that you could end up blowing yourself up...people took it seriously!

Well, now we had proof. The public were largely capable, and quite willing to some degree, to be fooled, and for others to be mildly entertained, by a new declaration of some out-of-the-blue fact that was just discovered…the sublime.

In the 80's my brother and I would catch what we humorously called "secret messages" in movies. A good example of that was in a movie called The Naked Gun. I love the movie for its humor but there is a scene that takes place in a meat packing plant that had a bunch of vats of poison used in processing. The movie makers didn't make a big point of the poison/meat thing it was meant to just go into the back door of your mind and change you thinking.

Then there was the egg. Really, one of God's great gifts to mankind…the incredible, edible and very versatile, fun, cheap egg was now bad for you. At this point it became common for people to be found opening a statement with "They say…" I.E. "They say riding a bicycle too much will make your nuts fall off" or "They say, pop-rocks make for a good birth control alternative if you ever get in a pinch…the girls seem to like it as well!" Stuff like that.

By now in 2017, these rumors, memes and full blown lies like health studies, bad foods, polls, government PSA's paid for by special interests, whole movie topics and designations by self-interested outfits like The Democracy index and much more, come at the public like a swarm of flies, often competing with each other, and all with one collective purpose and that is to assert that "You can't think for yourself, trust the most convincing of other people".

Well, I would be engaging in propaganda myself I were to expand on the idea but I am glad to say that "They say that the egg is now good for you to eat" as they have retired that old clunker of the Sublime.

U.S. downgraded from democracy to 'flawed democracy' due to a declining trust in the government

Jan 31, 2017 5:51 am

I was watching Fox News reruns from the night before when it was reported that Chuck Schumer proclaimed that the Democrats in the Senate will fight with "everything we have" if President Trump's Supreme Court nominee isn't "Mainstream".

That right there is when I was finally able to fold the edges of the tortilla over the big Burrito Supreme...that word "Mainstream".

That, and the partnering word which was uttered by a feller named David Harbour on Sunday night during some Hollywood award show, "Freaks" was uttered by one of the people on stage to describe themselves..."Mainstream Freaks"

We, and myself in particular, have been guilty of using that word "Mainstream" in describing the media...but that is incorrect. Many of the Republicans on the Hill are guilty of adopting as a reality the illusion, or better described as delusion, what exactly the Mainstream is and it isn't the major news outlets and, as David Harbour also added in describing themselves, the "Outcasts" in Hollywood.

Starting with the ragged and disenfranchised Hippies in the 60's and coming to full bloom in this last election, the Liberals have become successful in creating the public illusion that the Mainstream of America, regarding everything, is comprised of outcasts, freaks and undesirable immigrants...but that is not correct.

By its very definition, the "Mainstream" of America cannot possibly be identified by those who oppose America...the real America.

The fact is, what they really should be calling themselves by all accounts is the term "Pseudo Mainstream" because they are the opposite of what mainstream America is...kind of like what the character Bizzaro is to Superman.

Kind of funny isn't it, what was the Mainstream news media with the likes of Walter Cronkite and Peter Jennings has turned into an unwatched CNN and MSNBC and what was the Mainstream in film with the likes of "It's a Wonderful Life", "The Outlaw Josey Wales" and "Slingblade" has turned into a mish-mash of teenage level creativity, filled with unrecognizable

Soap Oprah actors and special effects.

But we ain't buying it. President Trump has been proven, against the utter onslaught of the "Pseudo Mainstream", just exactly who the real American mainstream are...and it ain't them.

They have been utterly rejected as the Standard Bearer of the mainstream and, my good Men and Women, they are going absolutely wild-eyed, ape feces throwing, screaming to the top of their lungs…nuts!

Those two words "Mainstream" and "Freaks" That describes them well.

Is Trump White House actually engineering a 'war on the media' — and is the press taking the bait?

Jan 31, 2017 6:17 am

That reminded me of the scene in "The Cowboys" when the character played by John Wayne rejected the character played by Bruce Dern as a hired hand.

Long Hair: "You're a hard man, Mr. Andersen!"

Mr. Andersen: "It's a hard life!"

BREAKING: Trump administration has dismissed and replaced acting Attorney General Sally Yates

Jan 31, 2017 6:31 am

Golly, Rubio and Scott…sitting in their tree house in nothing but shabby, loose fitting underwear hatching plans to be accepted by the popular people in school.

Senators Rubio, Scott issue joint statement on controversial Trump executive order

Jan 31, 2017 6:37 am

White folks routinely asked each other "What's your Nationality?" and white people always have an answer…either German, British, French etc…as well as the mixture of nationalities they might have.

But let me ask Peter Kim a question; are you able to tell what nationality all other Asians are when you see them?

Asian comedian: 'White supremacy' is when white people ask me, 'Where are you from?

Chapter 14

February 2017

Feb 1, 2017 5:51 am

I wonder how many people have thought long enough about just how significant the nomination of Neil Gorsuch is. For those on the Right it makes one want to behave well, for we are blessed. For those on the Left, they find themselves on a dirt road in the middle of the desert and their '62 Opel finally spilled spit out the last of the oil from the crankcase...the engine now seized.

And for those who never spend even one second pondering the ramifications in politics, you just happened to have strolled out of that brick building as it collapsed, the dust still on your heels, completely unbeknownst to you.
This really is the very best choice President Trump could have possibly made..not good, not will do, not a nerve-racker.....the best.

BREAKING: Trump announces his SCOTUS nominee pick, and Scalia would be proud

I predict that the Senate leadership will have to implement the Nuclear Option and they absolutely should if needed.

Remember this, Republicans in the Senate, the Democrats in the Senate wish you were dead.

'Democrats will not succeed in filibustering Judge Gorsuch' - Ted Cruz vows confirmation

Not even the glorious saint Obama could have made drive shaft out of a Slinky.

Report: Clinton mostly blames Obama for her loss

Aren't car wrecks also coincidence's?

"No officer, I was paying attention to my driving, it's just a coincidence that we were both heading for the exact same spot in the road at the same time!"

Budweiser ditches typical Super Bowl commercial in favor of expressing political views

The very best way to deal with these refugees in a humane way would be to take them back to a stable area in their original countries, give them a couple thousand dollars each and a nice sack lunch and the politely say "It's been good to meet ya, good luck"

Trump has a very good reason for not wanting to accept Australia's refugees

Someone needs to show these fellers a map of all the underground pipelines that traverse the country and ask them to identify the damage to nature (I don't call nature the "Environment" because that word defines a particular type of natural surrounding such as "Desert environment" vs a "Rain forest environment"...I learned that right thar in da school).

Over 70 protesters attempting to stop the Dakota Access Pipeline arrested at Standing Rock

Feb 3, 2017 5:05 am

I would have loved to see the looks on their faces after the police dug their way in. Here they thought they were totally barricaded in and then all of the sudden, Cops!

Prisoner: "How...how'd you get in here?!"

Police: "Tricky ain't we? And we brought some pretty assault rifles with us too!"

Delaware inmates take four prison guards hostage, blame the whole situation on Trump

Feb 3, 2017 5:43 am

President Trump will go down in history as the most profound President since Washington and Lincoln. It's just unreal all of these types of laws were ignored by so-called Conservatives in the past. Just what in the heck has been going on all these years? My guess is that you have to go all the way back to the Founding Fathers who didn't need the money or fame but did things for the good of the people and actually sacrificed themselves. All of our recent Presidents, except for Reagan, have become President for self-gain...and I mean dog-gone selfish reasons!

Ain't Trump one big ol' relief? Sometimes it's hard to believe that it's really happening...we have literally never seen it...well, people under 70 or so, anyway.

Report: White House drafts executive order to expand religious freedom protections

No matter what Mr. Trump, never, ever forget that we are still behind you and will always stand in support.

Remember, we still outnumber them by far.

Note to Republicans who are wanting to be a part of the Establishment Attack and creating unreasonable hurdles for Mr. Trump...we are keeping tabs!!! And we will not forget you come election time. You want to play hardball? You are playing against the will of millions...

WE WILL WIN!

Trump not backing down to 'outrageous' judge order to halt travel ban

I was having a discussion with a hippie friend of mine about the wall and the 7 country travel ban, he was bent against both strongly. I just wanted to ask a simple question and did "If the wall is built and illegal immigration from the southern border is greatly diminished to a crawl, what effect would that have on you that makes you take it so personally to a point of anger?" He couldn't answer for a while but then he just started to ramble off a bunch of unrelated reasons.

It would be interesting to ask these protesters that same question because the weirdest thing about these fake protests, and the organizers of them, is they are protesting fervently as though they are in danger of losing something personal, when in actuality they are looking to gain something. And the thing they are wanting to gain is more of themselves...weird!

CNN lists schedule of anti-Trump protests, brings journalistic integrity into question

I was talking to someone who called President Trump a "Narcissist" And so I said "That's impossible!" "Why?" he asked.

The answer is that narcissist's don't have any friends! Narcissism is the extreme view that the universe revolves around them and that everything somehow relates to them…as such, they are unable to establish a connection with people unless that person has something to offer the self-centered, they are worthless.

But Donald Trump has, as it seems, friends everywhere!….good friends! And now for the rest of the story…people who have many close friends from all walks of life are actually people that have the soundest of minds because they lack the flaws of self-centeredness and lack of self-reflection.

The Liberals are the ones who are insane!

Democratic congressman from California says Trump needs a 'mental health exam'

What's interesting to me is the startling fact that all of the platform concerns that the Democrats had only 20 years ago are……….gone!

Chuck Schumer gloats over judge's ruling on Trump's executive order: 'Trump should heed this ruling'

When you look at the efforts of these fake protests, guys like McCain's snotty saying that "Mexico isn't going to pay for that wall" others in congress now mysteriously wanting to escape the full overturning of Obamacare when only a week ago there was pretty much total consensus, judges overtly overstepping into legislative mode, is that it's like the quiet kid sitting at the corner of the classroom eating crayons and picking his nose just decided to, for no reasonable excuse, get up, start overturning desks and start shooting at everyone.

Iran defies Trump's new sanctions by holding military exercises

The Establishment isn't trying to escape "Dislike" by other countries, they are in full-blown and dedicated allegiance to the efforts of continuing to establish a New World Order at the expense of America and American's.

The Establishment stand's in deep regard and faces eastward with reverence, their backs to our nation, westward.

What do democrats and despots have in common?

It is a profound feat of trickery that today's liberals have somehow managed to convince a certain faction of the people that existing squarely in line with Lenin, 100 years ago, is somehow "progressive".

Bernie Sanders: Trump is a 'fraud'

And they don't realize that Global Warming and Climate Change are the same just as well.

Sometimes I wonder how it would be to be blissfully ignorant to things political...but then I always fear that everyone else might catch on and in three years, I would find myself standing in line during a snow storm with my bowl in hand, waiting for bark and leaves soup.

I'm pretty sure that Mr. Trump has better things to do than spend the day discussing the horny sex parts of different races and how we can all learn to break down in tears when they are prevented from getting it on in their cubicle's...on second thought, I'm most convincingly sure.

British House Speaker says he won't invite Trump to address Parliament over 'racism' and 'sexism'

The Republicans in Congress are still under the illusion that we are satisfied with being tossed a bone from time to time as the political marriage of both sides disappear through the tulips, in the garden of self-delight.

They should mind themselves and take seriously the people to whom they work for. Patience long gone and from our point of view, only President Trump demonstrates the only one there having an interest in our wellbeing.

We are taking names and making notes.

Clinton now dispatched with, along with Democrats nationwide, YOU Republicans unwilling to aggressively kill Obamacare, cut taxes and start planning an exodus from debt will become very visible and we don't have much for our political hands to do...

that is except, getting rid of those that are in the way.

And we aren't talking about the now fairly powerless Democrats.

That would be you Republican establishment types.

Trump supporter Matt Drudge now says Republicans 'should be sued for fraud'

This is important to note and that is that the argument here is whether or not this whole law is Constitutional.

It's so important that we are just going to have to be patient and wait for Gorsuch to be confirmed to want to argue this in the Supreme Court.

Here's why; The public has been nuanced into thinking that this is just about anti-Muslimism or some other quirky little thing but it is not, it's about our autonomy as a Country.

From the very beginning, our nation has always enjoyed our

280

autonomy from the world and have mercilessly and selfishly decided who comes into this country, and as it should be…we have absolutely no obligation to anyone else in the world to let anyone just waltz on in.

The George Soros' of the nirvana New World Order sect dream of border-less countries, because in that scenario, there is chaos and because of chaos, a heavy hand is indeed needed.

This law, that gives the President authority to disallow any individuals from entering our country based on whatever he deems necessary, if found to be unconstitutional will, by extension of a simple notion, would establish the premise that we are no longer able to crate or enforce any immigration law based on whatever we as a nation want…a bizarre contradiction that is self-imposed (?)

In short, if the law that is backing President Trump's immigration ban is found to be unconstitutional, it would be as if the United States itself, volunteered to have a third of its brain removed.

Ninth Circuit Court rules against Trump's travel ban

Feb 11, 2017 5:39 am

All of these gaily organized protests have long gone past being obvious and have moved into shear embarrassment. It's like "Dude, save at least some of your dignity!"

I suppose we shall soon witness an all-out crying and begging festival sometime around the corner.

A mob has gathered outside of Mitch McConnell's Kentucky home

Feb 11, 2017 6:40 am

And the congressmen said "What are these…strange things… that the working man say's about getting ass in gear, can you get dirty doing that?"

Sean Hannity puts 'spineless, gutless, timid' congressional Republicans on notice

My dear old Bronco II…he was one tough son-of-a-buck. It was only recently that he had to go to the rest home…still ran!

There was a period of time that he developed a ticking sound about the engine. I couldn't figure out what it was, maybe lifters or a gap in the exhaust manifold but he was old and I just learned to ignore it…that constant noise.

One day, about a year and a half later I discovered the culprit to all the noise and it turned out to be the most innocuous thing of all…a label that was wrapped around a piece of radiator hose that I replaced had partially come lose and was ticking and flapping against the radiator fan.

Sometimes a lot of racket, as it often turns out, is just that….a lot of racket.

'The Moral March on Raleigh' latest rally in support of left-leaning policy

I guess instead of draining the swamp in Sacramento they are getting ready for the entire thing to just simply get swept away.

When it's all over with I wonder if they will have the brains to re-think for even a minute how important those beetles were that held up so many dam proposals…meanwhile all that water so badly needed, slips into the sea.

Officials in central California order emergency evacuations amid imminent collapse of large dam

You got to wonder just how little someone has going on in their life…first be interested in going over one of the most brain bending things as a tax return as a form of entertainment but then also mooning a building because you can't get a hold of one.

I'm sure if they want, they could go on the internet and find a copy of an outdated corporate tax return...and they could even moon their computer while it's downloading!

Some people might not perceive well what I'm trying to say when I make comments regarding the distinct roles that women and men have...as well as the things that rightly belong in the male or female category of appropriateness.

The reason that there is this ongoing effort to mix women into everything male is the same evil at the roots of Climate Change.

And that is, if you can turn on its head even the most simple and basic understandings in life then you are able to go forward and freely distribute any and all complex lies from that point on due to a lack of mental structure in the people.

And you may have thought it was all about "Fairness"

As planned, it works out well...as the kitten is playing with the fuzzy little ball hanging from a string, he didn't even notice the approaching shadow of the hawk.

Good...it is well that government not get into discussions about Borats' sexy parts or anyone else's.

I mean…laws about the horny of humans? There just has to be many, many, many more priorities than that.

Trump administration takes big step back from Obama's transgender bathroom rules

Feb 16, 2017 6:22 am

Now, why on earth are Intel agencies that serve directly to the President acting autonomously?

The answer is that there are some individuals that are still serving a different President.

When there are efforts to determine the authenticity of unsigned art of old, aside from forensic and scientific analysis, one of the chief considerations always starts with subject matter. That is to say for instance, a question might be asked regarding a painting of a mouse in the style of Monet "Did Monet ever produce paintings of animals?" This initial process quickly edits out many would be and could be potential artists.

The hallmark subject matter related to the leaking of Flynn's conversation tells us much…it's the same subject matter that really began back last summer, Russia and Trump.

Those creating this meme blatantly show their brushstrokes obviously and it is as old as any Van Gogh. Trying to separate Trump from his supporters by trying to associate Trump with Russia.

The liberal Collective now tired and bereft of idea's, missing an ear, might just as well consider a life of leisure beyond the horizon of the path in the Wheatfield with Crows…it's getting old and we ain't falling for it.

Spies are withholding intelligence from Trump, says WSJ

Hillary's wretched, straw broom wielding chambermaid, sweeping the campaign stages with the frail and tattered hem of her dress, would be an absolute delight as she proudly proclaims with convincing vocal overtones that belong only to the despised, "Iiii…..am a naaaaaasty woman!"

Poll: If an election between Trump and Warren happened now, Trump would win

And millions of people across the country stood up and cheered or will be cheering when they file their taxes.

From this point going forward, the beautiful symbiosis of hundreds of millions of dollars going back into the economy as the illegitimate benefactors of those funds are being ushered to the border…it's music to my common sense.

Obamacare in trouble as IRS will no longer reject tax returns not answering healthcare questions

There comes a point when the little snot nosed kid (The media) that is screaming and begging for a nickel to put in the gumball machine, and is knocking down displays in the hardware store, to just put him in the back of the pickup and let the June bugs bounce off the back of his head all the way home.

Steve Bannon 'could care less' about repairing White House's relationship with media

Hmmm…Indian brave try hard but not consider veracity of "Reports"

Indian brave not going on buffalo hunt until moon get bright in head.

Spies are withholding intelligence from Trump, says WSJ

OH boy! Gonna freeze the arctic now…must be big boys now..gonna make you transformer (Which is more than meets the eye!) walk all the way across your bowl of Captain Crunch and pretend he swam the ocean!

Climate scientists propose refreezing the Arctic to combat global warming

I just back from running my friend around to the parts store in town looking for a connecting hose to an idler pulley on his car (I had no idea that some are water cooled) Something came up on the radio and he made a snappy comment about Trump and I said something that just came to my mind right away.

Of all the journalists, the pontificates, the politicians that analyze President Trump day and night trying to figure him out, the single most misunderstood and the single biggest motivation is wrapped up in this that I said to Larry…

"You may not like Trump, but he does like you"

Trump already gunning for 2020 with campaign rally in Florida

I think the thing Trump detractors hate the most is thousands in crowds, millions in support, of good ol' red-blooded Americans having a ball!

What we are seeing and perceiving well on the left are the self-focused, depressed and drab, gray hearted as a Soviet winter day people…just mad.

It's not even policy that's causing the chasm…have you noticed that? Nobody is arguing the merits of this or that, really, just fun happy people on one side…dreary on the other.

Trump brings supporter onstage during 'campaign rally' in Florida: 'A star is born'

Feb 19, 2017 6:17 am

Brought in on a pallet with a pallet jack, shrink wrapped, they cut off the cellophane and sat her in a chair. Over the years, Patricia McGuire sat on that chair as her ass cheeks expanded and enveloped the edges of it. Jabba McGuire, as she has become known, snorted in disapproval anything good...except food...if it moved even a little, she would eat it.

Unhappy still by being irrelevant, sees that a one time student had ascended the heights of success while all this time...she has only been lucky enough to achieve the height necessary to get out of that chair in order to grab another handful of lard from the 5 gallon bucket at the end of her desk.

Kellyanne Conway viciously attacked by the president of her alma mater in scathing letter

Feb 19, 2017 7:00 am

Only because Donald Trump was being a good guy and endorsed him, John McCain won his election. So, what does a good, loyal, military "hero" do to the one that saved his political life?

In John McCain's world, you wiz on his boots.

Arrogant...

'That's how dictators get started': John McCain rebukes Trump tweet

Feb 21, 2017 6:36 am

This is the very exact same battle that Chiropractors first ran into. I think that the horse massager's will eventually get their own designation.
I grew up in my junior and high school years on cutting horses, cutting cattle. I've never felt like massaging any of them but there were a few times with regard to younger ones that I felt like punching them in the nose.

Regulation madness: State agency threatens to jail and fine Tennessee woman if she touches a horse

This probably inadvertently swerves into the heart of the matter.

There is a very, very good reason why "Thou shalt not bear false witness against your neighbor" and "Thou shalt not kill" appear together in a very small list called the Ten Commandments.

When you lie to someone, you are doing the exact opposite of loving them or caring about their well-being…just like murder. It's not a stretch at all to say that by lying to people, you are at enmity with them.

You see, Chris Wallace and others, your position isn't to stand in correction and guidance to elected officials as is the common mindset and approach. Rather, the position of the news press is either give opinion or facts.

If you are deceptive to the people (I'm assuming that since they are looking at the people through a lens and telling them stuff) you are not caring about them and certainly not loving them because it's like someone who gives driving instructions that leads to the family station wagon roaring off a cliff instead of getting to McDonalds…see the difference?

Now, shall we asked the question "Who is it that has, and continues to, cross the line?"

Chris Wallace slams Trump for attacking media: He 'crossed an important line'

Not only does Maxine Waters have an acute understanding of morals, she is also a very respected prognosticator.

With an angry, shaky and bony finger of indignation, she stood at the podium and scorned Trump's voters by issuing a stern warning that Russia is going to invade a unified Korea.

While the rest of the world was stumped by such foresight, from that point on, every comment and observation that she issued was hailed by the Left as being the most exemplary display of the virtue of

discontented rebellion of reality and therefor crowned as their official standard bearer.

Maxine Waters says Trump's cabinet is full of 'scumbags'

Although having the death penalty is better than not, I have a particular problem with the way we go about it these days. One of the chief questions we find when discussing it is always "Does it deter crime?" As it is, not much...which I believe is its most useful purpose. If it is simply only considered punishment, I would say that it's worthless...you killed the guy, how can he experience the punishment inflicted by society's laws.

So, what happened? How did it go from being a deterrent (being less murder which is what we want) to simple euthanasia such as what occurs in the vet's offices?

The simple answer is that those who love evil things sought to protect themselves by being able to label hanging and the electric chair as "Cruel & unusual"...because hanging and being electrocuted to death publicly WERE effective deterrents.

But isn't it insidious that the death penalty is now implemented by some futuristic science fiction style of elimination, the likes that are reminiscent of "Soylent Green", by the quiet slipping of the needle in a quiet corner room by quiet people in lab coats?

To properly and effectively implement the death penalty, hanging by a rope in public is most effective. Outdoors, everyone invited. let the children out of school so that diligent and thoughtful parents can bring them along...a big lesson in life to be learned. Broadcast it on TV that those prone to violence and murder may SEE what's next by killing someone.

Outdoors, with a view of nature, before the hood is applied, the guilty given a chance to consider the Lord and ask for forgiveness and salvation.

If my suggestion makes one squeamish, then why doesn't the horrific

289

murders and slaughters that occur all the time make one squeamish? Because you don't see them, therefor it's not all that real and easy to ignore...which brings us right back to the effectiveness of public hanging as being the most efficient and purposeful form of Capital Punishment because all can SEE what happens next after murder.

Why these conservatives are making the case against the death penalty

Feb 24, 2017 7:25 am

Maybe the dolls will also come with a book: "My life as a transgender, the day I lost my 1 wood and the exhausting extremes it takes to look like a girl"

Even dolls are choosing to be transgender now

Feb 24, 2017 8:16 am

He's gonna sue because of what, medical malpractice? Just because they added another hole in his butt?

NYPD cops shot a burglar in the butt. Here's how he responded

Feb 24, 2017 9:19 am

I have been pointing this very real and hideous undercurrent for almost 20 years. It started to occur to me when I pondered why there was this "hidden rift" that I had with friends of mine that you would say are Liberal.

Politics used to be the act of debating how best to utilize public funds for the general welfare (That which benefits all equally and at the same time) of the people.

Now, it's become an act of creating division between people and creating acrimony between us...what else does this on whole?

Have you ever noticed what happens when the doors are opened to stores on the morning of Black Friday?

It's chaos and fighting between the people who only minutes earlier were just peacefully visiting with each other.

It should make one wonder why it is that Liberals want more and more of this division and hatred between Americans. You may want to conclude that it's either on purpose or just plain selfish stupidity but one thing is for sure, it perfectly serves as a strategy that a hostile nation would use as a tool of war against us.

How the government has changed the way we value our neighbors

I find something within Dan Rathers' comments very interesting and noteworthy, it's this " Mr. Trump is nearing or perhaps already beyond any hope of redemption."

When I read Rathers' expressed admonition and set it next to Hillary's admonition calling Trump supporters "irredeemable" a red flag in me goes up and I have to ask 'redeemed from what?'

That right there, the answer to that question, is very close to, if not THE root to, understanding where these Liberals are coming from.

The Merriam-Webster dictionary defines "redeem" as:

1 : to buy back : repurchase
a : to get or win back

2: to free from what distresses or harms: such as
a : to free from captivity by payment of ransom
b : to extricate from or help to overcome something detrimental
c : to release from blame or debt : clear
d : to free from the consequences of sin

Nowhere else in all of the religions of the world is this word "Redeem" used but in Christianity.
In fact, the word "Redeem" is barely used in common communication among people outside of talking about things like coupons and rebates.

God, the one that we would know by reading the Bible, invented that

291

word "Redeem". It is very, very specific to only one thing, and that is "Salvation" And that salvation is through Jesus who is God in the flesh.

Don't worry, I'm not going to dive into trying to convert anyone here with evangelizing and preaching.

I think that any reasonable people can agree that the premise of God saving, buying back or redeeming is exclusive to the God of the Bible, but then we must also conclude that there is an implied authority of "this God" to do so...He says this of himself in the Bible, just taking the Bible at face value.

Quite a thing to assert, isn't it?...having the power and authority to redeem people. Believe what the Bible says or not, the premise of having that kind of power would be so immense that you would also have to say that this God created everything (That we know).

Before I get too complicated, Dan Rather and Hillary Clinton have both asserted that they have that power or that they are, at least, a part of that power. To have that power and to speak of an ability to "redeem" you then have to have the authority to describe what people are redeemed from.

That to me is very, very insightful information when trying to see exactly where these folks are coming from. I didn't make the accusation, they themselves said it...just out of the blue.

What they are saying is "I have the power to describe and therefor judge, right and wrong" And then "I also have the power to save you, or redeem you from wrongdoing"...like a judge in a courtroom, he has the power to either put you in jail or set you free.

OK then, since they are asserting this ability, it would be reasonable to ask "What are the charges...sins that I have committed?"

Thus, THE world war.

A clash between a God as written in the Bible, asserting almighty power, and some people on earth who are simultaneously asserting that they somehow have the same power or at least are on the side of the one who has it.

If you are a sports fan and we would be sitting around analyzing teams that are going to play or are playing, we can have some fun looking at the differences in the two sides...God of the Bible VS Some People on Earth...the greatest showdown ever.

That right there, that's what all the fighting in America is all about right now.

Dan Rather calls Trump a 'threat to our democracy' after media ban

Feb 26, 2017 8:29 am

It is not only arrogant or naive, or just plain stupid, for people in the news business to think that "Freedom of the press" in the Constitution only refers to them. The Constitution is only making it clear that people can speak and print freely...not everything in life that could be printed by the people is the freak'n news. Maps, books, fliers, whatever...the Founders made sure that an individual can print anything they want!

Creepy arrogance!

What's freak'n next, freedom of speech only refers to the news?

Ari Fleischer criticizes 'hyperventilating' press after mainstream media outlets excluded from gaggle

Feb 27, 2017 5:59 am

Although we Trump supporters appreciate well his heart, ability, tenacity and courage, we are not just "Fan's" of a notable person being President Trump...it's because we have an ardent Fan of America and the American people as President.

Now to address borders. The borders of every country on earth has been established by acts

of war, going back to the earliest civilizations.

You have to be one droopy armed, bent legged, lobotomized with a drooling saggy lip moron to think and believe that it's possible to have a borderless world!

The reason we have borders everywhere is because it is a natural instinct for humans to breach them...even before they are drawn. Just try to sneak your hand past the hem of a newly acquainted girls' dress and up her thigh...you'll get the point when you see the stars.

Oscar nominated directors release statement condemning U.S. 'fanaticism' before the show

And the thing also wrote a book: "From girl to ape in 4 simple steps" Subtitled "I still can't pee very far away from me in a nice narrow stream, though"

Transgender teenager taking testosterone wins Texas state girls' wrestling tournament

Little bit late on that epiphany...just a few decades late. The only difference is that now-a-days, the President and a couple of other Republicans are actually fighting back.

There is something important to keep in mind when it comes to elections; The fact is, normal everyday red-blooded Americans are naturally nice people. Our Godly heritage compels us to love our neighbors. Many times, Conservatives that end up going into office simply don't understand that it's a brutal fight that they are walking into. The other side is a pack of ravenous wolves and the Republican just sits there going "Oh, my!" without fighting back.

At election time, vote for people who demonstrate the crude characteristic to fight back. Think of it like this, is it un-Christian to go into boxing? It's just a competition...and so is politics.

Politics should not be a discussion or an act of legislating issues regarding the heart...that's God's prerogative. Bill O'Reilly says acrimony between Trump and the media has escalated into 'war'

The very best way to approach a complicated problem is to simplify it. In the case of Obama care, when you have something so complex, confusing and containing multiple tentacles attached to so many other things, one could find themselves wasting time grooming and pruning climbing ivy instead of just pulling it out by the roots and aggressively pulling it off the building…keeping in mind that there will be some cleanup work to be done afterword's.

The complexity arises from the multiple crying mouths to be fed, mostly by politicians.

The full weight and burden of doing what's right is light and easy, but planning a bank robbery by tunneling through the basement walls and blowing through a safe is much, much more complicated…especially the part about having to get away with it.

This burden is specifically on the Republicans in Congress.

Trump says 'nobody knew health care could be so complicated'

Chapter 15

March 2017

Mar 1, 2017 6:08 am

A very, very well done speech! For all of those who were waiting for Trump to be Presidential, you just got what you were waiting for...and just might regret it!

He, and a bunch of others like me have always known that he could give a speech like this but Mr. Trump preferred not, rather to speak plainly instead. The well-dressed evening deserves the noble speak, the work day speak, deserving of Sailors.

I have to be honest, I think Clinton gave a speech like this as I remember thinking "Crap, that was effective" but it really hasn't been since Reagan that we were treated to the type of speech that was both noble and connected well with the people at the same time.

I did notice that the KKK caucus of the Democrat party sitting there either forgot their hoods or weren't allowed to wear them so that others in the back could see...probably the latter.

In his first address to Congress, Trump lays out his plan to 'make America great again'

Wow! a very memorable moment that will go down in history! And really, the country had a chance to render our respects to all of our servicemen and their families who lost their lives.

The whole evening absolutely shamed the Democrats and going forward, Americans now have a dramatic reference as to the contrast between President Trump and the Democrats stupid, immature and way out of touch words and actions...it was as if America was having a party and all they could do was peak through the windows while standing in the rain outside.

I was so happy to hear President Trump reference the Bible...it really is the very heart of our nation.

Here's the powerful moment from Trump's speech that left even Democrats stunned

I'm not going to say that manual work makes one smarter, but for many young men that don't grow up with a Father dedicated to the instruction and the development of sensibility of their boys, manual labor and having something to show for their work will help them leap forward in thinking.

There is just something special about moving and changing the molecules of things real that put's one's feet firmly on the ground and gives indifference to things silly and dreamy.

Watch: Mike Rowe has a plan for congress about how to fill 5.6 million jobs

I hate to be repetitive, but it really bugs me that these morons keep saying that Nazi's were Fascists...but if only they were to know that the Nazi's were officially named National Socialists and that Hitler and Mussolini, although allies and shared some common philosophy's, disagreed much on how to inflict tyranny.

For the dizzy young folks who throw Nazi and Fascist around loosely, they might consider well that any presence of fascism in the United States is evidenced by all of the regulations and mandates foisted upon the employers of their brand new shiny jobs...their health care, hours of work, "fair pay", behavior training etc... that there is your Fascism.

And that all of the presence of Socialism in the United States resides right smack dab in their vaunted and holy Democrat party.

An astonishing feat, whereas the people of Germany and Italy understood and followed the philosophy's of their leaders, the education system has managed to warp these protesters' minds so much that even while in midst of whole-hearted agreement and compliance to oppression, they go out and condemn their own thinking...odd.

University 'anti-fascist' group justifies violence and vandalism against peers

Mar 1, 2017 8:02 am

The one thing that has been scary to see over the years is that people were lacking the bravery to be honest, especially publicly...seems President Trump might be providing some much needed encouragement in this area!

Most Americans believe bathrooms should be linked to biological sex, new poll finds

Mar 1, 2017 8:09 am

And all the horns went WHA, Wha, wha...as they were all quietly lowered and placed to the side...O'Malley, red faced and looking down, toes of his shoes fidgeting, politely said "Well, it was just an idea...you can go now if you want."

Former Democratic presidential hopeful promotes festive Trump boycott

Fence sitting takes practice, balancing on the narrow boards between your butt cheeks, but when you become really good at it, people on both sides will clearly see you as being as half-assed as you don't think.

George W. Bush: I don't like the racism, name-calling in Trump era

And the orchestration of the colorful calliope of the Democrat party became erratic as a wooden wheel broke apart and fell off causing the buggy to veer sharply left and down the rocky hillside…hardly any discernible song could be recognized due to the calamitous racket, specked with toots of the whistles here and there, as it descended to the bottom and came to rest.

The horse that had broken free and was now discharged from his duties was taking advantage of some uncared for grass in the alley of two nearby buildings.

After a few moments of calm, the crowd could hear one last toot and then it faded indicating that it had resigned to its fate in life, and was now……kaput.

Liberal pundit Van Jones says Trump 'became the president' in his speech to Congress

Observing Pelosi's body language during the speech, she must be concluding that if you look like you are trying to choke down a piece of barbed wire and are trying to save face as she did, that must be the look of dignity.

Pelosi: 'I was very proud of the dignity' Democrats showed during Trump's address to Congress

Here's another question I have. let's suppose that we take the fantasy scenario that the Democrats are offering with regard to Sessions, or anybody else in the Trump Administration, that they were talking with Russians during the election.

If that is so, just what in the freak'n world would that conversation be about exactly?

The supposition here is that the Trump campaign was seeking help from Russia...help doing WHAT exactly? Voodoo the minds of the American people somehow? Hack into voting machines that aren't connected to the internet?

And since when would anyone in the US running for office solicit the advice or skills from a country or government that only has a scarce notion of what free elections are about...they even despise our system, and they have something special to offer?

What in the Dickens kind of help could the Russians possibly offer?

Democrats demand Sessions' resignation after Russian communications surface

Mar 5, 2017 8:02 am

Obama saying that his White House never "ordered" a wiretap and that they are "unable to issue a wiretap order" is a vacuous statement and childish in its oblivious recognition of the intelligence of the American people. Do they really think that we are ignorant enough not to know that a "Wink & Nod" to underlings is not just as effective as a direct order and is done to absolve them from guilt?

Obama spox says Obama never wiretapped a US citizen — immediately receives harsh history lesson

Mar 5, 2017 8:26 am

BIG GRIN! Now folks, remember that we have 4, and probably 8 more years of Governmental Pruning to be done...and pruning always makes the plants look so much more neat and pretty.

Report: Trump administration seeks to slash large chunks from climate agencies' budgets

For fear of being set up like a whiffle ball on that plastic yellow stand waiting to be whacked, I shall only make notations of facts with regard to all of the ambiguous circumstances going on right now.

Fact one, we now know exactly what it's like to be living in a Third World country and that fact is brought to us courtesy of one Barrack Hussein Obama. And, since Obama nation protesters always reference Hitler because Trump is half German, I shall then bring up the ironic fact that this Third World experience is brought to us by a dude who is half Kenyan.

We are now dealing with a bonafide underground war against us by an entity having the characteristics of a foreign country. Another fact is that we are in the initial stages of trying to find out just who exactly all the players are.

Of the people who are in the public limelight, we can tell if a certain person is part of the Coup because they wear it on their sleeve by what they DO…that is to say, if you want to know the exact species of particular tree, look at the fruit.

We know something else for a fact. Obama's intelligence officials are still largely in place and we also know that those officials are not acting on Mr. Trumps best behalf.

Now for a question, why are they still there?

Yet another, how and why is it that the intelligence community seems to act in utter autonomy as if it is something outlined in the Constitution as a separate and equal 4th branch of the government?

You would think that since they ultimately fall under the authority of the President, that he should be able to go in there a whoop'n and a whomping and throwing tables over…maybe that is something yet to come, I don't know.

We also know that certain factions in congress don't seem to mind this coup attempt…some are part of it by some turning a blind eye, the others by personal involvement.

Now for the most important fact of all: The individuals that are part of this attempt at a Third World like coup against the United States have a devastating lack of intelligence regarding the secret weapon, unbeknownst to them, that they are going to have to face if they persist...
The People of the United States of America.

James Clapper denies any wiretapping activity — instantly receives brutal fact check from conservatives

Mar 6, 2017 8:36 am

You mean to tell me that a prominent entity has created a major uproar by proffering a major story of great importance without sharing the details or presenting any evidence?

Byyyyy... gum, you don't say!

Watch: Trump spox schools Martha Raddatz over mainstream media's double standard on anonymous sources

Mar 6, 2017 8:50 am

Well by golly, the precious Liberals are so full of peace, love and understanding...let's all join hands across the sea and save the planet shall we?

Violent protesters beat pro-Trump demonstrators at Calif. rally, burn American flags & free speech signs

Mar 6, 2017 9:08 am

This headline coming from the very, very, least of ability to tell the truth in news.

I wonder what it would be like to be the dumbest kid in class...you would think embarrassed.

But then again, if you are indeed that dumb, you would of course be oblivious to everything...especially about oneself.

CNN quick to declare Obama innocent of wiretapping accusation — but Twitter says 'not so fast'

If I may, this may be a good time for me to see if I have anything to offer while we are in this current state of confusion and how to sort out what has become a clash between truth and falsehood. It's important because each side claims to have the truth and that the other side has falsehood.

What is it that makes a genius? And then likewise, why are there smart people and then not- smart people. It's relevant in this conversation because it would be reasonable to think that the smarter the person is, the more likely they are to lay claim to having the side with the truthful answers and the other side...not so much.

So, if we undertake the exorcise of discovering the differences between genius's and not, we would see that the most dramatic difference between them first, is the volume of questions that they ask throughout life. Because, to be simple about it, you can easily say that a genius has lots of facts, data and knowledge in their heads...the one who asks few questions would naturally have very little in the way of facts, data and knowledge.

But that's only half of it. The second and equal component is the answer that they accept to their questions. Because we are wondering who is smarter, it stands to reason that it's because when a genius accepts an answer to question, based on nothing but irrefutable, tangible fact, that he would be the smarter.

On the other hand, when the un-smart person want's answers, he jumps way ahead of the fact discovery process and replaces the answer with his wishes, dreams, preferences and other emotional things that makes him feel good. Thus, he's a nice guy, but dang, that boy's a moron.

"You mean to tell me that a genius is simply just a guy interested in the truth?"

Yep.

"You're stupid, you make me feel bad!"

"Why...thanks for volunteering to be today's audio/visual aid!"

303

If I remember right, it seems to me that every single so-called accomplishment that Obama had was done by unconventional means...even getting Obamacare passed with zero Republicans in favor of it.

If I'm right, one can easily conclude that Obama lives and works in the shadows that are outside of the conventional norms that we expect...as such, it stands to be easily concluded that wiretapping Trump is right down the middle of the alley of where Obama lives.

House Oversight chair: 'I have not seen anything directly' to support Trump's wiretapping claims

I am greatly encouraged that President Trump has indicated that the new Bill is out and available for negotiation. I have to admit, some things I have heard about the way it is now is very disturbing but for the sake of a gentleman's decorum during this negotiating period...let's think for a minute.

I sometimes wonder about the day I might be laying there on my deathbed and what my thoughts will be.

Coming from the side, if we were in some kind of starship a hundred million light years away and where warping through the universe, the skyscape seen would consist of nothing more than hot rocks, cold rocks, some bright one's too. There would be hot gasses, noxious one's. There would be black holes and asteroids, comets with moons...some without.

If we were headed in the direction of Earth, all of that vast sameness of nothingness would be astonishingly interrupted as this little blue marble approached. Getting closer, you start to see clouds and green. Landing there, a paradise...right smack dab in the middle of absolute NOWHERE.

Upon landing, a thoughtful man would have no other choice but to quickly conclude that this body in space has a purpose. And after seeing people, you would conclude that they too must also be a part of that purpose...in fact, a very special one.

If we were to approach that one laying on their deathbed here on this planet and see that soon he would be gone and ask him only one single question, how would he answer "Dude, you lucky feller, what did you do during your life here on this planet?"

Could he honestly answer that he was loving, noble and thoughtful of others and did well for good?

Or would squirm and have to admit, that upon having the chance of a lifetime to make a correction of long bad doing to people, he took the money and ran instead...and spent the rest of his life hiding in the shadows, the war drums constantly approaching.

If you are in politics, which way do you think you will be able to answer that question when that time comes?

Republicans release Obamacare replacement, the 'American Health Care Act'

Mar 8, 2017 7:43 am

I wonder if Chief Justice John Roberts now regrets his decision...all the absolute mess that has occurred, all the time wasted, all the money wasted with Obamacare.

Like something mounted a 1000 caliber machine gun in the sky above the middle of the country and it's just constantly fragging us...back and forth, up and down.

Mar 8, 2017 8:55 am

All I may be able to do is provide the big picture. Government hands in healthcare does something unique to us, but is very familiar to Communists and Socialists, and that is that through it, the government now becomes the owner of the people.

Let's see if I can make clear water as to how this works. When it comes to auto insurance, it's pretty easy to explain the reasons why everyone is made to have it...even citizens will agree because if they get run into by an idiot, he can get money for it whereas before he would have to go through a huge process to sue the offender. So, driving on the roads now becomes everyone's business.

That's okay, sounds reasonable. But do take note, the only reason it sounds reasonable is because the general public are all together on GOVERNMENT property…and as such, you're conduct is elemental to other peoples' lives.

By government being closely tied to healthcare, instead of letting the free market dictate its own interaction with its customers and pursuit of profit, the government would now have a vested interest in the customers and whatever profits.

Functionally, if you go to an investor for money to start a business, the investor now has a great deal of interest in your conduct. If you are a larger company with an operating line of credit, they OWN your ass until you balance out with them. Bigger companies aren't just audited by the IRS, they are also audited by banks in order to agree to keep that line of credit going. And when the banks audit, they go through EVERY single aspect of the company.

If you sell bedroom furniture, they might even check the drawers of the dressers on the shelves to see if there are any underwear in there to be counted…I'm exaggerating, but you get the point.

When government has a vested interest in healthcare, because people are so intimately involved, they now not only have an interest in the way the industry behaves but also, equally, how the people behave…because people are the second half of the two main elements that comprise the concept of something called health insurance.

With government having its hands in healthcare, the People now share an equal liability with the insurance companies as far as the government is concerned… they now have a vested interest IN YOU.

If you own a pit bull and it tears someone up, guess what? you go to jail right along with the dang dog.

The problem with the government now having a vested interest in you with regard to healthcare is this, your personal conduct, habits, lifestyles, what you eat etc… now becomes vitally important to an authority that can punish you.

And, like driving on the roads, your conduct assumes everyone else's business becomes yours.

Now, in that scenario…isn't it so, so, so much easier to make it seem reasonable that laws are created and agreed to that effect every single little thing about your life…even your underwear drawer?

Trump backs Obamacare replacement plan, says it follows his guidelines

Mar 8, 2017 12:57 pm

See, guys get stuff done right. Unlike "Revenge of the Nerd's", these clever cleavers don't even have to break in and mount secret camera's…they got themselves an inside dude with a body cam. Secretly mounted in those certain positions right in the middle of the fake boobs…camera on one side, microphone on the udder.

'A transgender woman is just as much of a woman as I am': Sorority to accept transgender students

Mar 9, 2017 6:42 am

And if you wanted to really slow down a plane, have everyone face backwards. The collective bodies looking forward at the past just seems to violate physics somehow.

Pat and Stu explain why jetliners haven't gotten any faster over the last 50 years

Mar 9, 2017 6:51 am

Am I the only one? Back when I was growing up, it would have been bizarre if older guys would have got in a fist-to-cuffs, but old ladies?

Great-grandmother repeatedly punched in face at Wal-Mart. You'll love how attacker gets identified.

307

The Lib's are like that one inept kid in the Cub Scouts that didn't take the time to glue the bottom fins on his rocket correctly.

At first it would take off well, but after a few yards in the air and the fins now fluttering back to earth, goes into a zany aeronautical stunt show that even flies wouldn't attempt.

It's a lesson for all, if you are in a tight situation or business relationship or anything similar and someone lies to you, even a made up story in the past, or if they are committing adultery…get them away from you.

There is just something about that characteristic that profoundly effects much of their thinking as they are always calculating how they can come out being the prime benefactor in the end and more importantly, it will tell you that this person is very selfish and will turn on you easily.

Mike Pence reacts to Mike Flynn filing as a 'foreign agent' advocating for Muslim country

I admit, I have been vacillating between the two arguments concerning healthcare…being preoccupied by learning how all the belts, levers and gears work and giving every one due deference. In these types of situations I tend to, as more often than not, fall back on character and their actions and in particular, the obvious lack of answers to the mystery's that seem to always come back to haunt you.

If the past combined agreement that was put before Obama before was good enough, why not now?

Why should we be stuck going through this process being throttled by the Bird Rule and having to act by reconciliation when we could get rid of that rule by Mitch McConnell?

I'm smelling once again, the intrepid nuances and sweaty going's on of the Establishment...foremost being the fact that there is no regard in total for the people.

And, most importantly, that certain peculiar lack of concern that passing this Bill as is, would greatly affect President Trump's clout with his crowd...<that one right there...that's the very concerning one to me.

Rand Paul introduces alternative to 'Obamacare Lite' bill that focuses on repeal

Mar 13, 2017 5:22 am

If you really want to save nature, or what some call the "environment", why would you ruin the actual look of it. If you cover any specified area with solar panels or wind turbines, you have essentially rendered that land useful only to the alternative energy industry...otherwise it's just a blight.

Which is exactly what liberalism does...ruins the good and replaces it with the ugly and unworkable.

Mar 14, 2017 9:30 am

Between schooling that spoils kids with false praise and parents who lack care for the development of character in their kids by rejecting the Word of God and therefore not raising them up with sound hearts, youngsters' souls are but a blank sheet of paper...waiting for the Devil to write.

'Scales are very triggering': Students weigh in on decision to remove scale from college's gym

Mar 15, 2017 8:33 am

This little incident was a bit of notable history in the news media world. Since Mr. Trump began his campaign it was the very first time that they had a chance to see themselves in the same way that audiences have been seeing them.

They may even now know what we have been laughing about............all of this time. Trump pulled the rug from underneath Rachel Maddow's great big tax scoop

I want a sanity break! For the last few months the Liberals have been touting a Trump/Russia "thing". The "thing" has also been called "ties", "collusion" and "meeting(s)" and paralleling that has been "what is the proof that the "thing" happened?"

But missing from it all is "Just what in the dickens IS the dang "thing" supposed to be?"

Furthermore, if the "thing" happened, what did it do?

Yeah, yeah…I've heard "something" about hacking the election but absent are the specifics.
Which leads me to my question, just what in the world, of all things, could a beleaguered clunker of a country possibly have to offer in the way of assistance to the Trump campaign?

No answer to that leaves me with an observation, it is absolutely possible for a human being to embark on a 6 month endeavor, work overtime to achieve it, exhaust oneself to tears and in the end, have nothing at all to show for their efforts.

Had they hedged their bet by planting even one little flower a day, they would have had at least SOMETHING to show…after all this time.

CNN: FBI Director Comey may go public on Trump-Russia probe…

And the husband, after all of this, transformed into a raving lunatic and dancing around the house wearing nothing but a sheet singing "Skip, skip, skip to my lou…".

Teen boy has been transitioning to a girl. Now Mom is becoming a man.

I saw this a good year ago, I never doubted that Mr. Trump's ACTIONS would look exactly like this.

That's what really sums up the Trump emergence altogether, we got freak'n sick and tired of being fed what Republicans wanted us to hear, only to have them get in office and completely ignore us.

For several reasons we love Trump, the biggest one is DOING...how did we know? Because we knew that he wouldn't embarrass himself by not doing.

Let this be the foregoing standard when voting for politicians!

Trump budget cut proposal has Glenn Beck declaring, 'I am so pro-Trump right now'

For decades, the Liberals have used this tactic. It's so easy for Sanders to say "thousands will die" if Obamacare is overturned because people are passing away all the time and because you can pick out several accusations of cause of death attributed to the death, legitimate or not.

Watch this, today, millions will die on earth if Sen. Sanders does not resign by 10:00 this morning.

By this time tomorrow, I will be able to pronounce that I was right and have a handful of confusing statistics as to why it was caused by Sanders not resigning.

Sanders asserts 'thousands' will die from Obamacare repeal, but refuses to offer evidence

Isn't it incredible, since the riots are all over with...the issue of races not liking each other goes away. Hm...everyone is getting along just fine...just like before they rioted.

Poll: Number of Americans worried about race relations reaches record high

We need a Secret Service director who can clean up that entire organization, top to bottom. It looks to be as ugly as the VA...especially in light of White House lawn breeches.

They can't even place relatively cheap ground sensors?

Old men with machetes can keep people off their lawns much better than we are getting!

Secret Service agent who said she wouldn't 'take a bullet' for Trump has finally learned her fate

With regard to Dr. Ezekial Emanuel, he's like an Agricultural Educator giving a lecture while proudly standing in his field that is completely over-run with weeds.

Fox News health care debate explodes when Karl Rove confronts Obamacare architect, Clinton ally

I was talking to a friend this weekend and he pointed to corporate corruption as a big problem. I responded by pointing out that outside of political lobbying, corporations can't afford efforts at corruption...it doesn't fit into their internal business model and it would be like throwing an entire tool box into the gears.

It's enough of an effort to run legitimately than to also operate a simultaneous and juxtaposing model.

And when they do try to integrate corruption...well, ask Enron how long you can pull that off.

Donald Trump would be nowhere if he had tried to embrace corruption in his organization, especially being privately owned.

CNN host bashes Trump: He got to the White House by 'bulls****ing' his way through life

All the resist stuff is nothing more than people with empty souls, while looking for a purpose, found the most emotional and plentiful one's offered by Liberals and embrace them as a way of having a meaning in life...

productivity wrought by effort being the foreign enemy and the evil rebel to their newly found self-righteous moral authority.

Watch: Liberal activists try to explain why they dislike Trump, hilarity ensues

Every time I see a picture of Sanders gripping about something with his mouth open makes me want to create a game whereby contestants try to toss eggs into his mouth without being cracked by hitting his bottom teeth.

Curious: Trump say wiretap 1 moon ago, trickling evidence true, Hume get embarrassed.

Establishment say Trump/Putin collude 8 moons ago, not even turd from ghost buffalo on ground, Hume not embarrassed.

Brave not think right...not go on buffalo hunt 8 times... 'till he get own ghost turds together.

Brit Hume says wiretap claims are a 'continuing embarrassment' to Trump

For those looking for "proof" in the Trump/Putin collusion claim, we have now found it.

Ironically it turns out, with regard to the investigators, we now have proof of THEIR collusion with the DC Establishment.

Wait a minute...that's like the same that the adults taught us as little kids, while you point one finger at someone else, there's three pointing right back at you...cool!

Mar 21, 2017 9:12 am

Regarding that poll, ain't nothing like watching someone trying to push a wet rope up a hill...just to make you laugh!

Mar 23, 2017 6:10 am

I'm always amazed at companies that were once positioned to crush any creeping competition and yet, they were instead, overwhelmed. They had so many options because they owned the brick & mortar properties and had exclusive brands but all they did was downsize and double wax the floors.

They failed because they lost their "fight".

Do we see any difference in Republican politics these days? Trump and a few others exist, but it looks to me like there are many who are still content with the mop & bucket approach.

Mar 25, 2017 8:46 am

I suspect that this guy got into a terrible bike accident as a kid and somehow got his sack yanked off in the spokes.

Mar 26, 2017 6:59 am

Boy, dem clamit chanje peipl is a smawrt bunctch!

So, what does a woman do when she looks like some kind of bad hybrid of Marty Feldman and Ruth Buzzi when she goes to the hairstylist?

She say's "Yeah, I know I look like thunder...now make me look scary!"

Dem congresswoman says GOP stands for 'Get Old People' — then promptly gets destroyed

I've been thinking about this for a while, I'd be in favor of offering financial rewards to whistle blowers in the government agencies...the people closest know the most.

Shocking: NSA whistleblower tells Tucker Carlson Trump, Supreme Court, Congress likely spied on

I was hoping that there would be a much greater resistance to bow down to political correctness due to Trump's influence by now...it's early yet.

People, it's very important not to bow down to the weaker elements of our society, even if you lose a couple of customers.

"Resist the Devil and he will flee" –The Holy Bible

Chelsea Clinton angry over billboard saying 'it's OK to throw rocks at girls.' But there's one problem.

I wonder if Schniff has considered the possibility that Hillary didn't need an ounce of help getting beat...she ought to be 50 points ahead by now, notwithstanding...cough, cough, cough, uuuhhhggg...

Schiff says intel committee is investigating Russian trolls and bots spreading 'fake news'

That is pure child abuse. Observe what the attempt here is, Satan hates God's Righteousness and has made a list of his own commandments for the purpose of dissuading people from recognizing the Lord.

The willing participants of Satan's effort dispense the teachings with a new set of castigation's.

They teach a new faith...no longer Love thy neighbor, Thou shalt not steal etc... they teach "Save the planet" (which is accursed of God), Kill the potential babies that might find the Lord, Holiness is evil, You are guilty and will never be saved, Seek your own, forget other people, Learn to fool yourself etc...

5-year-old girl suspended for playing with gun-like stick

Python: "OH crap! I forgot to get rid of the dudes lighter before swallowing him...and I have a huge fart welling up.....oh, please don't light it dude, there's nothing to see in there....please!

Python swallows man whole; video shows body inside cut-open snake

The bulk of Trump Voters, along with the newly registered ones, are way more on the Freedom Caucus' side.

Interesting to ponder a clever coup attempt...Ryan gets his way on H/C Bill and gets Trumps voters to leave.

Trump calls out Freedom Caucus Republicans by name on Twitter

A political point of view is not derived by what a person thinks...

it is derived by what a person thinks about themselves.

Chapter 16

April 2017

We would be very, very lucky if the mean temperature of earth increased. About 10,000 years ago the entire planet was a tropical paradise (skeptics: refer to palm branch fossils in arctic)

Question: Does a consistent warm region in nature abound in animal life?...see the Amazon.

Question: If the earth warmed and ALL of the ice melted, would the H2O remain liquid and flood the coasts, or would it evaporate and be retained in the atmosphere because of its new found, warmer capacity to hold it?

Question: If the atmosphere was moisture rich and free of cold temperatures would violent storms exist without clashes of hot and cold air masses?

Question: Since a higher mean earth temperature would lead to northern regions, that were useless, becoming flush with life and capable of raising crops resolve worldwide hunger and ease large metropolitan overcrowding...and would we have so much productive land, a lot of it, now make it possible that every person on the planet could easily have their own private 20 acres each?

We would be so lucky.

Apr 3, 2017 8:41 am

It used to be that the Left just took unreasonable pot shots at the Right or take silly stances like saving the whales etc..

Today is different and it's purposeful. Because the previous propaganda campaigns were easily ignored quickly and faded, the modern approach is much, much more aggressive in that, like the whales, they are trying to establish ownership of the basic tenants of life, of all things, even the atmosphere.

It is vitally important for them to gain ownership of the basics because the reality of the basics always eventually damaged their previous attempts at controlling thought and morality.

Just one example: If they can be successful in defining, legal and otherwise, the whole definition of gender, they would become the owners of it by default...and if the minds of people adopt this bizarre internal contradiction from what they see, would there be a greater lessening of foundations in the brain?

If somehow they were successful at convincing all people (Non-Christians) to adopt abstract notions of truth and reality have almost no ability whatsoever to have a good reason to think for themselves because they lack internal resources?

If the devil, Satan, left, whatever you want to call it, gains insurmountable power and control of thought, will it seem to them that embrace it feel like they have defeated God by establishing new universal laws?

319

The rest of us will be scratching our heads in perplexity as to why people would volunteer to undergo a spiritual lobotomy.

Canada considers controversial new 'gender identity' bill: 'This bill would cause fear'

Apr 3, 2017 8:55 am

Now, I wonder if the Liberals can understand why Mike Pence's no. 2 reason for not having private dinners with other women is to avoid all appearances of infidelity and not providing a platform for accusations?

Apr 5, 2017 8:04 am

It's a good lesson for a high profile person, but also for anyone…it's too easy for us guys to start getting instinctively flirtatious when we might not really be pursuing the sex.

Mike Pence's 'Billy Graham rule' has a long, proven history

Apr 4, 2017 8:26 am

It was a good idea, no one would know it was us.

We absolutely had to come up a plan to validate months of our accusations against the Trump team as having colluded with the Russians. You see, we were in a pretty good mess at the time with the whole DNC thing and a troubling Presidential candidate, and since Donald Trump ounce quipped a solicitation to Russia to find Hillary Clinton's emails, we thought "What a perfect gimmick to use to cast aspersions against Trump!"

At first we simply thought "Let's just roll out the accusations and create doubt…and make sure the media was on board"

Time went on and the public was becoming anxious about the Trump/Russia thing because it's normal for people to eventually need some kind of evidence…believe me, we were looking as the press kept the pot boiling for us.

Well, as everybody knows Trump won and we were absolutely

floored. We were convinced that we had signed up enough illegal aliens to vote in the key states (The SOB's were too afraid to show up!) and we still had in place our normal tally enhancement mechanism's in place...Trump still won!

We desperately wondered, what do we do now? How can we inflict a good dose of damage to Trump right from the get go?

I have to admit, I forget who it was at the time of the meeting that hatched the plan since the meeting was only me and Obama but we both stood up and did a high five!

Since we had already been spying on Trump by way of "Grey Knowledge" from Intel. for the past year, I would ask that the Trump text be unmasked.
And, since that information only went as far down as the FBI and we couldn't get Comey to get off the monkey bars, as usual, President Obama made an Executive Order that insured that the unmasked material from Intel. concerning Trump would be widely disseminated via the Order's directive to share these types of sensitive bits of information to 16 other agencies.

Bonanza! We had several well dedicated people, people who were well below the radar, throughout the agencies that were more than willing to cozy up to the press and try to put a little reality to a scheme hatched long ago.

As the press was being breast fed doses of material, we went as far as we could to find just one little bit of indictable material as we had already sent out the meme that Trump will be quickly impeached a couple of months earlier...we had to deliver!

SOB!............Nothing!

Susan Rice statement denies 'improper' unmasking, but appears to confirm accusation...

That!......is just fascinating!

Someone needs to install a new RAM drive in these guys...new releases have come out they ought to know. I think there is a new patch available as well if they can't afford one.

Susan Rice too, she can't clear her cache. When she was trying to explain why she was spying, she said she did it to save the country from the horrors of the "Trump/Russia" show.

Hard drives are full too and you can't store any new data...what system are they running on these idiots, Commodore Amiga 1000's?

Democrat on Intel Committee says people will go to jail for Trump-Russia collusion

The poor Left in the United States...they are now themselves a country without a "King" Or a Ruler...a Dictator.

Instead, they try to convert us to the oppression that they long for.

We ain't gonna do that...

Dem lawmakers say public schools are 'inappropriate place' for books written by 'climate deniers'

It's pretty obvious, but the next question is, will she finger Obama?...which is also obvious since he was the only one that could give her those marching orders.

Imagine, those spreadsheets physically sitting on his desk as Obama is pouring over them...Ufta!!

The coming year stands to present us both high hopes, prosperity, raised eyebrows and as usual...the full-blown comedy act's that the Liberals are sure to deliver.

Trump is asked if Susan Rice committed a crime - here's what he answered

I realize that whenever I site Biblical references to the end times and the allowing of demons to be released to heavily influence certain people that it's met with the rolling of eye's by some...some folk just don't want to imagine what it would be like if it were true and certainly don't want to live in that scenario.

We are living in that scenario, though.

Here's something to think about. If I say "Go or going Postal" only those who are roughly above 35-40 will instantly recognize that term for what it is, but especially have a real memory of when it first happened.

To us who know that term, it was a shocking event...but to Gen Y and Millennials "Going Postal" is an seemingly every day and expected occurrence.

Think of this if you will, Gen Y and Millennials can't even imagine what life would be like without all these people "Going Postal" all the time.

As well, terrorism was relatively nothing in the 70's, 80's and 90's except for pot shots here and there...now, we are in a full blown global war with them.

Not to be all negative and hopeless, Almighty and loving God has our back's and we will have eventual glory.

Black separatist kills three in Fresno, yells 'Allahu Akbar' at police

There, got that off my chest...for now anyway.

ABOUT THE AUTHOR

Born and largely raised on the High Plains of South Dakota and Nebraska, much of which on a ranch in Southwest Nebraska... an Evangelical Christian and Conservative from birth.

Catapults & Arresting Gear USS Constellation, Harvest Crews, an inadvertent Master of Upholstery, nicely seasoned with engagement in many areas of construction along the way.

www.ingramcontent.com/pod-product-compliance
Lightning Source LLC
Chambersburg PA
CBHW062124280526
45788CB00001B/49